W9-COA-199

Educational and Career Opportunities in Alternative Medicine

PRAISE FOR
Educational and Career Opportunities in Alternative Medicine

"What a great book! This will really help the aspiring alternative practitioner make sense of the multiple career paths available. I wish I would have had this when I applied to medical school."

—Brad Lichtenstein, N.D., cofounder, Natural Healing Arts Group

"This timely volume provides an excellent resource for individuals interested in opportunities to begin or advance their knowledge or skills in any of the major alternative and complementary medicine fields."

—Bruce Barrett, M.D., Ph.D., department of family medicine,
University of Wisconsin at Madison

"Teachers, career advisors, and guidance counselors are getting more and more questions from students about careers in alternative healthcare, and we haven't always known where to go for accurate, practical answers. This book fills a real need for complete and up-to-date information on a growing and highly rewarding field."

—Mary McGhee, M.S. Ed., dean of students,
Northwest Institute of Acupuncture & Oriental Medicine

"Rosemary Jones has contributed a much needed guide to the field of alternative healthcare education. I have found Rosemary's excellent research in this area to be comprehensive, intelligent, and a real time-saver."

—Katherine Parker, C.M.T.

Educational and Career Opportunities in Alternative Medicine

All You Need to Find Your Calling
in the Healing Professions

Rosemary Jones

PRIMA HEALTH   A Division of Prima Publishing

© 1998 by Rosemary Jones

All rights reserved. No part of this book may be reproduced or transmitted in any form or by any means, electronic or mechanical, including photocopying, recording, or by any information storage or retrieval system, without written permission from Prima Publishing, except for the inclusion of quotations in a review.

PRIMA HEALTH and colophon are trademarks of Prima Communications, Inc.

Information contained in this book has been obtained by Author from sources believed to be reliable. However, because of the possibility of human or mechanical error, or because such information may change after the publication of this book, the Author and Publisher do not guarantee the accuracy, adequacy, or completeness of such information and are not responsible for any errors or omission caused by the use of such information.

Library of Congress Cataloging-in-Publication Data

Jones, Rosemary (Rosemary L.)
    Educational and career opportunities in alternative medicine : all you need to find your calling in the healing profession / Rosemary Jones.
        p.   cm.
    Includes bibliographical references and index.
    ISBN 0-7615-1244-6
    1. Naturopathy—Vocational guidance.   I. Title.
RZ444.J66   1998   97-52165
615.5'023—dc21   CIP

98 99 00 01 DD 10 9 8 7 6 5 4 3 2 1
Printed in the United States of America

How to Order
Single copies may be ordered from Prima Publishing, P.O. Box 1260BK, Rocklin, CA 95677; telephone (916) 632-4400. Quantity discounts are also available. On your letterhead, include information concerning the intended use of the books and the number of books you wish to purchase.

www.primapublishing.com

ACKNOWLEDGMENTS

No author is an island. A book like this could never have been written without the contributions of the following:

Dave Molony at AAOM, for answering so many questions via e-mail.

Brett Kinsler, DC, for talking about Bridgeport and life as a chiropractic student.

James Sensenig, ND, and interim dean at UBCNM, who was very, very busy setting up a new program but still had the kindness to call back and chat one summer evening.

Miranda Castro, for her insights on homeopathy and her patience about the publication of her interview (postponed by this project).

7Song, for those last quick comments on herbalism.

Jack Kempt at Seattle Massage School, who thought he was calling a prospective student, not a crazed interviewer.

Cathy Kearns, public relations director at MSU, for sending so much extra material on osteopathy.

Bruce Rhodes, LMT, for the shoulder rubs (this book would never had been finished without them).

Henriette in Finland, for great herbal FAQs and information on English schools.

Kim Fabel and Ron Hobbs, ND, at Bastyr University, who also took time out of busy lives to answer more questions.

Chris Coates of Prima Publishing, for the coffee and insight on the book business for the last several years and pushing for more Canadian information. And Denise Sternad and Andi Reese Brady at Prima for the fine finishing touches on the manuscript.

Brad Lichtenstein, ND, and Christy Lee-Engel, ND, L.Ac., for being nice neighbors and helping out at the last minute.

Sabrina Urquhart, Kris Walberg, and Michael Hacker for technical and professional support.

Diane Jones, a marvelous mother, who also proofed this manuscript and provided her own insights from years of writing experience.

Robert Jones, an equally marvelous father, who gave up his computer for days on end because it had a faster modem.

The front desk staffs of numerous schools here and in Canada, who kept referring me on to the next school or organization (I apologize that I didn't keep all your names).

And finally, to all the customers who came into the store thinking they were going to buy a book and ended up discussing their lives as students and practitioners, my eternal gratitude.

The wisdom can be credited to these people, the errors to the author.

CONTENTS

PART 4   Learning from Home   269

PART 1

Researching Education

1

How to Use This Book

In the one city block where I work, there are three naturopathic doctors (two are also licensed acupuncturists), four or more licensed massage therapists, a dentist who uses aromatherapy, and a yoga studio. There used to be a midwife two blocks away, but her practice got so busy that she had to move to larger offices in another part of the city.

All of these people, and the vast number of other practitioners in North America, provide a needed service. Whether it is massaging the kinks in muscles, using osteopathic or chiropractic manipulations to treat a problem, prescribing herbs or homeopathy instead of chemical drugs, or helping a new mother experience natural childbirth, they are there to help. That's why students sweat through some very hard courses of study, practitioners keep educating themselves year after year far beyond the requirements of their licenses, and national associations spend a great deal of time, money, and debate on how to make their profession's brand of care the best possible.

Whether you are just beginning to think about a career in health care, or you've had several years of experience, you might be considering using natural therapies in your practice. The purpose of this book is to help you become aware of your options. Whether you are a student trying to find a school, a practitioner seeking to expand your therapeutic modalities, or a career counselor answering questions, the information provided here will help clarify the issues surrounding education and careers in this fast growing field of medicine.

✺EXPLORING THE RANGE OF NATURAL THERAPIES

During the last decade, natural medicine made the news in a big way. In 1992 the National Institutes of Health (NIH) added the Office of Alternative Medicine (OAM), which was directed by congressional mandate to study and evaluate various natural therapies. In 1993 the *New England Journal of Medicine* reported that one-third of all Americans have used some type of alternative medicine. More recently, a University of Maryland survey showed that 70 percent of the doctors questioned were interested in learning more about natural medicine, if only to answer their patients' questions. In November 1997 the NIH released a statement affirming that acupuncture is an effective treatment for treating pain after surgery or controlling nausea caused by chemotherapy or pregnancy. As one commentator put it, acupuncture could now be called "real medicine"—a statement that must have amused the millions of people who regularly use this 2,000-year-old therapy. In fact, many of the therapies discussed in this book have been used in other countries for hundreds of years—they are only "alternative" in North America.

Patient demand for natural therapies has created new recognition for practitioners and a more tolerant legal climate. Health insurance companies are increasingly willing to reimburse for these services. Integrated clinics that offer both allopathic and complementary services are becoming more common. Practitioners and schools in all fields are promoting research and forcing the adherents of allopathic medicine to take a serious look at the validity of their claims.

With all the attention focused on these therapies, you may be wondering which area makes the most sense for you. Part of your decision may come from where you are in school or your career, and from your area of interest. The chapters in part 2 address professional degrees or programs leading to licensing (chapters within each section are arranged in alphabetical order): Acupuncturist (L.Ac.), Doctor of Chiropractic (DC), Licensed Massage Therapist (LMT), Midwife (LM or CNM), Naturopathic Doctor (ND), and Osteopathic Doctor (DO). If you already have a career in health care, take a look at the end of each chapter to learn more about specific continuing education or career opportunities. If you would like a career that is similar to that of a medical doctor, consider the chiropractic, naturopathic, or osteopathic colleges. Chiropractic training emphasizes chiropractic and manipulative techniques, but also includes nutrition and other aspects of preventive medicine. If you like bodywork but want to do more than just massage, consider chiropractic medicine. Naturopathic physicians study many types of natural therapies, including herbs, homeopathy, and nutrition, and many choose to specialize in one of these areas. If you would like a career that is similar to that of a general practitioner, but without the allopathic training, the ND is a good choice. If you want the strongest possible grounding in allopathic medicine without becoming an MD, but with an emphasis on preventive care and family medicine, osteopathic schools will serve your needs.

Acupuncture and midwifery are more specialized. For example, acupuncturists treat many types of ailments, but generally use only techniques from traditional Chinese medicine (TCM). Midwives focus on one human condition—pregnancy and childbirth—but may use a variety of natural therapies.

If you want to have a lot of control over your hours or you would like to work part-time, massage therapy may be your field. You can begin to study massage straight from high school or from a completely unrelated career (a lot of massage professionals seem to be corporate escapees!). If you live in a major urban area, there's probably at least one good massage school close to your home—massage therapy has the most schools of any of the natural therapies.

If you're looking for specialized training in a particular therapy to enhance your current practice, read the chapters in part 3. Some of the programs listed there are geared toward practitioners in specific fields; others are open to all interested students. Most of the programs listed in part 3 offer certificates or diplomas of recognition rather than formal degrees. Some do satisfy continuing education credits for certain professions. Be sure to ask if you are in a profession that requires continuing education, as many of the programs listed are currently adding this type of certification to their courses.

LICENSING AND ACCREDITATION

Licensing laws can change, and the trend over the past few years has been to expand the licensing of several professions. The schools and professional organizations listed in part 2 can help you determine the current status of professional licensing in your state or province. Only the Doctor of Osteopathic Medicine (DO) and the Doctor of Chiropractic (DC) have uniform licensing throughout the United States, and the scope of the DC license varies slightly from state to state.

The "scope" of a profession refers to what a practitioner in that field can or cannot do. In health care this generally defines what types of problems can be treated and what types of treatments can be used. Board examinations for licensing usually include a section called "jurisprudence," which tests applicants on their knowledge of the laws pertaining to their profession.

Many licensing laws require an applicant to have graduated from a professionally accredited program. Accreditation in the United States can refer to general accreditation or to specialized accreditation. Specialized or professional accreditation is done by an independent professional body and concentrates on reviewing the academic program of an institution. To achieve accreditation, schools must demonstrate through written documentation and on-site inspection that their program and facilities meet the standards set by the profession for entry-level training (for example, if lab work is required, the school should have laboratories on campus).

General accreditation comes from an independent commission such as the Middle States Association of College and Schools, and denotes the accreditation of the institution as a whole rather than one particular program. Again, the college or university must submit to on-site inspections and provide written documentation of financial stability, facilities, teacher's credentials, and so on.

The United States Department of Education recognizes both regional and specialized accreditation organizations. Some financial aid programs require that the institution has achieved accreditation through a Department of Education–recognized body.

The accreditation bodies mentioned in part 2 are primarily the specialized ones whose accreditation may be necessary for licensing. Generally, a program has to operate for more than three years before a school can apply for accreditation. Before that, and during the review period, the accreditation bodies may choose to "recognize" a program, indicating that the students have the same status as students in an accredited programs (that is, they can sit board exams). All the schools listed in this book will provide, on request, information on their accreditation status and the accrediting bodies in their field.

The professional organizations and accrediting bodies listed in part 2 can also provide you with information. You can find more information on accrediting bodies recognized by the Department of Education in library reference works such as *Peterson's Register of Higher Education*.

✒ LENGTH AND COST OF TRAINING

Everything changes, and program length and tuition cost are no exception. As this book went to press, some schools were lengthening their programs from three to four years, and were offering new "accelerated" tracks that would allow students to complete the program in less time if they carried a heavier class load or worked through the summer. Many of the programs listed in part 3 are continuing education programs, geared to the working professional who wants to take further training in a particular skill, and completion time will vary from student to student.

The length of time it takes to complete a program and the average tuition is presented for general information only. Always check with the school for the most up-to-date enrollment information.

✒ ACADEMIC PREREQUISITES AND OTHER CONSIDERATIONS

The schools listed in part 2 have certain academic prerequisites that must be completed before entry into a program, such as two years of postsecondary education or a bachelor's degree.

For all the schools listed in part 2, admission depends on more than meeting the academic minimums. The applicant's commitment to the profession, their understanding of the demands of health care, their understanding of the particular profession, and their life experience are all components of the final decision.

All of the schools listed in part 2 also require that students be physically capable of completing clinical duties. For example, massage therapy can be physically demanding. If you have any concerns about this requirement, call the admissions departments. They will be happy to answer your questions.

✒ APPLICATION DEADLINES

Many of the schools in part 2, particularly the naturopathic colleges, midwifery schools, and osteopathic colleges, receive applications from many more students than they have space to admit. They address this problem in a variety of ways.

Some schools operate on "rolling" admissions—applications are accepted until the space is filled by qualified candidates. In these schools, you will improve your chances of acceptance by submitting your application as soon as possible. Other schools accept applications up to a deadline, then select the top candidates out of the pool. Many admissions directors who use this system expressed their frustration over great potential students who just miss the cut because of an incomplete form. Check and then double-check the school's application requirements before you apply. If you have questions, call the admissions department. Try to call early on, when the staff is less stressed. If you call the admissions department on the deadline day, you will likely spend considerable time on hold.

Schools that admit students throughout the year, such as acupuncture schools that enter students quarterly, may admit qualified applicants at the next opening. So, for example, you might apply for spring but end up entering in summer, when the next available space is open. In these situations the financial assistance deadlines may be even more important than when classes begin, as some financial aid programs only accept applicants once a year.

Again, programs change. The deadlines given in this book are meant only to give you an idea of what programs are available at what times of the year. Always check with the school as soon as possible for current deadlines.

🌿A FINAL WORD ABOUT THE SCHOOLS LISTED IN THIS BOOK

I know that somebody reading this book will want to ask: "But what do you believe? What's the best form of natural medicine?" The simple answer is that I don't think there is a "best" or even a "worst." The differences between the professions and therapies is often so great, that it would be like comparing "electrical engineering" to "computer programming." Thus I have made no attempt to rank or rate the schools or fields of study in this book.

When deciding which therapies to include in this book, I placed an emphasis on those concerned with correcting physical problems or promoting better physical health. No school was excluded deliberately. In many cases, I simply could not verify a school's existence (the envelope came back with "no forwarding address") or I learned about a program too late to even make the Appendix C: More Schools. In a few cases, I simply could not make the program fit into my parameters. So many schools and educational programs now include "natural therapies" that I had to draw some artificial boundaries. The emphasis in this book is on residential schools (that is, schools with classrooms and other academic facilities where people meet to learn) that have met the legally recognized professional accreditation standards.

I based the descriptions of the natural therapies in this book on standard historical reference works or material provided by the national associations. Be aware that there are many different forms of some of these therapies (acupuncture alone has about 2,000 years of written history and almost as many techniques), and many different schools of thought about the right and wrong way to practice them. At the end of every chapter, you'll find a recommended reading list that will let you explore these issues a little more. You'll also find a list of professional organizations, informational resources like mail-order bookstores, web sites, and Internet newsgroups, which can lead you to even more opinions.

I have based the descriptions of the schools on their catalogs, their web sites, or their written responses to my questionnaire. Sometimes the information I was sent was too long to fit into the book's format and I had to cut; sometimes the school was a little too modest in its responses. The word count of the description does not reflect the quality of the instruction. If a school sounds interesting to you, call, write, or check the web site for the latest information. Most will send out informational brochures for free. Full academic catalogs usually cost $3 to $5.

Some professions, such as midwifery and massage, are working to get their accreditation body recognized by the federal government. When their educational standards meet the educational standards of the licensure laws, I have listed the schools currently accredited or under review for accreditation by that body. I have also listed the other professional organizations in that field that can provide you with lists of their affiliated schools.

For areas where no licensure or accreditation exists, such as herbalism, I have emphasized schools that provide residential programs geared to health professionals (an applicant must be a medical student or practitioner) or those that include therapeutic courses meant to be used in working with sick as well as healthy people.

Some degrees largely exist within well-documented public institutions, such as a master's degree in nutrition. I've left those programs to the *Peterson's* guides and other college reference books unless they were specifically taught by a school already included in this book or had a definite relation to the professions listed in part 2. At the end of the book, you'll find lists of accreditation bodies and professional organizations to help you track down more programs.

A number of "service marked" therapies, such as Hellerwork, are the trademark of a specific school or teacher. Practitioners of these therapies are only allowed to call themselves by that name if they've received training from an instructor approved by that organization or corporation. I've listed several of the better known, especially those geared to health professionals, but there are many new programs being formed every day. Professional organizations, such as the International Healthcare Educators Alliance, may be able to help you track down a particular program. If you get stuck, or if you know of a great program I missed, send me a self-addressed envelope in care of Healing Pages Bookstore, 600 W. McGraw #2, Seattle, WA 98119, or send me e-mail at hpedu@aol.com.

Recommended Reading

By necessity, the descriptions of the therapies and professions in this book are deliberately brief. If you are intrigued, read on—literally thousands of books are available on these topics (and new ones are coming out every day). So, at the end of every chapter, you'll find a recommended reading list. These books are meant to serve as a general introduction to the concepts behind these therapies and in no way replace formal training.

Many of the therapies listed in this book have interesting legal and political histories, which tend to get forgotten in the books about how to practice a particular therapy. During Henry VIII's tenure on the throne of England, for example, Parliament issued a charter to protect the herbalists from frivolous lawsuits brought by surgeons. These lawsuits, according to the government, were inspired by malice and the loss of patients rather than any evidence of harm done by the herbalists. Chided for "minding only their own lucre" and not their patients' welfare, the surgeons were told to leave the herbalists alone. England still has Medical Herbalists today.

At the end of the eighteenth century and throughout the nineteenth century, there was a movement in Europe and North America to find a kinder form of medicine than the purging and bloodletting practiced by allopathic doctors. Homeopathic, osteopathic, and chiropractic therapies were all developed by men deeply disturbed by the trends of medicine that created cures almost more horrible than the diseases.

There is an ongoing academic debate in conventional medical schools that medical doctors need to understand the history of their type of medicine better. The historians argue that knowing the past helps to recharge enthusiasm as well as caution students about common errors. So at the end of many chapters in parts 2 and 3, you'll find not only books about the therapies, but also about the people who played an important part in their development.

Burroughs, Hugh and Mark Kastner. *Alternative Healing: The Complete A-Z Guide.* La Mesa, CA: Halcyon Publishing, 1993.

> There are fatter, heavier, and more illustrated books that cover the same topics, but this handy, quick guide explains more than 160 different types of natural and alternative therapies, including brief histories of their original teachers.

Bratman, Steven. *The Alternative Medicine Sourcebook.* Chicago: Lowell House, 1997.

> Bratman, an MD who uses natural therapies, gives a thoughtful, critical appraisal of many techniques based on his own clinical experiences.

PART 2

Professional Degrees or Programs Leading to Licensing

2

Licensed Acupuncturist (L.Ac.)

In its simplest form, acupuncture denotes the insertion of slender needles in various points along the human body to reduce pain or stimulate healing. Most acupuncturists in North America follow the complex system of traditional Chinese medicine (TCM), which traces its origins back to the reign of the Yellow Emperor, Huang-ti, 2697 to 2595 B.C. The *Huang-ti Nei-Ching (Yellow Emperor's Classic of Internal Medicine)* is one of the oldest existing medical texts describing acupuncture techniques. Acupuncture had spread throughout Asia by A.D. 1000, and many countries developed their own variations on the basic techniques.

Acupuncture slowly filtered back to Europe during the periods of exploration and expansion in the eighteenth and nineteenth centuries. French acupuncturist George Soulie de Morant is credited with translating many of the Chinese words into the terms used by Western acupuncturists today, such as "meridian" or "source point." Soulie de Morant was even nominated for the Nobel Prize in physiology in 1950, based on the publication of his major textbook of acupuncture, *L'Acuponcture Chinoise.*

Much of acupuncture's current popularity can be traced to President Richard Nixon's 1970 visit to China. During this trip the president's press secretary, James Reston, fell ill and required an emergency appendectomy, with the post-op treatment including acupuncture and favorable coverage by the press. Later that year the University of California Los Angeles medical school invited thirty Chinese acupuncturists to participate in a pain control program.

Today, acupuncturists treat a wide variety of physical ailments, going beyond the simple control of pain associated with acupuncture in Western medicine. Some acupuncturists specialize in the treatment of addictions such as alcohol, smoking, and cocaine.

In TCM, the acupuncturist diagnoses disease by specifically examining the pulse and the tongue, and by a general examination of the body, which is seen as a network of *meridians* and *points* along which flows *qi*, or vital energy. Treatment may be a combination of acupuncture, herbal medicines, and massage, among other techniques.

In modern China the government schools blend the concepts of acupuncture with that of Western medicine. New students are required to study both the basic biological sciences and the TCM model of the human body. In North America most schools conform to the Chinese model of acupuncture, although some teach the Japanese technique or other methods. In Europe the Vietnamese culture has had a strong influence on some French schools.

Most acupuncture programs combine lectures, labs, and clinical internships. Acupuncture students spend three to four years in a residential program. Besides studying acupuncture, they take classes in Western biological sciences, Oriental herbology, bodywork, and other holistic therapies. As their studies advance, students work in a college-affiliated clinic, treating patients under the supervision of trained acupuncturists.

Because many of the teachers originally trained in China, several schools have used their professional ties to establish student internships in Chinese hospitals. For two months or more, American or Canadian students work in Chinese hospitals or clinics with their Chinese counterparts. Participants describe these programs as extremely intensive, giving students a chance to observe a wider range of ailments and treatments than they would normally encounter in a North American clinic.

Upon graduation in the United States, students usually take the National Certification Commission for Acupuncture and Oriental Medicine (NCCAOM) written and practical examinations for acupuncture certification. Graduates may also be required to take other examinations to meet the requirements of their state or province licensure.

Depending on the legal requirements of the state or province in which they practice, acupuncturists work in independent practices or in clinics or hospitals under the supervision of doctors.

Income varies depending on type of practice and geographical location. Acupuncturists need a minimum of 500 patient visits per year to keep up their national certification. At an average charge of $50 per hour, that comes to approximately $25,000 a year, and most acupuncturists report having far more patient visits than their NCCAOM minimum. A 1993 survey by the California Acupuncture Association showed practitioners' gross annual income ranging from $30,000 per year to more than $100,000 per year.

✎COST OF EDUCATION

Tuition and books vary from $6,000 to $12,000 per year, depending on the structure of the program. The tuition costs listed for the schools below are the average tuition based on the schools' own budgets. These figures do not include costs of housing, commuting, or personal expenses.

Average tuition is based on full-time attendance. Many schools also offer part-time programs, which can increase your opportunities to work while in school. Many schools seem to participate in some type of federal or state aid program, but most financial assistance comes in the form of student loans.

✎LENGTH OF TRAINING

Most programs last three to four years, and require the students to attend classes at the school. The number of class and clinical hours actually needed for licensing varies from state to state. The schools tend to structure their programs to meet the general requirements of licensing as well as the specific requirements of their state. If you're planning to practice in a state other than where the school is located, be sure to check that your program will meet that state's requirements.

Most acupuncture schools follow a standard academic year with a summer break. Some allow a more intensive year-round approach, letting students accelerate the completion of their studies. Many schools can accommodate part-time students, but some do not. If you do not want or cannot afford to be in school full-time, ask before beginning the admissions process.

Students generally spend the first one or two years of their training in lectures and lab classes, with perhaps some clinical observation courses. Students then move into a mix of clinical internships and classes, where most of their time is spent treating patients under the supervision of a practicing acupuncturist.

✺ADMISSIONS PROCESS

Like most colleges, acupuncture schools require applicants to fill out a formal application form; provide proof of the fulfillment of prerequisites; and, possibly, participate in a personal interview with the admissions staff. Letters of reference or a personal essay may also be required.

At some point in the admissions process, applicants will probably be asked to pay a nonrefundable application fee. Most schools accept applications throughout the year, and many accept new students more than once a year.

✺UNDERGRADUATE PREREQUISITES

Many acupuncture schools do not require candidates to have a bachelor's or other undergraduate degree. However, most do require applicants to have completed at least two years of college-level courses.

Foreign students who do not speak English as their first language may be required to take an English proficiency test. A few schools offer programs in Chinese or Korean. Students entering these programs must demonstrate that they speak these languages at college-level proficiency.

Prerequisites shown for the schools date from 1996/97 entrance requirements, and should be regarded as the bare minimum needed. Check with the institution to make sure that these requirements have not changed.

✺LICENSING AND ACCREDITATION

UNITED STATES

Acupuncturists were licensed or allowed to practice in thirty-five states and the District of Columbia as of 1997, but licensing varies greatly from state to state. In some states acupuncturists are licensed to work independently of other medical supervision. In others, they are required to work under the supervision of a medical doctor or osteopathic doctor. Some states do not acknowledge acupuncture as a separate profession or restrict its practice to medical doctors.

In general, to become licensed, acupuncturists must successfully complete an acupuncture course of study in an accredited program. The exact number of class/clinical hours needed may vary. In 1995 New York required 4,050 clock hours of instruction and a clinical internship, while New Mexico required 2,400 clock hours of instruction. Check the requirements of the state where you plan to practice, and then check with your school to make sure that your academic program covers all needed course/clinical work.

Most states that license acupuncturists require applicants to pass the NCCAOM written and practical exams. Candidates may also have to pass a Clean Needle Technique (CNT) exam or other local state exams. Rather than licensing, some states certify or register acupuncturists, leading to such designations as C.Ac. (certified acupuncturist) or R.Ac.(registered acupuncturist).

The Accreditation Commission for Acupuncture and Oriental Medicine (ACAOM), formerly known as the National Accreditation Commission for Schools and Colleges of Acupuncture and Oriental Medicine (NACSCAOM), is the accreditation body recognized by the US Department of Education.

The National Acupuncture Foundation publishes a regularly updated book, *Acupuncture and Oriental Medicine Laws*, on the changes in state laws governing acupuncture.

National Certification Commission for Acupuncture
  and Oriental Medicine (NCCAOM)
PO Box 97075
Washington, D.C. 20090-7075
(202) 232-1404

CANADA

Acupuncture is regulated by province in Canada. At the time of publication, there was no national acupuncture organization in Canada, although there were many provincial groups. Prospective acupuncturists should contact the Health Professions Council or appropriate body in Health Ministry in their province. The schools listed in this chapter and in Appendix C should be able to help you contact professionals in your area or verify provincial requirements. Make sure that the number of hours offered in the educational program will satisfy the requirements of the province in which you plan to practice.

US Schools

The following schools were accredited or candidates for accreditation by the ACAOM at the time of publication.

Academy of Chinese Culture and Health Sciences
1601 Clay Street
Oakland, CA 94612
(510) 763-7787
http://www.acchs.edu

Program:
The master of sciences in traditional Chinese medicine takes three years to finish for full-time students. Classes include acupuncture, acupressure, herbology, and the entire philosophy of the Chinese medical approach.

Prerequisites:
Applicants should have two years of college or 60 units of undergraduate education from an accredited university or college. Prerequisites include communications, humanities, social sciences, and standard medical science courses (contact the school for current requirements).

Tuition:
In 1997 tuition and fees for a full-time student came to approximately $9,000 a year or $27,000 for the full program.

Financial Assistance:
The TERI loan alternative program is offered. The school was under application for the federal loan programs in 1997.

Application Deadline:
Applicants are only admitted in the fall. Applications are due by August 1.

Other Programs:
Contact the school for information about continuing education for licensed acupuncturists and registered nurses.

Academy of Oriental Medicine
PO Box 9446
Austin, TX 78766-9446
(512) 454-1188
http://www.holistic.com/listings/aom.htm

Program:
The master's of science in Oriental medicine includes: acupuncture, moxibustion, herbology, Oriental bodywork, internal martial arts, nutrition, and Western sciences. Although designed as an accelerated three-year program, part-time students may take up to six years to complete all requirements.

Prerequisites:
Applicants are required to have satisfactorily completed at least 60 semester hours or 90 quarter hours of general academic college-level classes. The school may also choose to interview students regarding their interest in acupuncture and Oriental medicine.

Tuition:
In 1996/97 tuition for full-time students was approximately $6,300 per year. Books, supplies, and fees such as intern's insurance were additional.

Financial Assistance:
The Academy of Oriental Medicine has been approved by the Veterans Administration to train veterans with VA benefits. It expects to be able to offer federal student loan programs by 1997/98.

Application Deadline:
The school accepts applications throughout the year. Beginning and transfer students may enter at the start of each semester and at the beginning of the summer session. Sessions begin in September, January, or July.

Other Programs:
The school also offers a 618-hour Oriental bodywork program approved by the American Oriental Bodywork Therapy Association (AOBTA).

American College of Acupuncture and Oriental Medicine
9100 Park West Drive
Houston, TX 77063
(713) 780-9777
http://www.acaom.edu

Program:
The program lasts four academic years and leads to a master's degree. Course work places an equal emphasis on Oriental medicine, acupuncture, and herbology. Part-time students have up to six years to complete the program.

Prerequisites:
Applicants need to have successfully completed a minimum of 60 college credits.

Tuition:
In 1997 full-time student tuition was approximately $5,500 per year.

Financial Assistance:
Applicants should contact the school for current payment plans and other financial assistance available.

Application Deadline:
Applications are due in December.

Other Programs:
The college offers seminars and continuing education courses.

American College of Traditional Chinese Medicine
455 Arkansas Street
San Francisco, CA 94107
(415) 282-7600
http://www.actcm.edu

Founded in 1980 as a nonprofit corporation, the American College of Traditional Chinese Medicine has a study abroad program that enables students to attend classes in several Chinese medical schools. The college also established an exchange program with Goto College of Medical Arts and Sciences in Tokyo, Japan, in 1990. In 1992 the college worked with the San Francisco Department of Public Health

AIDS Office to provide medical care to people with HIV using acupuncture and herbal medicine at the school's clinic.

Program:
The master of science in traditional Chinese medicine degree program lasts for three years (twelve quarters). The curriculum follows the licensure requirements of California with training in acupuncture and herbal medicine. Students can use the college's Study Abroad Program to complete the curriculum requirements of either the eleventh or twelfth quarters.

Prerequisites:
Applicants should have a BA or equivalent, including at least 22 quarter credits in general sciences. Check with the admissions office for specific course requirements. Applicants with deficiencies in the required areas may apply for provisional admittance.

Tuition:
In 1996/97, tuition was $122 per credit hour for didactic classes and $244 per credit hour for clinical classes. Qualified students may borrow up to $18,500 per academic year under the Stafford Loan program.

Financial Assistance:
The school participates in the Stafford and other federal loan programs.

Application Deadline:
Applications accepted throughout the year. Prospective students should inquire about current financial aid deadlines.

Other Programs:
The college has been approved by the California Board of Registered Nurses to offer continuing education units. It also has a continuing education program for acupuncturists.

Bastyr University
14500 Juanita Drive NE
Bothell, Washington 98011
(425) 823-1300
http://www.bastyr.edu

Bastyr, best known for its naturopathic doctor program, also offers two master's degrees in acupuncture. Classes take place at Bastyr's new campus in Bothell, Washington, about one hour's drive northeast of Seattle.

Program:
Bastyr offers two master's degrees in acupuncture and Oriental medicine. The three-and-a-half-year master of science in acupuncture and Oriental medicine (MSAOM) teaches Chinese herbal medicine and Chinese medical language in addition to the core theory, TCM diagnosis, TCM pathology, TCM techniques, acupuncture therapeutics, and clinical training. The shorter three-year master of science in acupuncture (MSA) is designed for medical professionals who desire advanced comprehensive training in acupuncture and Chinese herbal medicine.

Students may attend morning or evening programs. Clinical training is done at the Bastyr Natural Health Clinic. Students may also train at external clinic sites or complete clinical internship credits at the Chengdu University of Traditional Chinese Medicine in the People's Republic of China.

Prerequisites:
Applicants should have a bachelor's degree, with classes including algebra or pre-calculus, general chemistry, biology with lab, and general psychology. Applicants should check with the school for current minimum hours and grade point average (GPA) required.

Tuition:
In 1996/97 average full-time tuition and fees were $12,000 for the MSAOM and $11,000 for the MSA in the first year of study. Books and supplies will probably cost an additional $1,000.

Financial Assistance:
Students participate in state and federal financial aid programs, including the Washington State Need Grant, Washington State Education Opportunity Grant, Federal Pell Grant, Federal Supplemental Educational Opportunity Grant (FSEOG), Federal Stafford Student Loan, Federal Perkins Loan, and Federal Work-Study. The financial aid office recommends that applicants complete the application process by June 1, before starting school in September.

Application Deadline:
School begins in September, and applications should be in by February 1; late applications are accepted on a space-available basis.

Other Programs:
Bastyr also offers a bachelor of science (BS) degree and a master's degree in nutrition. The largest educational program at the university is the naturopathic doctor (ND) degree program.

Dongguk-Royal University of America
1125 West 6th Street
Los Angeles, CA 90017
(213) 482-6646

The school was founded in 1979 as the Royal University of America.

Program:
The master of science in Oriental medicine (2,500 hours) includes 1,690 hours of didactic course instruction and 810 hours of clinical instruction. The four-year program covers acupuncture, Oriental medicine theory, herbology, tui-na (Chinese massage therapy), Western sciences related to medicine (biology, chemistry, and so on), Western medicine, and pharmacology. Electives include Korean hand acupuncture, sa san constitutional medicine, and iridology.

Students may choose to satisfy 200 hours of the clinical internship practicing at a private medical clinic. These externships occur at clinics owned and operated by Dongguk-Royal alumni.

Prerequisites:
Applicants must have completed the minimum of two years (60 semester credits or 90 quarter credits) at an accredited college or university.

Tuition:
In 1997 the full program was approximately $21,000 (or $5,220 per year). Textbooks, medical supplies, and lab fees for the full program were approximately $1,000.

Financial Assistance:
Dongguk-Royal University participates in federal programs such as Pell Grants, Stafford Loans, Parents Loans for Undergraduate Students (PLUS), and veterans' benefits. The university also offers some scholarships based on academic merit, achievement, and financial need.

Application Deadline:
Applications are accepted throughout the year, and new students are admitted at the beginning of each quarter.

Other Programs:
The university offers the same program with instruction in Korean or Mandarin Chinese. A certificate course in tui-na has been available in the past.

Emperor's College of Traditional Oriental Medicine
1807-B Wilshire Boulevard
Santa Monica, CA 90403
(310) 453-8300
http://www.emperors.edu

Program:
The master of traditional Oriental medicine (MTOM) program may not be completed in less than three calendar years by full-time students. Part-time students may take up to six calendar years to complete this degree. Qualified health-care professionals such as medical doctors, registered nurses, or chiropractors may qualify for advanced placement. Emperor's College models its master's degree program on the type of training found at the Beijing and Shanghai Colleges of Traditional Chinese Medicine.

Since 1995, Emperor's College has offered an eight-week, pregraduate internship program. Students can elect to complete 320 hours of internship in a medical university hospital training program in the People's Republic of China.

Prerequisites:
Applicants must have satisfactorily completed 60 semester units (or 90 quarter units) of undergraduate course work from an accredited college.

Tuition:
In 1996/97 the entire program cost approximately $21,400 ($7,133 per year for full-time students). Students should also budget $300 to $400 per year for books and supplies.

Financial Assistance:
Emperor's College participates in the standard federal student loan programs and veterans' benefits. Students are encouraged to apply for assistance two to three months before registration.

Application Deadline:
Applications are accepted throughout the year. Following the completion of all applications paperwork, including academic records and letters of recommendation, student should allow time to arrange a personal interview and assistance with the financial aid application if necessary (see above).

Other Programs:
The college offers an acupressure and massage certification program. It also provides a Korean-language equivalent of its MTOM program in its night classes.

Five Branches Institute
College of Traditional Chinese Medicine
200 7th Avenue
Santa Cruz, CA 95062
(408) 476-9424
http://www.fivebranches.com

Program:
The Five Branches Institute's four-year program emphasizes acupuncture and herbology, but also allows students to explore the other branches of traditional Chinese medicine. The Five Branches of the school's name refer to qi gong energetics; dietary medicine; acupuncture; herbology; and bone medicine (traditional Chinese soft-tissue massage and structural adjustment).

The Institute works with TCM colleges in the People's Republic of China, and has established an ongoing research program.

Prerequisites:
All applicants must have the minimum education requirement of 60 semester units (two years or an associate degree) of general education

from a nationally accredited college. A bachelor's degree is not required. The 60 semester units need to include human anatomy and physiology, physics, chemistry, and biology (the physics, chemistry, and biology courses need not be designated for science majors). Other requirements are English/communications; arts and humanities; and social and behavioral sciences.

Tuition:
In 1997 the average tuition, books, and fees cost $6,285 for first-year students. These costs increase slightly every year, so estimated expenses for fourth-year students in the 1997/98 academic year totaled $6,665.

Financial Assistance:
The Stafford Loan programs are the primary source of aid for students. The school also participates in the Federal Pell Grants, which can be used for the first year of study if the student qualifies as an undergraduate.

Application Deadline:
Five Branches prefers that applicants request and read the catalog thoroughly; and then phone and schedule a pre-application interview. Prospective students are encouraged to tour the campus facilities; schedule a visit to sit in on a class lecture and talk with other students, or attend the Open House (held in the spring) to see the school and Santa Cruz. Applications are reviewed for admissions four times a year. Freshman classes enter in the February or August semester. Letters of acceptance are mailed in October and December for February entrance and April and June for August entrance.

Other Programs:
Five Branches was working on adding a doctor of traditional Chinese medicine degree (DTCM) at the time of publication.

International Institute of Chinese Medicine (IICM)
PO Box 4991
Santa Fe, NM 87502
(505) 473-5233

Branch Campus:
4600 Montgomery, NE, Bldg. 1, Suite 1
Albuquerque, NM 87109
(505) 883-5569

IICM holds classes three days a week with a day/evening/weekend schedule available at the Albuquerque campus.

Program:
This four-year, 2,400-hour master's degree program has an intensive clinical focus. By the last half of the second year, students work with a team partner to treat patients under the supervision of a licensed acupuncturist. In the third and fourth years, students independently provide health services to patients from the community in the supervised advanced student clinic. Advanced students can go on a summer study tour to China for intensive training at Chinese TCM colleges and hospitals. Part-time study is allowed, but students must complete the program in no more than eight years.

Prerequisites:
For admission into the master of Oriental medicine degree program, applicants must have completed at least 60 credit hours of general education at the postsecondary level from an accredited institution.

Tuition:
In 1996/97 tuition for full-time students (14 credits or more) was $145 per credit at the Santa Fe campus.

Financial Assistance:
Federal loan programs and work-study are available for qualified applicants.

Application Deadline:
Completed applications are due no later than three months before the desired entry date. IICM enters students in the fall and spring.

Other Programs:
The school offers continuing education programs for acupuncturists and other qualified health professionals. It recently added a t'ai chi certificate program.

Kyung San University
8322 Garden Grove Boulevard
Garden Grove, CA 92644
(714) 636-0337
http://www.kyungsan.edu

Program:

The master of science in Oriental medicine degree includes diagnostics, acupuncture, herbology, therapeutic massage, and other therapeutic methods in traditional Oriental medicine.

To meet the California Acupuncture Committee regulations, students must take a minimum of 1,548 class/lecture hours and 800 hours of clinical training. As organized by Kyung San University, the graduation requirements consist of didactic and clinical courses totaling 220 quarter units (2,600 hours), including 1,800 hours of classes and 800 hours of clinical experience. This program can be completed in a minimum of thirty-six months if the student is enrolled on a year-round, full-time basis.

Prerequisites:

Student must have successfully completed two years of undergraduate study at an accredited college or university.

Tuition:

In 1997 average cost was $21,000 for the four-year program.

Financial Assistance:

Loans are available through a private finance company.

Application Deadline:

Applications are accepted throughout the year, and students can enter at the start of any quarter.

Other Programs:

Student may also take the same program in Korean if they demonstrate college-level proficiency in that language.

Maryland Institute of Traditional Chinese Medicine
4641 Montgomery Avenue, Suite 415
Bethesda, MD 20814
(301) 718-7373

Program:

The three-year, 1,890-hour program consists of 990 hours of academic instruction and 900 hours of clinical training. The school limits class size to thirty participants for optimal teacher and student interaction.

Students are strongly encouraged to take NCCAOM exam even if it is not a requirement for licensure where they will practice. A preparation course for this exam is offered each fall as part of the regular course of study.

Course work places a special emphasis on yin-yang theory and application, advancing through different levels of traditional Chinese medical diagnostic theory, point location, needling technique and treatment. Western medical classes in pathophysiology and participation in a research project are also part of the program. Students begin their clinic work in the second or third year.

Prerequisites:
Applicants must have completed two years of undergraduate education including science credits in anatomy and physiology. MDs and other health professionals may not be required to take the Western medicine curriculum (see tuition below).

Tuition:
In 1996/97 full-time tuition was approximately $6,000 per year. MDs and health professionals who have already satisfied the Western medicine requirements pay approximately $5,000 per year.

Financial Assistance:
In 1997 the school only offered payment plans.

Application Deadline:
Call for a current catalog and calendar.

Other Programs:
The Institute offers t'ai chi courses for the public.

Meiji College of Oriental Medicine
1426 Fillmore Street, Suite 3
San Francisco, CA 94115
(415) 771-1019

Program:
The master of science degree in Oriental medicine includes comprehensive training in Traditional Chinese Medicine (TCM), comprised of acupuncture, herbology, and moxibustion, as well as instruction in Japanese needling techniques, abdominal diagnosis, and electrical acupuncture. Students learn both the traditional Chinese and the Western medical models of the human body.

Meiji College operates year-round on a quarterly basis. Classes are held on Tuesdays, Thursdays, and Saturdays, and can be attended on a full-time or part-time basis. The full program has 2,455 hours of classroom and clinical training. More than one-third of those hours are spent in the Meiji's student clinic. Students experience clinical practice throughout the program, with the greatest number of hours occurring in the third year.

Prerequisites:
Applicants should have a bachelor's degree or equivalent through an accredited college or university.

Tuition:
In 1996/97 quarterly tuition for full-time students was $1,650 ($6,600 annually). The cost of books, physical and diagnostic supplies, and fees are greatest for the first year ($560 maximum) and less for subsequent years ($250 maximum).

Financial Assistance:
Financial aid for full-time students is offered in the form of state student loan programs.

Application Deadline:
Early application is strongly encouraged by the financial aid office for students who need financial assistance. Check with the college for current deadlines.

Other Programs:
Check with the college for classes appropriate to continuing education.

Midwest Center for the Study of Oriental Medicine
6226 Bankers Road, Suites 5 and 6
Racine, WI 53403
(414) 554-2010
http://www.acupuncture.edu

This is one of the oldest acupuncture schools in the United States. In 1996 it was granted official affiliation with the Guangzhou Medical University in the People's Republic of China.

Program:
The four-academic-year program is located at the Racine campus, but first-academic-year classes in acupuncture and evening classes in bio-medicine are offered in auxiliary classrooms in Chicago.

Course work focuses on the Chinese eight-principle system of physiology, pathology, diagnosis, and treatment strategy. Classical herbal theories and traditions studied include Shang Han Lun, Wen Bing, and Zang Fu.

The required acupuncture internships (660 hours) take place at the school's student clinics or at off-campus internship sites working with approved clinicians.

Graduates earn a Master of Science in Oriental Medicine (MSOM) and are qualified to sit for both the acupuncture and herb examinations given by the NCCAOM.

Prerequisites:
Applicants must have an associates degree from an accredited college or two years postsecondary education (60 semester credits). Selection is based on previous academic achievement, professional experience, and an interview.

Tuition:
In 1997 the average tuition was $7,140 per year or $28,560 for the entire four-year program.

Financial Assistance:
Financial assistance is available for students attending the main campus in Wisconsin. Students who attend the Chicago campus need to check with the financial aid office about eligibility. Midwest participates in standard federal loan packages and the Pell Grant program.

Application Deadline:
Applications are accepted up to ten days before the beginning of the quarter.

Other Programs:
The school also offers a three-year acupuncture program that does not include the intensive herbal studies.

Minnesota Institute of Acupuncture and Herbal Studies
1821 University Avenue, Suite 278-S
Saint Paul, MN 55104
(612) 603-0994

MIAHS draws its program from a variety of national traditions, including the Chinese, Japanese, Korean, Vietnamese, and European styles of acupuncture and Oriental therapies.

Program:
The curriculum for the Professional Oriental Medicine program provides 2,400 hours over a period of four years. Flexibility is available for part-time students.

The program includes education and training in traditional Oriental medical concepts, acupuncture principles, and skills incorporating a variety of traditions and systems of thought: tui-na, traditional Chinese herbalism, Western medical concepts, Chinese culture and philosophical foundations of Oriental medicine, related Chinese studies (t'ai chi chuan, qi gong, and introductory Chinese language skills), and such holistic skills as counseling, nutrition, communication skills, bodywork, touch, and subtle energy therapies.

Prerequisites:
Applicants must have completed two years of undergraduate education at an accredited college or university.

Tuition:
In 1996/97 full-time tuition and fees were approximately $6,000 per year.

Financial Assistance:
State loans and work-study are available for eligible students.

Application Deadline:
Classes enter once a year in September, and space is limited.

Other Programs:
The school offers an acupuncture program, which does not include the herbal studies portion of the professional Oriental medicine program.

The New Center College for Wholistic Health Education
   and Research
6801 Jericho Turnpike
Syosset, NY 11791-4465
(516) 364-0808
http://www.newcenter.edu

The New Center College is the home of AMMA Therapy®, a system of Oriental bodywork therapy developed by co-founder Tina Sohn.

Program:

The acupuncture diploma program is a 2,790-clock-hour program that can be completed as a three-year full-time program or as a five-year part-time program. Upon completion of the program, graduates are eligible to sit for the New York State licensing exam in acupuncture and the NCCAOM acupuncture certification exam.

The diploma program in Oriental medicine integrates the study of acupuncture and Chinese herbal medicine. This comprehensive 3,210-clock-hour program meets the same requirements as the acupuncture diploma, but also qualifies graduates to take the NCCAOM certification exams in both acupuncture and Chinese herbal medicine.

The New Center Clinic provides professionally supervised internships for students as part of their clinical experience.

Prerequisites:

Applicants must have two years of undergraduate education, including biological sciences (check with the admissions department for current course and GPA standards).

Tuition:

In 1996/97 tuition ranged from $26,505 for the acupuncture diploma to $30,495 for the Oriental medicine diploma. Cost per year varies depending on the number and type of courses taken.

Financial Assistance:

The school participates in all the standard federal loan programs.

Application Deadline:

Prospective students seeking financial assistance should check with the financial aid office for current deadlines.

Other Programs:

Under its School for Oriental Medicine, New Center also offers a Chinese Herbal Medicine Program and AMMA Therapy® Program. New Center also has a School for Massage Therapy and a School for Wholistic Nursing.

The New England School of Acupuncture (NESA)
30 Common Street
Watertown, MA 02172
(617) 926-1788

Founded in 1975, the New England School of Acupuncture is the oldest acupuncture school in America.

Program:
The master of acupuncture degree program is designed to train students in the major aspects of Oriental medicine, with the primary focus on acupuncture and Chinese herbal medicine. Acupuncture styles and techniques from other traditions, such as Japanese acupuncture and the Five Element approach, are offered as electives. The clinical instruction concludes with a year-long internship in the NESA and off-site clinics.

NESA emphasizes that a significant portion of the master's degree curriculum is devoted to Western medicine and science. These courses include basic sciences, anatomy and physiology, pathophysiology, pharmacology, emergency medical conditions, and medical research techniques.

Most students attend full-time. Part-time students are accepted on a space-available basis only.

Prerequisites:
Applicants must have a bachelor's degree from an accredited institution, or be certified in a medical profession requiring at least the equivalent training of a bachelor's degree. NESA also requires applicants to have completed general biology (3 credits, 45 hours), anatomy and physiology (6 credits, 90 hours, including physiology lab), and general psychology (3 credits, 45 hours). Applicants without these science credits may be allowed to complete them during the first twelve months after entering NESA.

Tuition:
In 1996/97 full-time tuition was approximately $8,000 per year, not including books and supplies.

Financial Assistance:
NESA participates in the standard federal aid programs.

Application Deadline:
The school operates on a semester system. Students interested in financial assistance should contact the financial aid office for current application deadlines.

Other Programs:
The school offers a separate certificate program in traditional Chinese herbal medicine (see chapter 13, Herbalism and Aromatherapy).

Northwest Institute of Acupuncture and Oriental Medicine
(NIAOM)
1307 North 45th Street, Suite 300
Seattle, WA 98103
(206) 633-2419
http://www.halcyon.com/niaom

Founded in 1981, NIAOM operates its current classrooms and student clinic in the Wallingford neighborhood of Seattle. The school plans to move to a larger facility in 1998/99.

Program:
This three-year masters of acupuncture program focuses on the study of traditional Chinese medical theory, diagnosis, meridians and points, therapeutics, and techniques, as well as Western anatomy, physiology, pathology, and clinical sciences. Elective course sequences include Chinese dietary therapy, auricular medicine, medical qi gong, Chinese medical language, and tui-na.

Clinic work includes both observation of licensed acupuncturists and supervised clinical practice. NIAOM also maintains clinic externship connections with many schools in mainland China.

For students planning to practice in California, there is a herbal certificate program to meet the licensure requirements of that state.

Prerequisites:
NIAOM prefers applicants to have a bachelor's degree. Applicants need a minimum of three years of accredited college or university study (135 quarter credits or 90 semester credits) and must also have completed a course in general biology and a course in general psychology.

Tuition:
In 1996/97 the three-year program cost approximately $22,600 ($7,533 per year) for tuition alone.

Financial Assistance:
NIAOM participates in standard federal aid programs such as the Stafford Loan program.

Application Deadline:
The Institute accepts applications throughout the year. Students enter the program in the fall quarter. Space is limited, so early applications are encouraged.

Other Programs:
NIAOM's continuing education program offers approximately fifteen workshops per year conducted by nationally and internationally known practitioners. The school also offers certificate programs in qi gong and Chinese herbal medicine. These programs are open to students who are enrolled at NIAOM or are licensed acupuncturists. At the time of publication, NIAOM was working on additional certificate programs.

Oregon College of Oriental Medicine (OCOM)
10525 SE Cherry Blossom Drive
Portland, OR 97216
(503) 253-3443
http://www.infinite.org/oregon.acupuncture

OCOM was founded in 1983. In addition to the college's resources, students have library privileges at the Oregon Health Sciences University, the nearby National College of Naturopathic Medicine, and Western States Chiropractic College.

Program:
The master of acupuncture and oriental Medicine (M.Ac.O.M.) degree takes four academic years or three calendar years for full-time students. Course work and training covers the theory and practice of acupuncture, herbal medicine, traditional Chinese physiotherapy, exercise, and *qi*-cultivation. Courses in Western medicine include anatomy, physiology, pathology, pharmacology, and clinical diagnosis. The program places a strong emphasis on public and community health, clinical research, practice management, and practitioner/patient dynamics.

At the college clinic, student interns practice under the direct supervision of experienced acupuncturists, many from China, who are licensed in the state of Oregon. Students complete more than 900 hours of supervised clinical training before graduation. All students must also complete an internship rotation in a community health clinic.

Prerequisites:
Three years of college at an accredited institution are required (a minimum of 135 quarter credits, or 90 semester credits). OCOM recommends that incoming students have completed four years of college.

Tuition:
In 1996/97 the average tuition for full-time students was $7,800 for one academic year (three quarters) of enrollment. Books and medical supplies cost an additional $500 to $600 per academic year.

Financial Assistance:
Various forms of financial aid are available, including the federal Stafford Loan program, veterans' benefits, and the Federal College Work-Study program.

Other Programs:
A specialized certificate program in teacher training is offered for advanced students of qi gong.

Pacific College of Oriental Medicine
7445 Mission Valley Road, Suites 103–106
San Diego, CA 92108
(619) 574-6909
http://www.ormed.edu

Branch campus:
Pacific Institute of Oriental Medicine
915 Broadway, 3rd Floor
New York, NY 10010
(212) 982-3456

In general, the San Diego and New York programs of Pacific College of Oriental Medicine follow the same academic schedule. Differences in tuition and approach are noted below.

Program:
The master's of traditional Oriental medicine (San Diego) or the diploma of traditional Oriental medicine (New York) follow essentially the same curriculum. The fundamentals are introduced in the first academic year and include acupuncture, herbal medicine, anatomy, body therapy, biological sciences, and therapeutic exercise. Second-year classes include advanced needling techniques and

advanced herbal prescriptions. During the third and fourth year, discussion of clinical cases becomes an important part of the classroom experience. Students begin their clinical experience as part of a team at the college's community clinic, advancing to work as independent interns. Pacific College of Oriental Medicine, San Diego, received one of the National Institutes of Health Office of Alternative Medicine's original research grants. Among research projects done were the effects of Oriental medicine on premenstrual syndrome, acupuncture's effect on tinnitus, and body therapy's effect on the side effects of chemotherapy.

Prerequisites:
Applicants should have at least two years of undergraduate education (60 semester units or 90 quarter units). Additional biological science courses may be required for entry into the New York program (check for current minimum GPA and course descriptions).

Tuition:
In 1996/97 the total tuition for the master's of traditional Oriental medicine program offered in San Diego was $29,950 (approximately $9,983 per year). The tuition for the equivalent program offered in New York, the diploma of traditional Oriental medicine, was $32,534 ($10,845 per year).

Financial Assistance:
Pell Grants and Stafford Loans are available to eligible students.

Other Programs:
A diploma of acupuncture is offered at the New York branch. Contact Pacific Institute for more information.

Samra University of Oriental Medicine
600 St. Paul Avenue
Los Angeles, CA 90017-2014
(213) 482-8448
http://www.samra.edu

Samra University began as the Samra Institute of Healing Arts in 1969. Originally, it trained medical missionaries working in third world countries. By 1979, Samra was restructured as a university and became the first acupuncture school in California to be approved by the State Medical Board, Division of Allied Health Professions, and the first authorized by the State Department of Education to grant master's degrees in Oriental medicine.

Program:
Master of science in Oriental medicine covers acupuncture, herbology, and Oriental medicine in four academic years. This can be completed, in full-time study, in thirty-six months (the minimum required for licensure in California). Most full-time and part-time students attend classes year-round.

The master's program incorporates Asian medical traditions from Korea and Japan, as well as contemporary movements in acupuncture practiced in France, England, and America. Often the university will build seminars around study with nationally or internationally known acupuncturists to expose students to a wider range of techniques and specialties.

Samra also offers an honors master of science in Oriental medicine designed specifically to offer more intensive study in herbology and acupuncture as well as specialized training in research methodology. Each honors class is limited to twenty students.

Prerequisites:
Applicants to the regular program must have successfully completed two academic years (90 quarter units or 60 semester units) of undergraduate education.

Applicants to the honors program must have at least a bachelor's degree with a 3.0 GPA. Applicants must also sit for and achieve a strong score on Samra's own eligibility examination.

Tuition:
In 1996/97 full-time students paid approximately $5,025 per year for tuition and fees, plus an additional $700 for books and supplies. Tuition is higher for the honors program, but this program qualifies for special scholarships.

Financial Assistance:
Samra offers standard federal aid packages. The school also gives academic scholarships to participants in the honors program. These awards can range up to full equivalent of a year's tuition, and are based on academic excellence as well as need.

Application Deadline:
Quarters begin in October, January, April, and July. The program is structured so students may enter in any quarter.

Other Programs:
In addition to the honors' program described above, Samra University also has an undergraduate acupuncture internship program hosted by the Beijing College of Acupuncture and Orthopedics in Beijing. Instruction is also offered in Mandarin Chinese and Korean (students must demonstrate college-level proficiency in the foreign language as well as proficiency in English).

Santa Barbara College of Oriental Medicine
1919 State Street, Suite 204
Santa Barbara, CA 93101
(805) 898-1180

Santa Barbara College of Oriental Medicine began as the Santa Barbara branch of the California Acupuncture College. It has operated as an independent college since 1986.

Program:
The Master's Degree in Acupuncture and Oriental Medicine is a four-year academic program that can be completed in three calendar years by a full-time student. Classes include acupuncture theory and practice, Chinese herbs, Chinese nutrition, moxibustion, qi gong, and acupressure. Students also learn the fundamentals of Western medical science.

Clinical training includes one year of observation and one year of internship.

Prerequisites:
Applicants must have 60 semester units or 90 quarter units of undergraduate education, including humanities and social sciences. An anatomy course with a lab and a physiology course are required as well.

Tuition:
In 1997 the average tuition for a full-time student was $7,670 per year or $23,000 for the full program.

Financial Assistance:
The college participates in Stafford Loans, Pell Grants, and other forms of federal assistance.

Application Deadline:
Applications are due by June for entry in the fall.

Other Programs:
Due to the high level of demand for the masters program, the college was not offering any other certificate programs in 1997. Contact the college for information on continuing education.

Seattle Institute of Oriental Medicine (SIAOM)
916 NE 65th, Suite B
Seattle, WA 98115
(206) 517-4541

SIAOM is one of the newer schools. It stresses a hands-on, apprentice style of education, involving students in clinical observation from the first week of study.

Program:
This clinically based three-year program is focused on small group instruction with experienced practitioners in the school clinic. Course work includes differential diagnosis; points and palpation; *materia medica* of Chinese herbs; acupressure; qi gong; and nutrition and pharmacognosy. The acupuncture detox course taught in conjunction with work at the Evergreen Treatment Center qualifies students for National Acupuncture Detoxification Association (NADA) certification (see listing under Professional Organizations later in this chapter). SIAOM also teaches Chinese language and thought to prepare students to use Chinese medical literature.

The school has clinic and classes forty-five weeks out of the year, organized into three fifteen-week trimesters. Students spend an average of 20 hours in clinical training and didactic courses per week. All students are expected to enroll on a full-time basis.

Prerequisites:
Students must have three years of undergraduate education from an accredited college or university including human anatomy and physiology with a lab (120 hours minimum). SIAOM recommends that prospective students take at least one Western medical terminology course and one quarter of Chinese language study before starting the program.

Tuition:
In 1997 the tuition for the full program was approximately $26,250 ($8,750 per year).

Financial Assistance:
The school offered payment plans only for the 1997/98 academic year.

Application Deadline:
SIAOM enters students once a year in the fall. Due to the small class size, applicants should apply early.

Other Programs:
No other programs were listed for 1997/98.

South Baylo University (Keimyung Baylo)
1126 N. Brookhurst Street
Anaheim, CA 92801
(714) 533-1495
http://www.kbu.com

South Baylo also has a branch campus located in Los Angeles.

Program:
The master's of science degree in acupuncture and Oriental medicine is designed to meet the requirements of the California Acupuncture Committee. In addition to academic courses, students spend 840 hours in clinical training/internships. South Baylo has a study abroad program through the Beijing College of Traditional Chinese Medicine.

Prerequisites:
Applicants must have completed at least two years of undergraduate education (60 semester units or 90 quarter units).

Tuition:
In 1996/97 tuition for the entire program was $16,150 plus a $5,880 internship fee.

Financial Assistance:
The school participates in federal loan programs and work-study.

Application Deadline:
Inquiries are welcome at any time. Students seeking financial assistance should check with the financial aid office for current deadlines.

Other Programs:
Instruction is also offered in Chinese and Korean for students proficient in those languages.

Southwest Acupuncture College
325 Paseo de Peralta, Suite 500
Santa Fe, NM 87501
(505) 988-3538

Southwest has also offered classes in Albuquerque since 1993. Clinical facilities in Santa Fe include a low-cost public clinic as part of the college's commitment to broadening community exposure to acupuncture.

Program:
Students earn a master of science in Oriental medicine in 2,500 course hours (three to four years). Training emphasizes the five branches of Oriental medicine: acupuncture, herbal medicine, physical therapy, nutrition, and exercise/breathing therapy. Clinical education begins in the first term, and nearly half of the program hours are spent in the college clinic.

Students may choose between an accelerated, full-time, or part-time program. The accelerated program requires 20 to 23 hours of course work per week and can be completed in three calendar years.

The Santa Fe campus operates on a yearly schedule of two fifteen-week semesters and a ten-week summer session. The Albuquerque branch operates on a yearly schedule of three thirteen-week trimesters. Santa Fe offers only daytime classes. In Albuquerque, classes take place in the evening and on Saturday.

Prerequisites:
Applicants must be at least twenty years of age and have completed two years of general education at the college level.

Tuition:
In 1997, depending on whether students decided to take the accelerated or full-time program, costs ranged from $2,100 to $3,150 per semester. Tuition for the full program is approximately $26,439.

Financial Assistance:
The college is certified to participate in Title IV student aid programs; Stafford Loans are available to students enrolled in the master's degree program. Veteran's benefits are also available for qualified applicants.

Application Deadline:
A new program begins each fall at both the Santa Fe and Albuquerque campus. A program beginning in January may be available at the Santa Fe campus if the school receives sufficient interest from applicants.

Other Programs:
The college provides continuing education classes for the profession. Advanced clinical training programs in acupuncture and herbal medicine are held in both the summer and fall in Beijing, China, at the International Training Center of the Academy of Traditional Chinese Medicine.

Texas College of Traditional Chinese Medicine
4005 Manchaca Road, Suite 200
Austin, TX 78704
(512) 444-8082
http://www.ccsi.com/~texastcm

Texas College of Traditional Chinese Medicine emphasizes the traditional and classical understanding of Chinese medicine. Students study classical texts of Chinese medicine such as *Shan Han Lun, A Glimpse of the Golden Chamber,* and *Jin Yuan Si Da Jia.* Established in 1990, it is the oldest school of acupuncture in Texas.

Program:
The three-year (six-semester) program covers all aspects of traditional Oriental healing methodologies, with a special emphasis on acupuncture and herbology. Students spend the first year studying the fundamental integration of natural healing therapies, as well as scientific research. By the second year, students work as part of a clinical team that includes other assistants, interns, and certified acupuncturists.

Prerequisites:
Applicants must have completed at least 60 semester hours of accredited college-level course work, or hold an associates degree.

Tuition:
In 1996/97 tuition and fees were approximately $4,500 per year ($2,250 per semester) for the first year. Costs rise in the following years to approximately $2,900 per semester.

Financial Assistance:
Payment plans are available. The school began offering Foundation-based merit scholarships for eligible students in September 1997.

Application Deadline:
The school accepts applications throughout the year. New classes are entered with the beginning of each semester in mid-August or mid-February.

Other Programs:
No other programs are listed.

Tai Hsuan Foundation
Acupuncture and Herbal Medicine College
2600 S. King Street #206
Honolulu, HI 96726
(800) 942-4788 or (808) 949-1050

Mailing address:
PO Box 11130
Honolulu, HI 96728-0130

The Tai Hsuan Foundation was started by Taoist Master Chang Yi Hsiang (Dr. Lily Siou, Ph.D.) in 1970. Dr. Siou claims to be the sixty-fourth generation lineage holder of Heavenly Taoist Masters of Lung Hu Shan.

Program:
The college seeks to train professional acupuncturists and Oriental medicine practitioners by providing an integrated, disciplined, thorough education in the traditional Taoist healing arts.

The curriculum is structured to prepare individuals to pass the National Certification Exams in Acupuncture and Herbs as well as the Hawaii State Board of Acupuncture Licensing Exam.

Prerequisites:
Applicants need to have completed two years of undergraduate education from an accredited college or university.

Tuition:
In 1996/97 full-time tuition was approximately $6,600 per year.

Financial Assistance:
The college offers federal loans and veterans benefits to qualified students.

Application Deadline:
Students seeking financial assistance need to check with the college for current deadlines.

Other Programs:
The college is associated with the Tsai Hsuan Foundation, which offers various Taoist educational courses.

Traditional Acupuncture Institute (TAI) American City Building
10227 Wincopin Circle, Suite 100
Columbia, MD 21044-3422
(301) 596-6006

Program:
The M.Ac. degree can be earned in seven semesters (twenty-nine-month program) or ten semesters (forty-month program). Students must have over 500 hours of supervised clinical practice to graduate. They must also successfully complete studies in t'ai chi and qi gong as well as acupuncture.

Prerequisites:
Applicants must have a bachelor's degree from an accredited institution, 200 hours of clinical experience in a Western medical setting, and have completed studies of anatomy, physiology, and other subject areas. Check with the admissions office for a complete list of requirements.

Tuition:
In 1996/97 the total cost for the program was approximately $25,000. Cost per year varies depending on whether the student takes the seven-semester or ten-semester program.

Financial Assistance:
TAI participates in Federal financial assistance programs such as the subsidized and unsubsidized Stafford Loans.

Application Deadline:
Students seeking financial aid should check with TAI for current deadlines.

Other Programs:
TAI offers a special Chinese herbalism program, lasting two-and-half years for acupuncturists and students who have completed their third year.

Yo San University of Traditional Chinese Medicine (YSU)
1314 Second Street, Suite 200
Santa Monica, CA 90401
(310) 917-2202
http://www.yosan.edu

The founders of YSU followed the tenets of Taoism and Ni family instruction. The school's program seeks to have students blend the principles of Taoism into their practice.

Program:
The four-year program leads to a degree of master of acupuncture and traditional Chinese medicine. Students follow an integrated curriculum of traditional Chinese medicine including acupuncture, herbs, tui-na, Western science, biomedicine, and *qi* cultivation.

Students take approximately 16 units each trimester for the first three years and spend the last year in an internship in the teaching clinic.

Prerequisites:
Applicants must have two years of college general education (60 semester units or 90 quarter units) at an accredited undergraduate institution. YSU places a strong emphasis on the student's commitment to the intensive training needed to become a primary health-care provider of TCM.

Tuition:
In 1997 tuition was $29,485 for the full four-year program.

Financial Assistance:
Federal loans and work-study programs are available. Some scholarships may be available to qualified applicants.

Application Deadline:
Prospective students are encouraged to phone the admissions manager and schedule an informational interview as soon as possible. Classes begin in winter, spring, or fall.

Other Programs:
YSU offers a continuing education program for licensed acupuncturists.

Canadian Schools

Academy of Classical Oriental Sciences
533 Baker Street
Nelson, British Columbia V1L 5R2
(250) 352-5887 or (888) 333-8868 (toll-free)
http://www.acos.org

Mailing address:
PO Box 352
Nelson, British Columbia V1L 5R2

Nelson, British Columbia, is a city of 10,000 located close to major ski resorts and wilderness areas in the eastern side of the province, approximately eight hours from both Calgary and Vancouver.

Program:
The four-year program (3,500 hours) is geared to introducing students to the broad range of therapies found in the classical Chinese medical paradigm. First-year and second-year classes concentrate on introducing the students to the fundamental theories and concepts. In addition to such specific subjects as acupuncture points, herbs, and techniques of treatment, students also study the classical view of mental and emotional disharmony patterns and the effect on health.

Fourth-year studies emphasize the final preparation of students as independent practitioners of traditional Chinese medicine. Classes during the final year include business management and ethics, supervised clinical practice, research techniques, and a thesis project.

Prerequisites:
Students should have two years of postsecondary education. Some educational prerequisites may be waived for "mature students" (contact the admissions office for more information).

Tuition:
In 1996/97 tuition for the September to April program was $5,800 CDN per academic year.

Financial Assistance:
Financial aid may be available through the Canada Student Assistance program.

Application Deadline:
Applications are accepted from October 15 to July 15 for entrance into the September class. Applications received after July 15 are reviewed subject to availability of space. Preference is given to applicants interested in attending full-time, but some part-time applicants are accepted on a space-available basis.

Other Programs:
The school offers continuing education classes in the summer.

Canadian College of Acupuncture and Oriental Medicine
  (CCAOM)
855 Cormorant Street
Victoria, British Columbia V8W 1R2
(250) 384-2942

CCAOM started in 1985 as a part of the Canadian College for Chinese Studies. In 1991 it became a separate organization directed by the nonprofit East West Medical Society. CCAOM is registered with the Private Post Secondary Education Commission of British Columbia. The college bookstore, located at 853 Cormorant Street, is open to the public and provides books at a discount to students.

Program:
CCAOM offers a four-year, full-time course of study in traditional Chinese medicine (TCM). The core curriculum includes Chinese acupuncture and herbology, basic Western medical sciences, and related holistic therapies.

First-year instruction concentrates on giving students a grounding in the theory and philosophy of traditional Chinese medicine, point location, and introductory Chinese *materia medica* (herbology). Western anatomy and physiology (as well as surface anatomy) are also taught during this time. Other classes include t'ai chi and basic Jin Shin Do acupressure. First-year students have one semester of clinical observation.

By the second year, students receive more instruction in TCM diagnosis and syndromes, point energetics and location, acupuncture therapeutics and techniques, and classical herbal prescriptions. Students study Western pathology, receive training in basic counseling and communication skills, and participate in two semesters of clinical observation.

At the college's clinic, clinical interns treat patients for a wide variety of conditions under faculty supervision. Other courses include comparative East/West medicine and clinical lectures.

Prerequisites:
Students must have at least two years of postsecondary education, including course work in anatomy and physiology (check with the college for current hours requirements).

Tuition:
In 1997 tuition was $5,500 CDN per year. An extra $500 to $600 may be spent on books and supplies in the first year.

Financial Assistance:
Full-time students may qualify for assistance under the guidelines of the Canada Student Loan Program.

Application Deadline:
Applications close on June 30. Prospective students should apply early. Classes begin in September.

Other Programs:
Some continuing education classes are offered.

Ontario College of Acupuncture and Chinese Medicine
658 Danforth Avenue, Suite 413
Toronto, Ontario M4J 1L1
(416) 560-2340

The Ontario College of Acupuncture and Chinese Medicine is registered with the Ontario Ministry of Education for the purpose of establishing and maintaining the professional standards for the use of acupuncture and Chinese herbal medicine.

Program:
This advanced professional training program takes approximately eighteen months to complete. Students attend part-time in the evening. The program was designed to provide students with solid

background in acupuncture and Chinese herbal therapy. The program has a total of 560 hours including 260 hours of home-study. An optional study program in China may be available to qualified students.

Although acupuncture was not regulated in Ontario at the time of publication, the college will help students prepare for licensing examinations through in-class teaching and homework.

Prerequisites:
Applicants must have completed a postsecondary education in humanities or sciences. Applicants who do not meet these academic requirements but have related training or experience will be considered on an individual basis.

Tuition:
In 1996/97 the entire program cost approximately $4,500 CDN, not including books, supplies, and miscellaneous fees.

Financial Assistance:
Check with the admissions office.

Application Deadline:
Applications must be made before August 15 to begin in September.

Other Programs:
Some classes are open to the public. Contact the college about continuing education classes.

PROFESSIONAL ORGANIZATIONS AND OTHER EDUCATIONAL RESOURCES

American Association of Oriental Medicine
433 Front Street
Catasauqua, PA 18032
(610) 266-1433

The American Association of Oriental Medicine, formerly known as the American Association of Acupuncture and Oriental Medicine, holds annual conferences and works on issues pertaining to Oriental medicine.

National Acupuncture Detoxification Association
3220 N Street NW, Suite 275
Washington, DC 20007
(503) 222-1362

The National Acupuncture Detoxification Association (NADA) promotes the use of acupuncture as a detoxification technique through public education; training and certification of professionals; consultation on the establishment of treatment sites; and distribution of NADA-approved literature, audiotapes, and videotapes. Clinicians who wish to become certified in the NADA protocols must work under a NADA Registered Teacher, participating in a 30-hour classroom/didactic training course followed by 40 hours of hands-on work in a clinic. To find out more about certification or to locate a Registered Teacher, contact NADA.

National Acupuncture and Oriental Medicine Alliance
14637 Starr Road SE
Olalla, WA 98359
(206) 851-6896

The National Acupuncture and Oriental Medicine Alliance was formed in 1993 to represent the diversity of practitioners of acupuncture and Oriental medicine in the United States. Voting membership in the National Alliance is restricted to individuals who are state licensed, registered, or certified to practice acupuncture or Oriental medicine based on standards of competency, who are nationally certified in acupuncture or Oriental medicine by the NCCAOM, or who have graduated from an Accreditation Commission for Acupuncture and Oriental Medicine (ACAOM) accredited or candidacy program and are now practicing in an unregulated state. Consumers, schools, other health-care providers, organizations, corporate sponsors, and others may join as nonvoting members.

✨CONTINUING EDUCATION

Many states require acupuncturists to take continuing education courses to maintain their license. Most of the schools listed above offer continuing education classes and seminars for practitioners. For additional training in a particular field, such as herbology or shiatsu, refer to the chapters in part 3.

Blue Poppy Seminars
c/o Blue Poppy Press Inc.
1775 Linden Avenue
Boulder, CO 80304
(800) 448-8372
e-mail: bpsem@aol.com

Blue Poppy Press is well-known as one of the larger publishers of TCM books in the United States. In 1997 and 1998 it offered a variety of seminars throughout the United States on topics ranging from allergies to TCM pediatrics. The weekend seminars were approved as NCCAOM continuing education units (CEUs). Contact Blue Poppy for a current calendar.

✂ ADDING ACUPUNCTURE TO AN ESTABLISHED PRACTICE

UNITED STATES

In many states, MDs, DOs, and DCs are allowed to practice acupuncture under their current license and they do not have to take the NCCAOM exams. Often, they need to take far fewer hours of training than a three-year or four-year acupuncture program offers before adding acupuncture to their practice. The number of hours of training required varies, and the practitioner should check with the appropriate state medical boards.

Many of the US schools listed in this chapter offer night classes or part-time programs designed for health professionals to receive training in acupuncture without disrupting their current practice. The American Academy of Medical Acupuncture also provides training classes for physicians.

The American Academy of Medical Acupuncture
5820 Wilshire Boulevard, Suite 500
Los Angeles, CA 90036

CANADA

The Canadian Medical Acupuncture Society has developed a Certificate Program in Medical Acupuncture (CPMA) designed for physicians, dentists, physical therapists, and other eligible health-care professionals. The 200-hour program teaches the fundamentals and clinical applications of acupuncture for health professionals who wish to add this type of therapy to their practice.

The program has been recognized by the College of Physicians and Surgeons of Alberta, British Columbia, Saskatchewan, and the Yukon, as well as by the College of Family Physicians of Canada. For more information, contact the Canadian Medical Acupuncture Society.

Canadian Medical Acupuncture Society
9904-106 Street NW
Edmonton, Alberta T5K 1C4
(403) 426-2760

✌Recommended Reading

Eckman, Peter. *In the Footsteps of the Yellow Emperor.* San Francisco: Cypress Book Company, 1996.

> This fascinating history traces the development of several different types of acupuncture in the East and the development of Five Elements acupuncture in the West. Those interested in Five Elements or Worsley methods of acupuncture will especially enjoy this book.

Kaptchuk, Ted J. *The Web That Has No Weaver: Understanding Chinese Medicine.* Chicago: Congdon & Weed, 1983.

> Kaptchuk explains the basic theories behind Traditional Chinese Medicine in an unusually lucid fashion. Students of the Eight Principles or TCM type of acupuncture generally read this in their first year of study.

National Acupuncture Foundation. *Acupuncture and Oriental Medicine Laws,* updated annually.

> This book is available through the National Acupuncture Foundation, 1718 M Street, Suite 195, Washington, D.C. 20036,(202) 332-5794. The text reviews laws pertaining to acupuncture in the United States.

3

Chiropractic Doctor (DC)

Chiropractic health care focuses on the relationship between the spinal column and the nervous system. Chiropractors learn how to make adjustments to the spine to alleviate problems caused by "subluxations," or misalignment of the vertebrae.

Many chiropractors today use other therapeutic techniques besides spinal manipulation. These techniques may include soft tissue manipulation, counseling patients on ergonomics, giving advice on nutrition, or teaching various forms of stress reduction. Some chiropractors use therapies such as water, light, ultrasound, electric, or heat. Chiropractic doctors do not prescribe drugs or perform surgery.

The American Chiropractic Association (ACA) estimates that approximately 50,000 chiropractic doctors saw more than 19 million patients in 1996, making it one of the largest and best-known forms of natural health care available in the United States. Chiropractic doctors surveyed by the ACA say that muscular, nervous system, and skeletal problems account for approximately 85 percent of all conditions treated. The other 15 percent includes visceromotor, vascular-related, and metabolic/nutritional problems.

Chiropractic colleges date back to 1897, when the first college was founded in Davenport, Iowa, by D. D. Palmer (1845–1913). Today there are fifteen colleges in the United States and one Canadian college recognized by the Council on Chiropractic Education. Chiropractic students study basic life sciences as well as various chiropractic and related therapies. Different schools emphasize different branches of chiropractic philosophy, but all structure their programs to satisfy the national licensing requirements.

To become licensed, students must pass a three- or four-part national exam administered by the National Board of Chiropractic Examiners (NBCE). Sections of this exam are taken during the student's tenure at school, and passing may be required before the student can advance to the next level of study.

Parts 1 and 2 of the National Board Exam cover the basic science subjects (general anatomy, spinal anatomy, physiology, pathology, chemistry, microbiology, and public health) and the clinical sciences (general diagnosis, neuromusculoskeletal diagnosis, X-ray, principles of chiropractic, chiropractic practice, and associated clinical sciences). Physiotherapy is an elective subject, and may be taken with either part 1 or 2.

Parts 3 and 4 are usually taken after graduation, but students within six months of graduation may take the exam. Part 3 is a written clinical competency examination covering such topics as case history, physical examination, clinical lab, neuromusculoskeletal examination, roentgenologic examination, special studies examination, diagnosis and clinical impression, chiropractic techniques, and case management.

Part 4 is a practical examination developed to test the candidate's clinical performance. It includes such sections as X-ray interpretation as well as an observed examination of "patients" played by actors. Some states now use part 4 instead of an individual state exam for licensure.

Upon graduation, students receive a doctor of chiropractic (DC) degree. They must also complete those sections of national board exams not yet taken as well as various written or oral examinations, according to the licensing requirements of their state or province.

As with other natural medicine professions, most chiropractic doctors choose to establish their own practice, although the large number of chiropractic clinics in North America makes it reasonably easy for the newly licensed chiropractor to find work in an established practice.

Unlike some of the other natural medicine professions, most federal and state worker compensation plans recognize and reimburse for chiropractic treatments. Many insurance plans also recognize this type of treatment.

The ACA reports that chiropractic doctors enjoy income levels equivalent to that of any primary care physician. In 1994 the average income was $75,000 after expenses, with the lowest 10 percent earning $28,000 or less and the highest 10 percent earning $150,000 or more. The typical practitioner works five days a week.

Chiropractic doctors may also take advanced certification in a variety of areas, including chiropractic orthopedics, nutrition, thermology, and sports injuries. Continuing education programs vary from college to college, ranging from specialized certification programs to continuing education credits designed to keep chiropractic doctors up-to-date and satisfy the requirements of licensing.

For those interested in research work, all of the colleges have some type of research facility, and many offer research grants to both faculty and students. The American Spinal Research Foundation in the United States, and the Chiropractic Foundation for Spinal Research in Canada, both fund chiropractic research. The Foundation for Chiropractic Education and Research also funds research fellowships for chiropractic doctors seeking research training or advanced degrees in the basic sciences or health related areas.

The majority of students at the chiropractic colleges are male and in their mid-twenties. In 1996 the ACA reported that only 30 percent of all chiropractic students were women, but that this figure was expected to rise.

COST OF EDUCATION

You should budget between $11,000 and $20,000 per year for your education. The wide variance in cost comes from number of credit hours taken during a calendar year rather than a wide range in tuition fees.

Some programs are structured along the four-quarter academic year; others follow a trimester system with three trimesters per calendar year. Many colleges offer an intensive program that allows students to stay in school throughout the year. Although an intensive program allows students to complete school more quickly, the tuition bills are concentrated in three years rather than spread out over four or five years.

Like most medical students, chiropractic students find the academic requirements of the DC degree do not leave much time for outside employment. Also, many schools will only accept full-time students.

Most of the American chiropractic colleges provide a mix of financial aid, including federally funded grants and loans; state-funded grants and loans; private foundation grants and loans; state chiropractic association or auxiliary scholarships; and college and alumni association-funded scholarships. A specialized loan program called ChiroLoan is designed for chiropractic students and available through most of the schools. Some also provide special financial aid packages for foreign students.

Students work with the financial aid officer at their institution to determine the financial aid package appropriate for their situation. As with the other professions, students generally finance their education through a mix of loans, work, and aid from their families.

There are chiropractic colleges in every region of the United States. If you don't live near a college, you will need to factor the cost of housing into your education. Some colleges have dormitory space available, while others provide information on student housing off-campus.

Following graduation and licensing, chiropractors may set up a new practice, purchase an established one, or enter into partnership with an established practitioner. These costs vary from region to region, and most colleges offer some counseling in this area. Some schools provide intensive business courses in the senior year to lessen the impact of moving into private practice.

Tuition figures listed below are based on the average cost of attending the school in a given year, and should be used for general comparison only. Contact the school's admission office for current tuition requirements as well as any additional expenses, such as lab fees, equipment costs, and even graduation fees.

LENGTH OF TRAINING

Most chiropractic programs require a minimum of four academic years of professional resident study. Some, such as the Cleveland College program, can be completed in three years.

In a four-year program, the structure and function of the human body in health and disease is taught through a combination of lectures and lab courses during the first two years of study. These classes emphasize the biological and basic sciences as well as the clinical disciplines. The final two years emphasize practical or clinical studies dealing with the diagnosis and treatment of disease, and students spend approximately half their time in college clinics or internships at chiropractic practices. A number of colleges also add special seminars during the senior year on establishing a business; and some colleges also require final-year students to complete a paper based on a chiropractic research project.

✌ADMISSIONS PROCESS

The length of time that an applicant should allow for the admission process varies widely from institution to institution. Colleges that admit classes only once a year suggest starting the application process at least a year before the desired admission date. Schools that enter classes at the beginning of each semester or trimester generally set their admissions deadlines six to nine months before the desired admissions date.

In addition to the standard application form, candidates may be required to write a personal essay or provide letters of reference. Some schools require a personal interview. Check with the college's admissions department. Most colleges do require a nonrefundable applications fee.

✌UNDERGRADUATE PREREQUISITES

Traditionally, chiropractic colleges required students to have a minimum of two years of undergraduate education. However, by 1993, approximately 40 percent of entering students had bachelor's degrees or better. Recent articles on chiropractic education indicate that four years of undergraduate education with an entering grade point average (GPA) of more than 3.0 is becoming the norm. In fact, some states require that chiropractic doctors have a four-year bachelor's degree as well as the doctor of chiropractic degree in order to qualify for a license. Some chiropractic colleges also offer a bachelor of sciences degree, which can be taken concurrently with the chiropractic program.

Many state and community colleges have developed pre-chiropractic programs similar to premed programs to satisfy the requirements of the chiropractic colleges. Your local undergraduate institution may have such a program, or may be able to recommend one in your area.

Prerequisites shown for the schools date from 1996/97 entrance requirements. These should be regarded as the bare minimum needed, and you should also check with the institution to make sure that these requirements have not changed. Many of the colleges increased the minimum GPA required in 1997 for 1998 entrance.

✌LICENSING AND ACCREDITATION

UNITED STATES

Chiropractic doctors may be licensed to practice chiropractic medicine in all fifty states and the District of Columbia. To qualify for licensure, students must graduate from an accredited college and pass both national and state boards. All licensed chiropractors are usually entitled to use either the title of doctor of chiropractic (DC) and/or chiropractic physician.

Most states also require that chiropractors complete a specified number of continuing education credits each year. These classes are offered by the colleges as well as the state chiropractic associations. The exact scope of the chiropractic license varies from state to state. To learn more about your state's regulations, contact the Federation of Chiropractic Licensing Boards. The Council on Chiropractic Education (CCE) and its Commission on Accreditation are recognized by the US Department of Education as the accrediting body for chiropractic colleges.

Council on Chiropractic Education (CCE)
7975 North Ayden Road, #A-210
Scottsdale, AZ 85258

Federation of Chiropractic Licensing Boards
901 54th Avenue #101
Greeley, CO 80634

CANADA

Chiropractic doctors have licensing in all provinces in Canada. Check with the Canadian Council on Chiropractic Education for provincial requirements and local organizations. There is only one chiropractic college in Canada, which was under review for reciprocal accreditation from the United States' Council on Chiropractic Education in 1996/97.

Canadian Council on Chiropractic Education
130-10100 Shellbridge Way
Richmond, British Columbia V6W 2W7
(604) 270-1332

OTHER COUNTRIES

Chiropractic doctors are also regulated or licensed in Australia, Bolivia, Cyprus, Guam, Iceland, Liechtenstein, Mexico, New Zealand, Norway, Panama, Puerto Rico, Sweden, Switzerland, South Africa, West Germany, and Zimbabwe. The profession is also acknowledged, but not licensed at the time of publication, in Bermuda, the British Isles, Denmark, Israel, Italy, Japan, Peru, Singapore, and Venezuela.

US Schools

The following colleges are accredited by the CCE or are candidates for accreditation at the time of publication. Many of the chiropractic colleges have also achieved regional accreditation.

Cleveland Chiropractic College, Kansas City (KC)
6401 Rockhill Road
Kansas City, MO 64131
(816) 333-8230 or (800) 467-CCKC (toll-free)

Branch Campus:
Cleveland Chiropractic College, Los Angeles (LA)
590 North Vermont Avenue
Los Angeles, CA 90004
(213) 660-6166 or (800) 466-CCLA (toll-free)
http://www.clevelandchiropractic.edu

Cleveland Chiropractic College maintains campuses in Kansas City, Missouri, and Los Angeles, California. Both grant the doctor of chiropractic (DC) degree. Cleveland (LA) was established in 1950 by the Cleveland family.

Program:
The Cleveland (KC) degree program allows the students to choose between a twelve-trimester program (four years) or a nine-trimester program (three years). The Cleveland (LA) degree program can be finished in ten trimesters (forty months). The final trimesters at each institution are devoted primarily to clinical practice under the supervision of licensed doctors of chiropractic.

Cleveland (KC) divides the curriculum into two main areas: basic sciences (anatomy, physiology, chemistry and pathology, microbiology, and public health) and clinical sciences (diagnosis, radiology, and principles and practice). The Cleveland (LA) curriculum is separated into three departments: basic sciences (anatomy, physiology, microbiology, chemistry, and public health), clinical sciences (diagnosis and radiology), and chiropractic sciences.

Both campuses maintain public clinics that provide practical experience for the students. Research facilities at both campuses create opportunities for clinical and basic science research. Students may participate in research in cooperation with faculty and may be eligible for further financial assistance for research.

Prerequisites:
Students must have completed a minimum of 60 semester units or 90 quarter units of undergraduate education, including English/communications, humanities/social sciences, psychology, and biological sciences. Check with the schools for more information, such as lab requirements and types of courses considered acceptable.

Tuition:
In 1996/97 Cleveland (KC) charged $156 per contact hour. The tuition at Cleveland (LA) was $4,800 per trimester for the ten-trimester program ($14,400 per year) based on full-time enrollment. The campuses do not charge additional out-of-state, laboratory, or graduation fees.

Financial Assistance:
Cleveland Chiropractic College offers the standard federal loan programs as well as private loan programs including TERI Loans, Professional Education Program Loan, Grad Excel, Option 4, ChiroLoan, and Ultimate Graduate Loan. Students should also inquire about private grants and scholarships.

Application Deadline:
Cleveland (LA) suggests prospective students apply no later than nine months before the desired starting date. Cleveland (LA) admits three classes per year starting in January, May, or September. Cleveland (KC) accepts inquiries throughout the year; check with the admissions office for current deadlines.

Other Programs:
Cleveland (KC) offers a bachelor of science degree in human biology.

Life College
1269 Barclay Circle
Marietta, GA 30060
(770) 426-2884 or (800) 543-3202 (toll-free)

Life College underwent a $14-million modernization of the campus in 1989, followed by a $37-million expansion begun in 1996. The Nell K. Williams Learning Resource Center on the campus has a collection of 70,000 books, periodicals, and audiovisual aids. The college is also accredited by the Southern Association of Colleges and Schools.

Program:
The chiropractic doctor degree requires fourteen academic quarters of study and includes courses in basic and clinical sciences and other health-related subjects, as well as an internship at one of three outpatient clinics. Unlike some other colleges, patient care can begin as soon as the seventh quarter. Special emphasis is placed on the relationship between structural and neurological aspects of the body in health and disease.

Students participate in research designed not only to provide data about chiropractic phenomena but to also develop the students' natural talents and encourage them to accept roles of health-care leadership.

Prerequisites:
Applicants must have completed a minimum of 60 semester hours or 90 quarter hours of undergraduate college classes, including organic chemistry, inorganic chemistry, physics, biology, English, psychology, and humanities/social sciences. Science courses must have a lab component.

Tuition:
In 1997 tuition was approximately $3,200 per quarter, or $152 per quarter hour. Laboratory fees vary by course.

Financial Assistance:
Life participates in the various federal programs including work-study, Perkins Loan, and the Stafford Student Loan. Contact the financial aid office for more information about the Life College Foreign Student Loan, other scholarships, and various state loan programs.

Application Deadline:
Prospective students are encouraged to apply four to six months before the desired admissions date. Four classes are admitted each year starting in January, April, July, or October.

Other Programs:
Life College also offers a BS nutrition for chiropractic science; a BS dietetics; and a bachelor of business administration.

Life Chiropractic College West
2005 Via Barrett
San Lorenzo, CA 94580
(510) 276-9013 or (800) 788-4476 (toll-free)
http://www.lifewest.edu

This school was founded in 1976 as Pacific States Chiropractic College. It became Life Chiropractic College West in 1981.

Program:
The program lasts for four academic years, but can be completed in three calendar years. Although course work covers all the basic medical sciences, the college emphasizes the teaching of chiropractic technique and philosophy as "envisioned by the founders of our profession."

The first two years concentrate on the biological sciences related to chiropractic medicine. The last two years (quarters seven through twelve) deal primarily with clinical training, diagnosis, and treatment techniques. The student clinic sees 1,500 to 1,600 patients per week.

Prerequisites:
Applicants must have completed at least 60 semester hours of under-graduate college work including course work in biology, physics, organic chemistry, inorganic chemistry, English, psychology, and social sciences/humanities. Applicants should contact the college for the current minimum GPA and lab requirements.

Tuition:
In 1997 tuition was $16,000 per year ($4,000 per quarter).

Financial Assistance:
The college offers all normal forms of financial aid, including federal loan programs, work-study, and veterans' benefits.

Application Deadline:
Applications are due by February 1 for entrance in the spring quarter, May 1 for summer, August 1 for fall, and November 1 for winter. Quarters begin in April, July, October, and January.

Other Programs:
The college offers continuing education, license renewal courses, and certification in specific areas of treatment for chiropractic doctors.

Logan College of Chiropractic
1851 Schoettler Road
PO Box 1065
Chesterfield, MO 63006-1065
(314) 227-2100 or (800) 533-9210 (toll-free)

Logan is accredited by the CCE, and by the Commission on Institutions of Higher Education of the North Central Association of Colleges and Schools. Recently, the college built a new $3.1 million science and research building with state-of-the-art laboratories. The outpatient health center participates in the clinical research program, using its patient population, treatment rooms, clinical lab, and computer facility.

Program:
Students should plan on taking ten trimesters or five academic years to complete the doctor of chiropractic degree. A minimum of three trimesters is spent in outpatient work either at the college or at one of the satellite health centers. The last trimester in residence includes an intern associate program that is open to all qualified students in residence.

The curriculum provides courses in special chiropractic techniques, including the Logan system of body mechanics. Adjunctive procedures, including physical therapy, office procedures and patient management, and diagnostic and case management, plus specialized courses in chiropractic general studies, are an important part of the curriculum.

All students must prepare and complete a research project under the direction of the Research Department. Logan College also offers a special on-campus competitive residency program in roentgenology, which requires specific research.

Prerequisites:
Applicants must have successfully completed a minimum of 60 semester hours at an accredited college or university. Subject areas must include biology, general and organic chemistry, physics, psychology, communication arts, and social sciences/humanities.

Tuition:
In 1997 tuition averaged $13,380 per year ($4,460 per trimester), and books cost approximately $945 per academic year.

Financial Assistance:
In addition to the standard federal and state aid packages, Logan College also has available scholarships and grants provided by alumni and friends. Special stipends are granted to students participating in the residency programs. Information about financial aid is sent to prospective students.

Application Deadline:
Logan has a rolling applications system. Students may enter in January, May, or September. The admissions department recommends completing the applications process at least two months in advance of desired entry date. Students needing financial aid may need to begin the process much earlier.

Other Programs:
The Postdoctoral and Related Education Department offers special programs for continuing education credit at the license-renewal level. At the undergraduate level, students may earn a bachelor of science degree in human biology.

Los Angeles College of Chiropractic (LACC)
16200 East Amber Valley Drive
PO Box 1166
Whittier, CA 90609-1166
(310) 947-8755 or (800) 221-5222 (toll-free)

LACC was founded in 1911 in Los Angeles, but later moved to its present thirty-nine acre campus in Whittier, approximately fifteen miles southeast of Los Angeles.

Program:
In 1990, LACC remodeled its program to emphasize patient care experiences for students from their first year on. Most students complete the program in approximately three years. The integrated approach to adjustive procedures includes Gonstead, Cox/flexion and distraction, Thompson, sacro-occipital technique, Nimmo, muscle energy, and soft tissue procedures. In addition to clinic internships, some hospital rotations with observations are available through the Coast Plaza Doctors Hospital and Whittier Hospital Medical Center.

Prerequisites:
The following undergraduate science courses should be the equivalent of one academic year, and include a lab component: biological science, inorganic chemistry, organic chemistry, and general physics. Botany or marine biology are not acceptable substitutes for the biological sciences requirement. Students also need 6 semester units of English/ communications; 3 semester units of psychology; and 15 semester units of social sciences/humanities.

Tuition:
In 1997 the average tuition for full-time students was $5,311 per trimester or $15,933 per year.

Financial Assistance:
The school participates in the standard federal loan programs and has endowment scholarships available for eligible applicants.

Application Deadline:
Prospective students should submit applications no less than twelve months before the desired admissions date. Students may start in January or September. A personal interview is required, but out-of-state or regional interviews might be available.

Other Programs:
LACC provides continuing education and postgraduate courses.

National College of Chiropractic
200 East Roosevelt Road
Lombard, IL 60148-4583
(630) 629-2000 or (800) 826-NATL (toll-free)

Founded in 1906, the 32-acre suburban campus is located near Chicago, Illinois.

Program:
National's program leads to the doctor of chiropractic degree, and also gives the student the option of earning a bachelor of science in human biology. All students are full-time.

The ten-trimester program lasts for five academic years, but can be finished in three and one-third calendar years. The total number of credit hours for the chiropractic course of study is approximately 240. Students take an average number of 25 credit hours per trimester.

The basic curriculum is divided between problem-base, and practical instruction in the basic and clinical sciences, and an intensive clinical internship in one of seven college-operated modern health-care facilities.

Besides meeting the requirements of state licensing boards, the college will also help prepare students to sit for international board examinations.

National offers five training residencies for students in clinical practice, clinical research, family practice, radiology and diagnostic imaging, and orthopedics.

Prerequisites:
Students need to take the following science courses with a lab component: chemistry, organic chemistry, physics, and biological sciences. Hours required vary depending on whether the classes are held on a quarter or semester basis. Other required courses include English/communications, humanities/social sciences, and psychology.

Tuition:
In 1997 tuition was approximately $5,500 per trimester or $16,500 per year. Students should also budget extra for books, diagnostic instruments, and supplies.

Financial Assistance:
The financial aid office offers assistance with traditional federal and state grants and loans as well as scholarships and employment on campus.

Application Deadline:
Prospective students should begin the applications process at least twelve months before the desired entrance date. Classes are admitted in January, May, and September.

Other Programs:
Continuing education classes offered through National's postgraduate and continuing education division are held throughout the United States. National also offers a B.Sc. in human biology for chiropractic students.

New York Chiropractic College (NYCC)
2360 Route 89
Seneca Falls, NY 13148-0800
(315) 568-3040 or (800) 234-6922 (toll-free)

Originally established in 1919 as the Columbia College of Chiropractic, NYCC now operates a fifty acre facility, largely renovated in 1991, in Seneca Falls, New York. The college is also accredited by the Middle States Association of Colleges.

Program:
The five-year academic program lasts for ten trimesters, and is open only to full-time students. Since the college offers classes throughout the year, students can complete the program in forty months of continuous study. Students spend two trimesters as interns at one of NYCC's three outpatient clinics.

Prerequisites:
Approximately 60 percent of the entering student body had a BA/BS degree. Prerequisite science courses include biology, chemistry, organic chemistry, and physics. Other prerequisites include English, psychology, and humanities/social sciences.

Tuition:
In 1997 the average tuition and fees for the calendar year (three trimesters) were estimated at $15,140. Textbooks, equipment, and supplies can add up to $2,100 per year ($700 per trimester).

Financial Assistance:
Besides federal sources of aid, limited grants are available under New York State's Tuition Assistance Program (TAP). Students may also compete for scholarships offered by chiropractic associations, private foundations, and NYCC.

Application Deadline:
Prospective students should begin the admissions process at least twelve months before the desired starting date. NYCC starts new classes in January, May, and September.

Other Programs:
Continuing education is offered through the college's postgraduate division for the professional development of chiropractors and to satisfy the license renewal requirements of various states. The college also has several 3+1 BS/DC agreements with other institutions in New York so that students can save a year in the completion of the two degrees. Call the college's admission office for more information on this program.

Northwestern College of Chiropractic (NWCC)
2501 West 84th Street
Bloomington, Ma 55431
(612) 888-4777 or (800) 888-4777 (toll-free)

NWCC was established in 1941, and was one of the earliest colleges to use field clinicians to tutor students during the last term of enrollment. The college holds to a total enrollment of not more than 600 students to insure as much individual instruction as possible.

Program:
NWCC offers a ten-trimester (three terms per year) program. Students may also pursue a concurrent bachelor of science degree in human biology.

NWCC divides the chiropractic curriculum into three parts: basic sciences, clinical sciences (including diagnosis, radiology, and chiropractic principles and integrated methods), and clinical (intern) experience in one of the five clinics.

Students may gain more in-depth clinical experience through the chiropractic physician's associate program by spending their last academic term as associates in private practices of participating doctors of chiropractic.

Prerequisites:
Students must have the following science courses with lab: biology, inorganic chemistry, organic chemistry, and physics. Students must also have completed classes in English/communication arts, psychology, and humanities/social sciences. Check with the college's admissions department for total number of hours required.

Tuition:
In 1997 the average tuition for a full-time student was approximately $4,800 per trimester ($14,400 per year). Students should also budget approximately $1,100 per year for books and equipment. Other incidental fees may occur.

Financial Assistance:
Standard federal and state loans and grant programs, as well as assistance in finding state and private scholarships, are available through NWCC's financial aid office.

Application Deadline:
Students should apply nine to twelve months before the desired starting date. Classes are admitted in January, April, and September.

Other Programs:
NWCC offers a bachelor of science degree for chiropractic students.

Palmer College of Chiropractic
1000 Brady Street
Davenport, IA 52803
(319) 326-9656 or (800) 722-3648 (toll-free)

Palmer, founded in 1897, is the oldest college of chiropractic in the United States. The library probably has the largest collection of chiropractic publications in the world. In 1991, Palmer joined with its sister college in California to form the Palmer Chiropractic University System. Both colleges maintain that chiropractic care should focus primarily on chiropractic adjustment and such therapies as exercise, nutrition, ergonomics and posture, physiotherapy/ancillary procedures, extremity adjustments, patient education, case management, and participation in coordinated care. The colleges do not accept certain practices or procedures as an appropriate form of chiropractic care including drugs, surgery, acupuncture, colonic irrigation, obstetrics, reduction of fractures, and manipulation or adjustment under anesthesia.

Program:
The ten-trimester doctor of chiropractic program can be completed in three years and four months if the student enrolls in three terms each year. Trimesters begin in October, February, and July.

Palmer College strongly encourages student involvement in faculty research activity to ensure that its graduates are familiar with the most recent developments in the field of chiropractic.

Course work is divided generally into the basic sciences (anatomy, physiology, pathology, and chemistry); preclinical subjects (X-ray, diagnosis, and chiropractic technique), and clinical training. Palmer emphasizes the philosophy of chiropractic throughout all of its courses.

Prerequisites:
Applicants must have a minimum of 60 semester hours completed at an accredited college or university, including courses in the usual premedical sciences, social sciences, and humanities.

Tuition:
In 1997 tuition was $14,460 per year ($4,820 per trimester), not including books, supplies, and other fees.

Financial Assistance:
The financial planning office offers help with federal grants and loans as well as Iowa Tuition Grants (Iowa residents only), Palmer College scholarships, and a variety of scholarships offered at the state or association level.

Application Deadline:
The admissions office suggests beginning the process up to a year in advance of the desired starting date. Classes enter in March, July, or October.

Other Programs:
A bachelor of science degree in general science is conferred independently of but in conjunction with the doctor of chiropractic degree.

Palmer College of Chiropractic West
90 East Tasman Drive
San Jose, Ca 95134
(408) 944-6024 or (800) 442-4476 (toll-free)
http://www.palmer.edu

Palmer College of Chiropractic West, the sister college of Palmer College of Chiropractic, was founded in 1980 and received full accreditation in 1985 from the CCE. In 1991, the two colleges formed the Palmer Chiropractic University System (see above).

Program:
The basic sciences are emphasized in the first half of this four-year program (thirteen quarters). The clinical sciences are the primary focus in the second half. Chiropractic principles and procedures are taught throughout the curriculum.

The curriculum is generally organized into three areas: life sciences (anatomy, chemistry, physics, and physiology); diagnosis (geriatrics, laboratory diagnosis, microbiology, obstetrics, pathology, pediatrics, physical diagnosis, and roentgenology); and practice (clinical practice, principles and philosophy, and therapeutic procedures).

Students may choose from an elective program of various chiropractic procedures and related subjects. These are also required to complete two research courses.

Students spend their ninth to twelfth quarters of study treating patients in the college's community clinics. One facility is based on campus, and there are two satellite clinics located in San Jose and Santa Clara.

In the thirteenth quarter, students participate in a preceptorship program to gain real-world experience by working in chiropractic offices. During this practice development quarter, students also attend a state board review course and seminars on patient and practice management.

Prerequisites:
Applicants must have completed a minimum of 60 semester units at an accredited college or university. Required courses include biology (environmental biology or botany are not acceptable); general chemistry, organic chemistry (combined organic-biochemistry classes are not acceptable); physics; English or communication arts (at least one English composition course required); psychology; and humanities/ social sciences. In 1997, the minimum GPA was raised to 2.5 GPA on a 4.0 scale for entry in fall 1998 or later.

Tuition:
In 1997 the average tuition was estimated at $4,070 per quarter, with additional book costs of $450 per quarter. Equipment purchases for the entire course of study generally do not exceed $600.

Financial Assistance:
Standard federal and state sources of financial aid are available. Students may also qualify for the institutional student work program. Palmer West also certifies eligibility for veterans' benefits and provides information on state and private donor scholarships.

Application Deadline:
The college admits new students in January, March, July, and September. Check with the college for current financial aid deadlines.

Other Programs:
Palmer West offers continuing education classes and seminars for chiropractic doctors.

Parker College of Chiropractic
2500 Walnut Hill Lane
Dallas, Texas 75229-5668
(214) 438-6932 or (800) GET-MY-DC (toll-free)
http://www.parkercc.edu

Parker College of Chiropractic is also accredited by the Commission on Colleges of the Southern Association of Colleges and Schools.

Program:
The four-year academic program (three calendar years of nine trimesters) strongly reflects the philosophy of its founder, Dr. James W. Parker, who developed "Seminars of the Parker School for Professional Success (PSPS)." These seminars are included in students' basic education. Along with regular training in the science, philosophy, and art of chiropractic, course work covers the basic and clinical sciences, jurisprudence issues, office procedure, and business management.

Prerequisites:
A BA is preferred for entering students. Applicants must show 6 semester hours or 9 quarter hours in the following sciences: biological sciences, chemistry, organic chemistry, and physics. All science courses must include a lab. Other prerequisites include English, psychology, and humanities/social sciences.

Tuition:
In 1997 the average tuition was $4,500 per trimester. Books and lab fees add approximately $618 per trimester.

Financial Assistance:
In addition to the standard federal, state, and scholarship programs, students also have access to the ChiroLoan program, available specifically to chiropractic students.

Application Deadline:
Prospective students are encouraged to apply twelve months before the desired starting date, and applications must be received no later than three months before the admissions date. New classes enter in January, May, and September.

Other Programs:
A concurrent bachelor of science degree in anatomy is available.

Sherman College of Straight Chiropractic
PO Box 1452
Spartanburg, SC 29304
(803) 578-8770 or (800) 849-8771 (toll-free)

Since 1973, Sherman College of Straight Chiropractic has concentrated on developing primary health-care providers within the boundaries of chiropractic medicine.

Program:
The thirteen-quarter program may be completed in thirty-nine months. The normal course load is 360 class and laboratory hours per quarter. Courses cover the biological sciences, but most of the curriculum is concerned directly with the art and philosophy of "straight" chiropractic, which the college defines as concentrating on the adjustment of the spine to correct subluxation. Electives expose students to a variety of techniques and additional areas of particular interest. Students also serve an internship in the Sherman's health center. In the thirteenth quarter, seniors may also choose an externship with a member of the Sherman College extern faculty in the United States or abroad.

Prerequisites:
Applicants must have a minimum of 60 semester units of undergraduate education, including biology, general and organic chemistry, physics, English or communication arts, and psychology.

Tuition:
In 1997 the average tuition per quarter was $3,610 with some additional fees varying from $20 to $25 per quarter. Books and supplies cost approximately $300 per quarter.

Financial Assistance:
Federal student financial aid funds are available as well as the Chiro-Loan program. The college also has scholarships for international and minority students.

Application Deadline:
Applications should be received approximately one year to six months before the desired starting date. Classes enter in January, April, July, and October.

Other Programs:
The college offers continuing education classes for licensure renewal and postdoctoral programs for the enhancement of professional skills.

Texas Chiropractic College
5912 Spencer Highway
Pasadena, TX 77505
(713) 487-1170 or (800) GO-TO-TEX (toll-free)

Texas Chiropractic College (TCC) was founded in 1908. It moved to its present location in 1965.

Program:
The ten-trimester program covers biological sciences, chiropractic technique, diagnosis, and treatment. Students move into clinical work by their third year. The tenth trimester is spent in clinic or preceptorships.

Prerequisites:
Applicants must have completed two years of undergraduate education (60 semester hours or 90 quarter hours) with a minimum 2.5 GPA, including biological sciences, inorganic chemistry, organic chemistry, physics, English, psychology, and humanities/social sciences. Sciences must have a lab component.

Tuition:
In 1997 average tuition was $13,500 ($4,500 per trimester), not including books, supplies, and other fees.

Financial Assistance:
TCC participates in the standard federal and state loan and financial aid programs.

Application Deadline:
TCC accepts applications throughout the year. The admissions office recommends submitting applications at least six months before the desired starting date. Classes are admitted three times per year.

Other Programs:
The college offers continuing education courses.

University of Bridgeport
College of Chiropractic
75 Linden Avenue
Bridgeport, CT 06601
(203) 576-4352 or (888) UB-CHIRO (toll-free)
http://www.bridgeport.edu/ubpage/chiro

The University of Bridgeport College of Chiropractic was the first chiropractic college to be associated with a larger university program.

Program:

The program is a full-time course of study lasting four academic years (eight semesters), including a clinical internship. Each academic year has two semesters (August through December and January through May).

The curriculum includes regular science courses such as anatomy, biochemistry, pathology, physiology, microbiology, radiology, diagnosis, orthopedics, neurology, and nutrition. Chiropractic courses include biomechanics, chiropractic technique procedures, physiotherapy and rehabilitation, and chiropractic principles and practice.

The curriculum emphasizes the body as an integrated unit. Students are taught how the neuromusculoskeletal system can affect the functioning of other systems and how these systems can affect the neuromusculoskeletal system. The state-of-the-art chiropractic clinic is located on the campus.

Prerequisites:

Applicants must have completed a minimum of three years of undergraduate education at an accredited university or college including science classes in general chemistry, organic chemistry, physics, and biology. Other required courses include English or communication arts, psychology, and humanities. A bachelor of arts or bachelor of science degree is recommended.

Tuition:

In 1997 average tuition was $5,900 per semester. Textbooks, equipment, and fees, are approximately $500 per semester.

Financial Assistance:

Financial aid includes federal Stafford Student Loans, residence hall directorships, and assistant hall directorships. UBC also participates in the ChiroLoan program for qualified chiropractic students.

Application Deadline:

Applications should be sent no later than May 1 for entry in the fall or August 1 for entry in January.

Other Programs:

The university also offered a doctor of naturopathic medicine degree (ND) starting in 1997 through its college of naturopathic medicine. Pre-chiropractic bachelor's programs and a master of science degree in human nutrition may be taken concurrently with the DC program.

Western States Chiropractic College (WSCC)
2900 NE 132nd Avenue
Portland, OR 97230
(503) 256-5723 or (800) 641-5641 (toll-free)
http://www.wschiro.edu

In 1994, WSCC became the first chiropractic college to be awarded a federal grant for research. The grant from the Department of Health and Human Services funded a collaborative study with Oregon Health Sciences University's Department of Family Medicine, and is cited by WSCC as typical of its interest in integrating chiropractic with other disciplines. The college is also accredited by the Northwest Association of Schools and Colleges.

Program:
WSCC gears its twelve-quarter program towards producing holistic chiropractic physicians, who are comfortable with therapies such as nutrition and lifestyle management as well as chiropractic techniques, and ready to deliver quality care within the integrated managed-care system. During the four-year (or three-year accelerated) DC program, students receive instruction in adjustive techniques every quarter while working with licensed chiropractic physicians in classes, technique labs, and campus clinics.

During their clinical internships, students can work with both chiropractic and medical physicians to gain the experience typical of a managed care setting. Students are also involved in a clinical research practicum during their last year.

Prerequisites:
Applicants must have completed two years (60 semester or 90 quarter credits) of college-level courses including biological sciences, general chemistry, organic chemistry, physics, English composition or communication skills, psychology, and other humanities classes. The admissions office will provide counseling on preprofessional course selection for undergraduate students.

Tuition:
In 1997 the average tuition was $4,325 per quarter with other fees, books, and supplies costing approximately $496 per quarter.

Financial Assistance:
The financial aid office supplies loan applications and information for US federal loan programs as well as provincial and national Canadian

loan programs. A financial aid adviser is available for individual consultation. Students interested in financial aid can contact the financial aid office before or during the admission process.

Application Deadline:
The college enters two classes each year in September and January. Applicants are encouraged to begin the formal application process up to twelve months in advance of their desired entry date.

Other Programs:
Students may also earn a bachelor of science (BS) degree in human biology concurrently with the DC degree. In 1997, the college offered its first 36-hour certification program in botanical medicine, co-sponsored by the University of Colorado Health Science Center—College of Pharmacy.

Canadian Schools

Canadian Memorial Chiropractic College
1900 Bayview Avenue
Toronto, Ontario, M4G 3E6
(416) 482-2340

Canadian Memorial was started in the 1940s, and the name was selected as a tribute to D. D. Palmer, the Canadian-born founder of chiropractic medicine. The college moved in 1968 to its present facilities. The college holds a reciprocal accreditation agreement with the CCE.

Program:
The four-year program is divided between biological sciences, chiropractic sciences, clinical sciences, clinical experience at the college's clinic, and research. The majority of Canada's chiropractic doctors are graduates of CMCC.

Prerequisites:
A baccalaureate degree is preferred but not required. Prospective students should have completed at least three years of university study (fifteen full courses; 90 credit hours). Science courses with lab should include organic chemistry and biology, as well as introductive psychology and other humanities/social sciences. Check with the admissions office for a full description of courses needed. A personal

interview is also required, but arrangements may be made for out-of-province interviews.

Tuition:
In 1997 tuition for full-time students was approximately $11,000 CDN per year. Books, diagnostic equipment, library and laboratory fees, and other education expenses can add up to $2,000 per year. Foreign students are charged a higher tuition rate.

Financial Assistance:
Contact the college for information on the Canada student loan program, provincial student loans, and private scholarships.

Application Deadline:
The college enters one class per year in September. Applications should be received approximately one year in advance of the desired starting date. The deadline for September 1998 was November 30, 1997.

Other Programs:
The college offers continuing education classes for licensure requirements and extension classes for chiropractic support staff and the general public.

PROFESSIONAL ORGANIZATIONS AND OTHER EDUCATIONAL RESOURCES

Contact the following professional organizations for more information on the profession, financial assistance, or chiropractic education. All the colleges listed offer extensive continuing education programs for chiropractors. Some bodywork and manipulative techniques listed in part 3 may also qualify for continuing education credits.

American Chiropractic Association
1701 Clarendon Boulevard
Arlington, VA 22209
(703) 276-8800

Canadian Chiropractic Association
1396 Eglinton Avenue W.
Toronto, Ontario M6R 2H2

Foundation for Chiropractic Education and Research
1701 Clarendon Boulevard
Arlington, VA 22209
(703) 276-7445

✺OTHER CAREER OPPORTUNITIES

Chiropractic Paraprofessional Assistant

Recently, some chiropractic colleges and liberal arts colleges in the United States have developed programs to train chiropractic assistants (CAs). Under the supervision of a chiropractic doctor, the chiropractic assistant works as a professional aide, performing various technical duties as well as helping in the preparation, control, and care of patients.

At the time of publication, there were no national licensing provisions for chiropractic assistants in the United States, although such licensure was under consideration in several states. State and national chiropractic organizations, along with the chiropractic colleges, were also working on ways to establish national standards for this type of training.

Life College (Marietta, Georgia), Life Chiropractic College West (San Lorenzo, California), Los Angles College of Chiropractic (Whittier, California), and National College (Lombard, Illinois) all offer a CA program in the United States. Canadian Memorial also offers a CA program in Canada.

National and International Volunteer Work:

The Christian Chiropractors Association has organized work by chiropractic missionaries in Indonesia, Peru, Quebec, Bolivia, Ethiopia, Monaco, Israel, Hong Kong, Mexico, and the United States. For more information, contact the Worldwide Christian Chiropractors Association, 3200 South LeMay Avenue, Fort Collins, CO 80525.

✺Recommended Reading:

McNamee, Kevin P., DC. *The Chiropractic College Directory*. Los Angeles: KM Enterprises, 1997.

> This annual overview of chiropractic education lists several US and foreign chiropractic colleges as well as full descriptions of the typical

pre-chiropractic curriculum, information on studying overseas, and the addresses of the state and international chiropractic associations. This book is particularly useful for undergraduate students looking for more information on how to prepare for a chiropractic education.

Wardell, William. *Chiropractic: A History and Evolution.* St. Louis: Year Book Medical Publications, 1992.

Wardell's history covers the development of the profession from D. D. Palmer to the present.

4

Licensed Massage Therapist (LMT)

Massage practitioners manipulate the soft tissues of the body to relieve stress or pain and correct muscle imbalances. One of the most common techniques is called Swedish massage, after the country where this form of massage was developed. With the strong influence of Eastern therapies, many massage schools now teach Asian techniques such as shiatsu or acupressure (see chapter 8). Other types of massage focus on treating specific needs: Sports massage concentrates on the needs of athletes; clinical massage treats specific recurrent or acute muscular problems.

Academic courses include physiology, anatomy or cadaver anatomy, plus hands-on techniques courses in several modalities, such as basic Swedish, neuromuscular, sports, or prenatal massage. Other standard classes include CPR and first aid; hydrotherapy; kinesiology; pathology; and training in the business skills needed to establish a massage practice. Didactic classes usually comprise one-third of credit hours, and hands-on classes the other two-thirds. Students gain clinical experience in school clinics or through internships at massage practices, rest homes, hospices, or hospitals.

Some schools add training in related natural therapies such as aromatherapy or energy work. Training in these therapies is not needed for licensing or national certification as a massage therapist. Other schools emphasize a specific form of massage developed by their founders, such as the Harold J. Reilly School of Massotherapy, which teaches the therapies developed by Dr. Reilly during his work with psychic healer Edgar Cayce. Because of the wide range of massage techniques, schools often allow students to pick a particular area of specialization such as sports massage or body/mind work depending on their interests and where they want to work after graduation.

Students who have completed their training must pass a state or national licensing exam. Many states also require practitioners to take a certain number of continuing education courses each year to maintain their license. Licensed massage professionals may use the designation of Licensed Massage Therapist (LMT) or Licensed Massage Practitioner (LMP).

After licensing, many practitioners choose to specialize in a specific form of bodywork such as Rolfing or Hellerwork. These techniques and the training involved are discussed more fully in part 3.

The professional standards for this field have undergone serious changes during the last five years. In the past massage therapists were required to take 100 hours to 300 hours of training; but some professionals are now predicting that 1,000 hours of training will become the norm within the next few years. Currently, the average training is 500 hours.

As with most of the natural therapies, massage schools report a rising number of applicants as well as applicants of a younger age. In fact, it is not unusual for students to choose massage school after finishing high school. Today the schools have a wide range of ages in their classes, from eighteen-year-olds starting on their first career to fifty-year-olds leaving corporate life for self-employment. Women tend to outnumber men at the massage schools.

Employment opportunities and potential income varies greatly depending on how the LMP decides to practice massage. Practitioners in private practice can charge between $40 and $70 per hour depending on the going rate for massage in their area. As with most forms of self-employment, earned income depends on overhead expenses and the number of hours a practitioner wants to work. Some massage therapists are comfortable doing seven to eight full hours in a day; others find that their physical limit is three or four full hours.

Third-party reimbursement for massage, such as insurance payments, is now available for the treatment of certain injuries. Often the therapist needs to get a referral from a physician or prior approval from the insurance carrier. Some therapists specialize in the treatment of labor and industry (L&I) injuries.

Massage therapists who do not want to be self-employed can work in chiropractic and osteopathic clinics, sports facilities and health clubs, spas, hotels, cruise ships, ski resorts, and many other places. This type of employment seems to work well for younger therapists, particularly those who go straight from high school to massage school, because it gives them extra time to gain the experience and business skills needed to establish a private practice.

Hourly wages for therapists employed by others depend on the type of practice. Ski resorts and other vacation destinations tend to pay on the low end of the scale, but therapists can earn tips and use the resort facilities. Hourly wages in medical clinics usually range from $15 to $20 per hour.

✁COST OF EDUCATION

Prospective students should budget between $4,000 to $7,000 for a 500- to 700-hour massage program. Costs vary greatly depending on the number of hours required as well as the location of the school. Books usually cost between $100 and $200 for a full one-year program, and a massage table costs $200 to $800.

Financial assistance can be limited to the schools arranging for payment plans. More schools in the United States are qualified to take Veterans Administration benefits than any other type of federal assistance. Many programs are geared to part-time or evening students, making it easier to work while taking classes.

Since most programs last one year or less, the average tuition listed is for the completion of the entire program. Check with the school for current tuition, fees, and other costs.

✁LENGTH OF TRAINING

The amount of training time needed to qualify for a license varies greatly in the United States. Many massage programs can be completed in one year; some schools offer a six-month intensive program. You may be able to complete all requirements in 350 course hours, or you may need to take 1,000 hours. Massage instructors and students interviewed for this book stress the importance of knowing your state's requirements. Even an experienced massage therapist may have to complete more courses after moving to another state.

Sometimes a school's accreditation can make a difference in the amount of training time needed. For example, in 1997 Rhode Island required 500 hours education at a school approved by the Commission on Massage Training Accreditation/Approval (COMTAA) or 1,000 hours of training at a non-COMTAA school.

The trend in recent years has been to increase the number of hours needed to qualify as a licensed massage therapist. At the time of publication, the American Massage Therapy Association (AMTA) recommended taking a program with a minimum of 500 hours of supervised training.

ADMISSIONS PROCESS

The admissions process for massage schools may include a personal interview or an entrance exam to demonstrate your interest and knowledge about this career field. During interviews, admissions directors look for good communication skills, genuine interest in massage therapy, and the maturity to handle course work requirements. Many schools hold an open house during which prospective students can tour the facility and experience a massage session.

Most schools accept applicants until the class is full, and some schools start classes several times during the year. Many admissions directors report that the increasing number of applications in the last few years have caused classes to fill well before the starting date.

UNDERGRADUATE PREREQUISITES

To enter most massage schools, you must have completed high school or demonstrate an equivalent education and be over eighteen years of age. Massage schools have become an increasingly popular choice for high school graduates who are not interested in pursuing a typical college undergraduate program.

Many schools also require applicants to have experienced at least two professional massage therapy sessions. If you don't know a massage therapist in your area, the schools will supply recommendations.

Because of the intensely physical nature of massage work, all massage schools require applicants to be physically and emotionally capable of performing and receiving massage from people of both sexes. A number of schools offer an introductory or novice course to help both the applicant and the school evaluate readiness to embark on a massage career.

Prerequisites listed here are the academic minimums required by the schools. If you're interested in a program, be sure to request a complete list of entrance requirements.

✍LICENSING AND ACCREDITATION

UNITED STATES

The following states regulated massage in 1997: Alabama, Arkansas, Connecticut, Delaware, District of Columbia, Florida, Hawaii, Iowa, Louisiana, Maine, Maryland, Nebraska, New Hampshire, New Mexico, New York, North Dakota, Ohio, Oregon, Rhode Island, South Carolina, Tennessee, Texas, Utah, Virginia, Washington, and West Virginia.

In states that did not license massage therapy, massage therapists may be regulated by municipal or county codes. Check with the local government where you plan to practice. In some areas you may need to satisfy both state and local law. The state organizations of the American Massage Therapy Association and other groups can usually help you establish the requirements of your area.

Many states have adopted the National Certification Exam as their written test for licensing. Some states require that applicants for licensure have attended a COMTAA-accredited school. Others simply require that the applicant have successfully completed a minimum number of hours of supervised training. Still other states, like Washington, require that the school be approved by the state board of massage.

The number of class hours required for a license varies widely from state to state, from a high of 1,000 hours to a low of 300 hours. If you take your training in a state other than the one in which you plan to practice, check with your school to make sure that their program will satisfy your state's requirements. The number of training hours required as well as the continuing education requirements for maintaining a license seem to be increasing in several states.

In 1994 the massage school accreditation program, COMTAA, became an independent affiliate of the American Massage Therapy Association. Its standards have been incorporated in some state laws regulating massage therapists. The American Massage Therapy Association is one of four professional organizations for massage therapists and bodyworkers in the United States (see Professional Organizations at the end of this chapter).

The National Certification Board for Therapeutic Massage and Bodywork (NCBTMB) also provides standardized competency tests for massage therapists and bodyworkers, as well as approval of continuing education units (CEU) offered by many schools. NCBTMB certification may not be necessary for licensing.

National Certification Board for Therapeutic Massage
   and Bodywork (NCBTMB)
8201 Greensboro Drive, Suite 300
McLean, VA 22102
(703) 610-9015 or (800) 296-0664 (toll-free)
http://www.ncbtmb.com

Commission on Massage Training Accreditation/
   Approval (COMTAA)
820 Davis Street, Suite 100
Evanston, IL 60201-4444
(847) 864-0123

CANADA

Regulation of massage therapy in Canada varies by province. Contact your provincial massage therapy association for current regulations and educational requirements (see Appendix B: Organizations).

US Schools

By late 1997 the following independent schools had achieved COMTAA accreditation or had been approved by the AMTA by demonstrating the provision of 500 or more supervised hours in their program. See also Appendix C.

Alexandria School of Scientific Therapeutics (ASST)
809 S. Harrison
Alexandria, IN 46001
(317) 724-9152

Program:
ASST specializes in Swedish massage therapy, but students also take classes in polarity techniques, iridology, color therapy, acupressure, shiatsu, craniopathy infant massage, manual lymph drainage, sports massage, and geriatric massage. The program lasts for 656 course hours, meeting for forty-one weeks, two days per week. Part-time students were not accepted in 1997.

Prerequisites:
Students must have a high school diploma or equivalent, be at least eighteen years of age, and go through an admissions interview.

Tuition:
In 1997/98 the full program (forty-one weeks) cost approximately $5,200.

Financial Assistance:
Financial assistance was not available at the time of publication.

Application Deadline:
Applications must be completed no later than July 15.

Other Programs:
The school also offers postgraduate courses in Pfrimmer Technique deep muscle therapy, and classes in animal massage including equine massage.

American Institute of Massage Therapy, Inc.
2156 Newport Boulevard
Costa Mesa, CA 92627
(714) 642-0735

Program:
Students at the American Institute of Massage Therapy may choose between certification as a massage therapist (624 hours) or as a sports massage therapist (1,029 hours). The school also offers a specialized associate degree program (1,269 hours).

The massage therapist program covers anatomy, physiology, and pathology; nutrition and supplementation; hydrotherapy and electrotherapy; specialized massage modalities such as shiatsu, Russian techniques, Thailand stretches, and myofascial release; psychology and philosophy; and other supplementary courses. The sports massage therapy program includes pre-event and post-event massage, training and conditioning, and restoration/rehabilitation.

Prerequisites:
Applicants must have a high school diploma or equivalent and may be asked to take an entrance exam.

Tuition:
Tuition varies depending on the number of course hours taken. In 1997/98 students had to budget a minimum of $6,000 for tuition, books, massage table, and other expenses.

Financial Assistance:
The school provides a monthly payment plan.

Application Deadline:
Evening classes begin in January and July, and day classes start in April. The school holds an open house every four to six weeks to allow prospective students to take a sample massage lesson and discuss the various programs.

Other Programs:
The institute offers training as a massage therapy instructor. Interested students should contact the school for current prerequisites.

Asten Center of Natural Therapeutics
797 N. Grove Road, Suite 101
Richardson, TX 75081-2761
(972) 669-3245

Program:
Asten's basic massage therapy program is 300 hours. After completion, students may advance to specialized massage therapy (250 hours), which includes sports massage, trigger point therapy, clinical applications, reflexology, and focus classes on specific techniques and health issues.

Prerequisites:
Candidates for the basic massage therapy program must complete an admission application, participate in an interview, and tour the facility.

Tuition:
In 1997/98 the average tuition for the basic massage program was $2,630; the specialized massage program cost $2,456.

Financial Assistance:
The school provides payment plans.

Application Deadline:
Asten has an open admissions policy. Day classes begin January, May, and September; evening classes begin in February and August.

Other Programs:
No other programs are listed.

Atlanta School of Massage
2300 Peachford Road, Suite 3200
Atlanta, GA 30338
(770) 454-7167

The Atlanta School of Massage has been accredited by the Accrediting Commission of Career Schools and Colleges of Technology (ACCSCT) since 1988.

Program:
The school offers both a 620-hour professional massage therapy program and 620-hour clinical sports massage program. Students may also choose to specialize in spa therapy and treatments.

Prerequisites:
Applicants must be at least eighteen years of age and have a high school diploma or equivalent.

Tuition:
Costs vary depending on which program or specialty that students select. In 1996/97 the professional massage program cost approximately $6,875.

Financial Assistance:
Federal loan packages and payment plans should be available through the school's financial assistance office. Contact them for application deadlines.

Application Deadline:
New classes are admitted throughout the year.

Other Programs:
No other programs are listed.

Baltimore School of Massage (BSOM)
6401 Dogwood Road
Baltimore, MD 21207
(410) 944-8855
http://www.bsom.com

BSOM was established in 1981, and is connected with the Virginia School of Massage. Its professional program was approved by the Maryland Higher Education Commission.

Program:
The 500-hour professional massage training program emphasizes the transformational approach to bodywork. Students attend part-time, and the course takes approximately eighteen months to complete.

Prerequisites:
Applicants must have a high school diploma or equivalent.

Tuition:
In 1997/98 the cost for the entire program was approximately $4,350.

Financial Assistance:
Check with the school at time of application.

Application Deadline:
The school accepts applications throughout the year.

Other Programs:
BSOM also offers a 100-hour vocational program in massage.

Bancroft School of Massage Therapy
333 Shrewsbury Street
Worcester, MA 01604
(508) 757-7923
http://members.aol.com/bsmttank/bsmtcontents.htm

Bancroft was established in 1950 by massage therapist Henry LaFleur. The school was the first of its type to achieve licensing from the Massachusetts Department of Education. It has also been accredited by the Commission of Career Schools and College of Technology (CCSCT).

Program:
The 800-hour program takes seventeen months to complete for full-time students and twenty-two months for part-time students. Swedish massage therapy is emphasized, and students also receive training in adjunct therapies such as sports massage, reflexology, and Oriental massage therapy. Academic courses are limited to class

size of thirty, and massage therapy classes are limited to twenty-four students.

Prerequisites:
Students must have a high school diploma or GED.

Tuition:
In 1997/98 the average cost for full-time students was $9,950. Students should also budget $1,200 for equipment and supplies.

Financial Assistance:
Bancroft participates in the federal Stafford Loan program and offers payment plans.

Application Deadline:
Applications must be received at least two months before classes start. Day classes begin in January, April, and September; evening classes begin in September.

Other Programs:
No other programs are listed.

Body Therapy Institute (BTI)
South Wind Farm
300 South Wind Road
Siler City, NC 27344
(919) 663-3111 or (888) 500-4500 (toll-free)

The Body Therapy Institute (BTI) moved to 150-acre South Wind Farm in Chatham County in 1995, and new education buildings were designed specially to meet the needs of massage therapy classes. Besides accreditation by AMTA/COMTAA, the school has been licensed as a proprietary school by the North Carolina Department of Community Colleges and has been approved by the Florida State Board of Massage.

Program:
Full-time students can complete the 650-hour program in eight to eleven months. The program can be taken in a two-semester daytime format or a three-semester evening/weekend format. Course work is a synthesis of Eastern and Western traditions of bodywork. Students learn about the mind/body connection, energetics, structural organization, body mechanics, and movement.

Prerequisites:
Students need a high school diploma or equivalent, must be at least nineteen years old, and must have experienced at least two professional massage/bodywork sessions (the school will provide a list of practitioners, if needed). Applicants must also take a basic introductory massage class or workshop.

Tuition:
In 1997/98 the average tuition for a full-time student was $6,500.

Financial Assistance:
Payment plans are provided by the school.

Application Deadline:
Applications for the spring program should be received by the end of February; applications for the fall program should be received by the beginning of July. Applications are accepted after deadlines on a space-available basis.

Other Programs:
BTI offers a variety of continuing education classes.

Boulder School of Massage Therapy
6255 Longbow Drive
Boulder, CO 80301
(303) 443-5131 or (800) 442-5131 (toll-free)

The Boulder School of Massage Therapy was incorporated as a not-for-profit education corporation in the 1970s, and received approval from the Colorado State Board of Community Colleges and Occupational Education. Today, the student clinic provides over 6,000 massages a year to the general public.

Program:
The diploma program takes four quarters and involves 982 hours of in-class supervised instruction, 10 hours of internship activities, and 70 hours of supervised clinic sessions. Students learn shiatsu, Swedish therapeutic massage, Anatomiken System, structural and clinical kinesiology, and therapeutic integrative massage, as well as modalities. The school also provides many elective courses to allow students to focus on particular massage techniques. The day program takes one

calendar year to complete in four ten-week quarters. The evening program takes two calendar years (four twenty-week quarters).

Prerequisites:
Applicants must be at least twenty-one years of age by the date of enrollment; have a high school diploma or GED certificate; and have received at least two professional massage therapy sessions. The school holds information sessions on the third Monday of each month.

Tuition:
In 1997/98 the average tuition was $7,725. Students should also budget an additional $2,000 for supplies and school fees.

Financial Assistance:
The school participates in federal student loan programs and the Pell Grant program.

Application Deadline:
The day program is offered four times per year, and the evening program is offered twice a year. Applications deadline is two weeks before the orientation date of each new quarter. The school recommends submitting applications three to six months before the desired starting date.

Other Programs:
The school offers students, graduates and other qualified individuals continuing education through workshops, lectures, and seminars.

Brenneke School of Massage
160 Roy Street
Seattle, WA 98109
(206) 282-1233

Program:
Brenneke offers a 650-hour 12-month Professional Licensing Program (PLP) or a 1,000-hour twelve-month Extended Professional Licensing Program (ELP). Each program is divided into four terms of approximately eleven weeks each. The core curriculum includes Swedish massage; anatomy and physiology; kinesiology; and advanced massage integration, including hydrotherapy. Students chose 84 hours of elective courses including advanced myofascial work; advanced sports massage; movement awareness; introduction to craniosacral

therapy; foot reflexology; Lomi Lomi and Loku Lomi; lymphatic massage; introduction to polarity therapy; pregnancy massage; reiki (first degree); shiatsu; introduction to Therapeutic Touch; trigger point therapy; and others.

The ELP adds extended supervised skill honing; expanded teaching clinics for increased exposure to the professional clinical setting; interaction with other health-care professionals through field training; and community outreach.

Prerequisites:
Applicants must be at least eighteen years of age; hold a high school diploma or GED; and successfully complete a Brenneke novice class. The director of admissions interviews applicants regarding academic and financial readiness as well as professional attitude, motivation, and goals.

Tuition:
In 1997/98 total tuition for the 650-hour program was $6,350, or $9,500 for the 1,000-hour program.

Financial Assistance:
The school has been approved for federal programs including Stafford Loans, PLUS, and Pell Grants. The school also offers payment plans. Students may also be eligible for financial support through the Commission for the Blind, Veterans Administration, Employment Security, the L&I retraining program, or other programs. Contact the financial aid office for more information.

Application Deadline:
The 650-hour program starts in March or September. The 1,000 hour program starts in January. Allow time to schedule an appointment with the admissions director and to attend the novice class.

Other Programs:
Brenneke offers continuing education workshops to licensed massage practitioners and specialized in-depth training programs in areas such as lymph drainage, sports massage, and myofascial training.

Brian Utting School of Massage
900 Thomas Street
Seattle, WA 98109
(206) 292-8055 or (800) 842-8731

Program:
Brian Utting's 1,000-hour course exceeds the licensure requirements in Washington state and emphasizes in-depth understanding of soft tissue work by giving students a background in biological sciences related to massage and their applications. This class work includes anatomy and physiology, kinesiology, and pathology and pathophysiology. Students also take a cadaver anatomy course.

Bodywork techniques taught include Swedish massage, deep tissue massage, circulatory massage, art and technique of deep touching, deep muscle therapy, clinical massage, injury evaluation and treatment, connective tissue massage, neuromuscular technique, foot reflexology, pregnancy massage, and sports massage.

Students meet either three or four days a week depending on which program they take. All the programs include one or two full-day workshops each month. The entire program, whether day or evening, takes approximately fifteen months to complete.

Prerequisites:
Besides basic entrance requirements, such as a high school diploma or equivalent, students must participate in an introductory workshop before application acceptance.

Tuition:
Tuition for the 1,000-hour spring program was $8,100 as of January 1998. The school also suggests budgeting an additional $1,200 for books, massage table, supplies, and other expenses.

Financial Assistance:
The school is approved for veteran's training benefits. Students have also received funding through the Washington Department of Labor and Industries or personal loans arranged through a local bank (contact the school for the bank's name and phone number). Brian Utting also has four different payment plans.

Application Deadline:
Applications are due at least four weeks before the start of class. Late applications may be accepted on a space-available basis. The school has two daytime programs, starting in January or April, and an evening program, starting in January.

Other Programs:
Brian Utting also offers an optional introductory anatomy course to prepare students for any professional massage study. It provides continuing education classes and post-graduate training.

Career Training Academy
ExpoMart
105 Mall Boulevard., Suite 300 W
Monroeville, PA 15146-2230
(412) 372-3900 or (800) 491-3470 (toll-free)
http://www.careerta.com

This vocational school also has a New Kensington, Pennsylvania, branch. Call (412) 337-1000 for information.

Program:
The Career Training Academy offers both a Swedish massage practitioner program and a therapeutic massage technician program. In the 300-hour Swedish massage program, students perform hands-on massage and study human anatomy, physiology, and kinesiology. This course is adequate for qualifying to practice massage in the state of Pennsylvania, which has no formal requirements for massage practitioners.

The 600-hour therapeutic massage technician program covers advanced Swedish massage with an emphasis on therapeutic techniques. Students are trained to perform an extensive therapeutic massage.

Maximum class sizes are twenty-five students. The 300-hour program takes approximately five months to complete. The 600-hour program takes almost ten months to complete.

Prerequisites:
Applicants are interviewed by a school representative and may, if recommended by the school administration, be required to complete an aptitude test. The purpose of the test is to determine the applicant's suitability for the program. Testing may also be necessary for students whose high school grade point average (GPA) or GED scores fall below the norm.

Tuition:
In 1996/97 tuition ranged from $1,750 for the 300-hour program to $3,500 for the 600-hour program, not including supplies, books, and incidental fees.

Financial Assistance:
Students qualify for the standard federal loans and veteran's benefits. Contact the school for other sources of financial assistance such as vocational rehabilitation credits.

Other Programs:
The school also offers a shiatsu technician program (see chapter 8).

Carlson College of Massage Therapy
11809 Country Road
Box 28
Anamosa, IA 52205
(319) 462-3402
e-mail: carlc@inav.net

The school's country setting includes walking trails, volleyball court, basketball court, and an herb garden.

Program:
Students receive a Diploma of Massage Therapy after completing 625 supervised classroom hours. The foundations of the program are anatomy and physiology, Swedish massage, and deep tissue specific massage. Students also take classes on sports massage, on-site chair massage, reflexology, shiatsu, therapeutic touch, polarity therapy, and herbology. Part-time students were not accepted at the time of publication.

Prerequisites:
Students must have a high school diploma or equivalent.

Tuition:
In 1997 the entire course cost approximately $4,500.

Financial Assistance:
The school did not provide financial assistance in 1997.

Application Deadline:
Applications are due in March and September.

Other Programs:
No other programs are listed.

Carolina School of Massage Therapy (CSMT)
103 W. Weaver Street
Carrboro, NC 27510
(919) 933-2212

Program:
The CSMT program mixes Western and Eastern therapeutic massage modalities, including Swedish massage, deep muscle massage, sports and joint mobilization, polarity therapy, and Five Elements acupressure. Other courses include standard anatomical studies, and somatic or body-centered awareness in healing.

Students receive a Certificate of Completion after finishing 650 hours of instruction. Classes are limited to a maximum of twenty students, and most hands-on classes include a teaching assistant as well as the instructor. This program can be completed in six months for a full-time student, using the weekday intensive program, or in twelve months for a part-time student.

Prerequisites:
Students must be high school graduates.

Tuition:
In 1997/98 the average cost for the full program was $6,275 .

Financial Assistance:
Payment plans are available.

Application Deadline:
The school holds two weekday intensive programs each year. Applications for the spring 1998 program were due by March 6, and for the fall 1998 program by August 31.

Other Programs:
The school also provides community education and extended education for bodyworkers and allied health-care professionals.

Central Ohio School of Massage (COSM)
1120 Morse Road, Suite 250
Columbus, OH 43229
(614) 841-1122
http://www.cosm.org

Founded in 1964, the COSM was established to fill a need in the community for a facility to train professional massage therapists. The program was the first Ohio program to be approved by the AMTA Commission on Massage Training Accreditation/Approval.

Program:
The eighteen-month program is designed to qualify students to take the Ohio State Medical Board examination for licensure as a Massage Therapist in the State of Ohio.

Students are trained in the techniques of massage: its uses, limitations, and the physiological effects of massage on the function of the human body and each of its individual systems. They also study the application of massage to health and the ability of massage to aid the body in its recovery from illness and injury. Senior students are required to perform practice massages and prepare responses to many proposed health problems including the evaluation of a described set of symptoms and preparation of a course of therapy for the client described.

Additional studies include anatomy, physiology, ethics, business practices, patient approach, uses of heat and cold, restorative exercises, and others. Students are also required to complete a course in basic life support and first aid.

Prerequisites:
Applicants must have a high school education or equivalent and complete a massage preliminary education form for the state medical board.

Tuition:
In 1997/98 the average tuition was $6,300 for the eighteen-month program, with an additional $300 budgeted for books.

Financial Assistance:
COSM provides payment plans for students.

Application Deadline:
Applications for spring 1998 were due by February 15. Applications for fall 1998 are due by August 1. Check with the school for current applications' deadlines. Any applications postmarked after the listed deadline must include a $10 late application fee to be processed.

Other Programs:
The school offers a myofascial therapy course for licensed massage therapists and other health professionals (see chapter 11).

Colorado Institute of Massage Therapy (CIMT)
2601 E. St. Vrain
Colorado Springs, CO 80909
(888) 634-7347 or 719-634-7347
http://www.coimt.com

The Colorado Institute of Massage Therapy teaches Neuromuscular Therapy (CIMT Method), a system of deep tissue massage therapy developed by Togi Kinnaman, the president and founder of the institute. According to the school's web site, the ultimate goal of Neuromuscular Therapy (CIMT Method) is to facilitate through massage therapy an "internal climate" that encourages "the body to utilize all of its God-given ability and power to heal itself from within."

Program:
The 1150-hour program includes classes in holistic health and bodywork concepts; massage theory and movements in Swedish massage; deep tissue massage; reflexology; anatomy and physiology; structural kinesiology; pathology as it relates to massage therapy; sports massage; geriatric massage; applied massage for common physical complaints; and related therapies.

To gain clinical experience, students are required to fulfill forty-eight appointments over 16 weeks in the student clinic. This clinical work begins in the twenty-eighth week of the program. Students may also apply for a hospital internship in an outpatient rehabilitative center or a community internship with a health-care professional such as a doctor, or at a health club or massage therapy center.

Workshops are required in the course of the program and they are usually scheduled one weekend per month.

Prerequisites:
Applicants must be at least twenty-one years old unless special permission of the admissions committee is granted. A high school diploma, or equivalent, or special permission is also required.

Tuition:
In 1997 average total tuition was $5,500, not including books, supplies, and other fees.

Financial Assistance:
CIMT offers its own student loan program with three- to four-year student loans and payments under $200 per month.

Other Programs:
CIMT offers a variety of workshops and other continuing education classes.

Core Institute
223 W. Carolina Street
Tallahassee, FL 32301
(850) 222-8673

Program:
The 500-hour program includes 97 hours of other modalities including sports massage, polarity therapy, traditional Oriental medicine, shiatsu, and neuromuscular therapy. Students also take 15 hours of instruction in hydrotherapy.

The course takes six months to complete for full-time students. Part-time students are accepted.

Prerequisites:
Students must be at least twenty years old and have completed two years of college or have the equivalent life experience.

Tuition:
In 1997/98 the average tuition for full-time students was $4,250.

Financial Assistance:
The program is eligible for veteran's benefits and work-study grants.

Application Deadline:
Applications are accepted throughout the year.

Other Programs:
No other programs were offered at the time of publication.

Desert Institute of the Healing Arts (DIHA)
639 N. 6th Avenue
Tucson, AZ 85705
(520) 882-0899 or (800) 733-8098 (toll-free)
http://www.fcinet.com/diha

DIHA is also accredited by the Accrediting Commission of Career Schools and Colleges of Technology (ACCCT), licensed by the Arizona State Board for Private Post-secondary Education since 1982, and is a member of the American Oriental Bodywork Therapy Association (AOBTA).

Program:

The 1,000-hour massage therapy certificate program prepares students for entry-level positions as professional massage therapists through integrating theory, technique, anatomy and physiology, practical experience, and personal and professional development. The program may be completed in three trimesters, with a fourth-trimester option available by petition only. The schedule consists of fourteen-week trimesters with three- or four-week breaks in between.

Classes include massage theory and practice; hydrotherapy; movement; anatomy and physiology; massage and wellness; communications; and massage electives in specialized areas of study.

Prerequisites:

Applicants should be at least twenty-one years of age with a high school diploma or equivalent. Waivers of age requirement may be available with parental consent and prior approval from the school.

Tuition:

In 1997 average tuition for the full program was $8,700.

Financial Assistance:

The school is approved for Federal Pell Grants, the Federal Direct Loan and Federal PLUS Program, and veteran's benefits for qualified students.

Application Deadline:

Applications are accepted throughout the year. Check with DIHA for current financial aid deadlines.

Other Programs:

DIHA is a NCBTMB approved continuing education provider for massage therapists. The school also offers a shiatsu therapist program (see chapter 8).

Downeast School of Massage (DSM)
PO Box 24
99 Moose Meadow Lane
Waldoboro, ME 04572
(207) 832-5531
e-mail: dsm@midcoast.com

The school is located on a 100-acre campus in rural, mid-coast Maine.

Program:
DSM offers three programs: Swedish and sports (607 hours); Swedish and shiatsu (682 hours); and Swedish and body/mind (601 hours). Full-time students can complete required course work in ten months. Part-time students may take two years to complete.

Core curriculum includes treatment of chronic pain; neuromuscular techniques; hydrotherapy; kinesiology; pregnancy massage; and other courses geared to the professional practice of massage therapy.

Prerequisites:
Students must be at least eighteen years of age and have a high school diploma or equivalent. An admissions interview is required.

Tuition:
In 1997/98 average tuition ranged from $5,825 to $6,625 depending on the program selected.

Financial Assistance:
The school provides payment plans and accepts credit cards.

Application Deadline:
Applications are due August 1 or November 30, depending on desired entry date.

Other Programs:
The school provides continuing education classes.

East-West College of the Healing Arts
4531 SE Belmont Street
Portland, OR 97215-1635
(800) 635-9141 or (503) 231-1500

Program:
The diploma program can cover 529 or 661 hours (nine to eighteen months). Geared to state licensure requirements, the subjects include anatomy, physiology, kinesiology, pathology, Swedish massage, deep tissue, sports massage, shiatsu, polarity therapy, and injury care.

Prerequisites:
Applicants must have a high school diploma or equivalent.

Tuition:
In 1997 tuition, fees, books, and supplies for a full-time student cost approximately $5,500.

Financial Assistance:
Some in-house financing is available.

Application Deadline:
Applications are accepted throughout the year for classes starting in January, April, July, and October.

Other Programs:
No other programs were offered at time of publication.

Florida College of Natural Health
2001 W. Sample Road, Suite 100
Pompano Beach, FL 33064
(954) 975-6400 or (800)541-9299 (toll-free)
http://www.nhtc.com

Formerly known as the Florida Institute, the school has also received approval from the Florida State Board of Independent Colleges and Universities for degrees in massage therapy. The school has campuses in Ft. Lauderdale, Miami, and Orlando.

Program:
The therapeutic massage program provides 624 hours of training. The advanced massage therapy program (900 hours) adds in-depth study of musculoskeletal disorders and sports related injuries. Basic classes include therapeutic massage, hydrotherapy, and introduction to allied modalities.

Prerequisites:
Students must have a high school diploma or equivalent. Depending on the program, students may be required to take an entrance examination.

Tuition:
In 1997/98 the average tuition for the therapeutic massage program was $4,350, and average tuition for the advanced therapeutic massage training program was $6,050.

Financial Assistance:
The college participates in various federal aid and loan programs.

Application Deadline:
Applications are accepted throughout the year. Check with the school for class dates for the individual campuses.

Other Programs:
The college offers a skin care/esthetics program, an electrolysis training program, advanced clinical training for massage therapists, and an associate of science degree in natural health. These programs can be combined with massage therapy training.

Florida School of Massage
6421 SW 13th Street
Gainesville, FL 32608
(352) 378-7891

Program:
The certificate program can be completed in 705 hours, but students have the option to expand the program up to 1,000 hours. Full-time students can complete basic classes in six months.

The massage modalities taught include Swedish; connective tissue massage; neuromuscular therapy (NMT); polarity therapy; sports massage, reflexology, and Awareness Integrated Massage (AIM).

Prerequisites:
Applicants must have a high school diploma or GED certificate.

Tuition:
In January 1998 average tuition for a full-time student was $5,150.

Financial Assistance:
None offered at the time of publication.

Application Deadline:
The school accepts applications throughout the year, but recommends completing applications at least two months before the desired starting date.

Other Programs:
Advanced training and workshops are offered throughout the year.

Harold J. Reilly School of Massotherapy
215 67th Street
Virginia Beach, VA 23451
(757) 437-7202
http://www.are-cayce.com
e-mail: are@are-cayce.com

The Harold J. Reilly School of Massotherapy is a department of the Association for Research and Enlightenment, Inc., a nonprofit organization inspired by the readings of Edgar Cayce. Reilly, a medical doctor who worked with Cayce, developed the massage therapies suggested by the Cayce readings. The school is also licensed by the Virginia Department of Education.

Program:
The 600-hour program takes six to seven months to complete for full-time students. Emphasis is given to the personal growth of students as healers, including personal journals, dream work, and the opportunity for daily meditation.

Cayce/Reilly Massotherapy is the primary modality taught, but students also study sports massage, therapeutic massage, chair massage, foot reflexology, and Jin Shin Do acupressure. Home remedies recommended by Cayce, such as castor oil packs, colon hydrotherapy, and the Cayce diet, are taught in one course.

Prerequisites:
Students must have a high school diploma or GED certificate.

Tuition:
In 1997/98 the average tuition for a full-time student was $4,500.

Financial Assistance:
Contact the financial aid office for information about Veterans Administration education benefits and need scholarships. Payment plans are also available.

Application Deadline:
Applications are accepted until registration on a space-available basis. Classes begin in January and September.

Other Programs:
The school offers continuing education in Vodder manual lymph drainage, Jin Shin Do, and advanced Cayce/Reilly massage.

Healing Hands Institute for Massage Therapy
41 Bergenline Avenue
Westwood, NJ 07675
(201) 722-0099
e-mail: HH1@aol.com

The Healing Hands Institute is approved by the New Jersey Department of Education.

Program:
The 580-hour program can be completed in six months by full-time students or in one year by part-time students. Studies include therapeutic massage, Swedish massage, Oriental massage, neuromuscular massage, reflexology, deep tissue bodywork, and sports massage.

Prerequisites:
Applicants must have a high school diploma or GED certificate.

Tuition:
In 1997/98 the average tuition for a full-time student was $4,800.

Financial Assistance:
The school participates in the Veterans Administration program. Call for more information on financial aid.

Application Deadline:
Applications are due in May, August, or January.

Other Programs:
Healing Hands also offers cancer massage certification; continuing education in geriatric, medical, trigger point, and baby's first massage; and holistic certification programs.

Heartwood Institute
220 Harmony Lane
Garberville, CA 95542
(707) 923-5000
http://www.heartwoodinstitute.com

Heartwood is a residential vocational school located in a mountainous, wooded region of Northern California. Students live at Heartwood during their training. The school's training in polarity therapy is approved by the American Polarity Therapy Association (see chapter 12).

Program:
Heartwood offers two choices of traditional massage therapy training: the six-month (two-quarter) massage therapist program and the nine-month (three-quarter) advanced massage therapist program. In the longer program, students may add energy work to their training by choosing either polarity therapy or Zen shiatsu acupressure training.

Heartwood believes that effective bodywork requires the scientific understanding of the human body, knowledge of muscle movement and function, and skilled assessment of the client's needs. The human sciences classes teach anatomy and physiology from a bodywork perspective. This section is divided into five classes: musculoskeletal anatomy, introduction to body systems, body systems 2, kinesiology, and pathology.

The clinical practicum occurs during the final quarter of study, when students work at the Heartwood Student Clinic. Students are expected to schedule and confirm their clients, greet them and do intake interviews, work with people they've never met, and collect payment for sessions.

Prerequisites:
Applicants must have a high school diploma or equivalent.

Tuition:
In 1997/98 the average cost for the massage therapist program was $4,990. The advanced massage therapist program cost $6,565.

Financial Assistance
Heartwood provides payment plans. Eligible applicants may qualify for veterans benefits for certain programs.

Application Deadline:
Students can enter in any quarter. Quarters begin in August, November, February, and May.

Other Programs:
Heartwood also offers a holistic health practitioner program, which combines 1,000 hours of bodywork and associated classes, including all the classes in the advanced massage therapist program, polarity, and shiatsu, plus a choice of additional healing modalities. The school holds a range of one- to four-week intensive classes, including contin-

uing and advanced education for bodyworkers. Some courses may qualify for continuing education credits for nurses.

Honolulu School of Massage, Inc.
1123 11th Avenue, Suite 102
Honolulu, HI 96816
(808) 733-0000
e-mail: hsminc@msn.com

The Honolulu School of Massage (HSM) holds a private vocational school license from the Hawaii Department of Education.

Program:
The full HSM program provides professional massage therapy training, including Eastern, Western, and Pacific bodywork modalities. The 630-hour program can be completed in eight months by full-time students.

Prerequisites:
Applicants must have a high school diploma or equivalent and be eighteen years of age or older.

Tuition:
In 1997 the average tuition for the full program was $6,550.

Financial Assistance:
The program is approved for Veterans Administration educational benefits.

Other Programs:
HSM offered community education courses, reiki first degree, and Feldenkrais Method workshops during the fall 1997 semester.

International Professional School of Bodywork (IPSB)
1366 Hornblend Street
San Diego, CA 92109
(619) 272-4142 or (800) 748-6497 (toll-free)
http://www.webcom.com/ipsb

Founded in 1977, the IPSB is affiliated with the Reidman Center in Tel Aviv, Israel, and certain IPSB classes are offered in Montana,

Montreal, and elsewhere. The school is also a member of AOBTA and is approved as a vocational school by the California State Council for Private Postsecondary and Vocational Education.

Program:
The three-month program includes instruction in massage techniques, movement education, anatomy and physiology, self-maintenance skills (t'ai chi, yoga, qi gong, meditation), communication and assessment skills, body psychology training, and the bodyworker as healer. The school offers elective courses in areas such as Alexander Technique, Feldenkrais Awareness Through Movement, sports massage, foot reflexology, tui-na massage, lymphatic massage, Jin Shin Acutouch, and Thailand massage.

Prerequisites:
Applicants must be at least eighteen years of age and have a high school diploma or equivalent.

Tuition:
In 1996/97 the cost for a basic massage program (150 hours to 330 hours) ranged from $900 to $1,980, depending on the number of hours involved.

Financial Assistance:
IPSB provides payment plans.

Application Deadline:
Applications are accepted throughout the year.

Other Programs:
The IPSB offers a variety of programs in holistic health, occupational studies, somatics, and humanities. Contact the school for a current catalog and status of degree programs.

Lauterstein-Conway Massage School and Clinic
4701-B Burnet Road
Austin, TX 78756
(512) 374-9222 or (800) 474-0852 (toll-free)

Program:
A diploma is issued for the completion of the AMTA–COMTAA-accredited program (two semesters, 550 hours). Students or currently

practicing therapists can also take a third semester of advanced training.

The first semester is 300 hours of professional massage therapy, and students can qualify to become Registered Massage Therapists in Texas upon completion. Courses include Swedish massage and hydrotherapy. The second semester includes sports massage, structural bodywork, deep massage Zen shiatsu, and advanced anatomy.

Prerequisites:
Applicants must have a high school diploma or equivalent.

Tuition:
In 1997/98, tuition was $2,450 per semester or $4,900 for the full year.

Financial Assistance:
One $500 scholarship is available for each semester 1 class. The school also offers a payment plan.

Application Deadline:
The school recommends sending applications approximately six weeks before class starts, although late applications are accepted on a space-available basis. New classes enter in March, June, September, and November.

Other Programs:
The school offers advanced training workshops in craniosacral work, Zero Balancing, deep massage, pregnancy massage, and myofascial release.

Massage Institute of New England, Inc.
22 McGrath Highway, Suite 11
Somerville, MA 02143
(617) 666-3700

Program:
The 680-hour course covers classic Swedish technique as well as Eastern and Western models. Students are encouraged to define their individual style within a holistic approach. Full-time students can complete their training in eight months.

Prerequisites:
Applicants must have a high school diploma or equivalent.

Tuition:
In 1997 tuition for a full-time student was approximately $6,900.

Financial Assistance:
Contact the school for information.

Application Deadline:
The school accepts applications throughout the year.

Other Programs:
The school offers continuing education classes, including sports massage and Zero Balancing.

Muscular Therapy Institute (MTI)
122 Rindge Avenue
Cambridge, MA 02140
(617) 576-1300
http://www.mtti.com

MTI was founded in 1974. At MTI students learn the Benjamin System of Muscular Therapy, a combination of massage treatment and client education that promotes physical health by helping reduce stress, pain, and muscular tension.

Program:
The intensive professional training in muscular therapy is a 900-hour program. It includes extensive instruction in the sciences, business development, and therapeutic relationships, and hands-on experience.

Each student experiences the entire MTI program with the same group, called a cluster. MTI expects the cluster to set a foundation for future professional support and networking. Students also receive fifteen private coaching sessions with a faculty member to practice and refine hands-on massage techniques. A class adviser is assigned to each class group for private consultations regarding educational or personal issues.

Prerequisites:
MTI requires applicants to take an introductory workshop as a prerequisite for enrollment.

Tuition:
In 1996/97 tuition was approximately $12,500, not including fees, supplies, and books.

Financial Assistance:

Financial aid is available to qualified applicants.

Application Deadline:

Applications are accepted throughout the year. The school uses a semester system, and introductory workshops are available throughout the year.

Other Programs:

The Touch Therapy Institute, offering programs in touch therapy, is located at the same address.

Mueller College of Holistic Studies
4607 Park Boulevard
San Diego, CA 92116-2630
(619) 291-9811 or (800) 245-1976 (toll-free)
http://www.fcinet.com/mueller

Founded in 1976, Mueller was the first school in California and the fourteenth in the United States to receive curriculum approval from the American Massage Therapy Association. Mueller has been active in influencing regulation of massage and body therapies in San Diego by supporting ordinances on testing, dress code, and the development of the Holistic Health Practitioner career path. The American Oriental Bodywork Therapy Association (AOBTA) has approved the school's acupressurist curriculum (see chapter 8). Mueller is recognized as a vocational school by the State of California Council for Private Postsecondary and Vocational Education.

Program:

Students must first complete a 100-hour massage technician course before taking the more advanced 512-hour massage therapist certificate. Full-time students may complete the massage therapist program in a minimum of six months.

Students who live outside the San Diego area may choose to take accelerated trainings. These include intensive hands-on bodywork courses taught in five or ten consecutive days, depending on the class. Students taking the intensive training may transfer academic courses in anatomy and physiology, kinesiology, pathology, business and cells/nutrition from a four-year college, junior college, or correspondence school with Mueller's advance approval of the school and its course descriptions. Mueller allows out-of-town guests to stay at the school at a charge of $5 per night in a bring-your-sleeping-bag "student hostel situation" (see the web site for more information).

Prerequisites:
Applicants must complete an enrollment packet that includes writing a contract addressing individual needs, developing a payment plan, and completing the qualifying process. Mueller's qualifying process may vary depending on the program.

Tuition:
In 1996/97 the massage therapist program cost $3,600 plus supplies.

Financial Assistance:
Payment plans, veteran's benefits, and California vocational assistance for qualified students are all available.

Application Deadline:
In order to complete the massage therapist program in six months, full-time students must start the program during the first or third quarter.

Other Programs:
Mueller also offers a 1000-hour program called holistic health practitioner. The school is approved to offer continuing education credits by the California Board of Registered Nursing and the National Certification Board for Therapeutic Massage and Bodywork (NCBTMB).

National Holistic Institute (NHI)
5900 Hollis Street, Suite J
Emeryville, CA 94608-2008
(510) 547-6442
Fax (510) 547-6621
http://www.nhimassage.com

NHI's massage therapy and health educator program is designed to provide students with professional skills and to be successful even if they did not do well in school in the past. NHI is also approved or accredited by the State of California Council for Private Postsecondary and Vocational Education (CPPVE) and the Accrediting Council for Continuing Education and Training (ACCET).

Program:
The massage program concentrates on five areas: massage theory and practice; anatomy, physiology, kinesiology, and pathology; practice management; student clinic; and externship/community service. Massage techniques taught include Swedish massage; acupressure/ shiatsu massage; sports massage; massage for pregnant women; massage for people with injuries; seated massage; foot reflexology; deep tissue massage; energy massage; joint mobilization; rocking and shaking massage; professional draping procedures; body mechanics for the therapist; and assessment and customization of massage sessions.

Prerequisites:
Applicants should have a high school education or equivalent. A state-required entrance examination may be necessary. Applicants are encouraged to schedule an appointment for an interview and a tour of the facilities.

Tuition:
In 1996/97 tuition for full-time students (approximately ten months) was approximately $6,050, plus fees and supplies.

Financial Assistance:
Federal financial aid programs available through the school include Federal Pell Grants, Federal Stafford Loans, Federal Parents Loans for Undergraduate Students (PLUS), Federal Supplemental Education Opportunity Grants (SEOG), and Federal Work-Study (FWS).

Application Deadline:
NHI accepts applications throughout the year. Allow enough time for the interview process and financial aid applications, if necessary.

Other Programs:
NHI is approved by the Board of Registered nursing and the AMTA for continuing education credits.

New Center College for Wholistic Health, Education and
 Research
6801 Jericho Turnpike, Suite 300
Syosset, NY 11791-4413
(516) 364-0808
http://www.newcenter.edu

New Center teaches AMMA Therapy®, a system of Oriental bodywork therapy developed by New Center's co-founder Tina Sohn.

Program:
In September 1996 the Board of Regents of the University of the State of New York granted approval to The New Center College to award a 63-credit Associate of Occupational Studies (AOS) degree with a major in Massage Therapy, the first of its kind in the United States. Graduates of this degree program are trained in both European massage therapy and AMMA Therapy® Graduates are eligible for licensing as massage therapists, and may also sit for the National Certification Commission for Acupuncture and Oriental Medicine (NCCAOM) national certification examination in Oriental Bodywork Therapy.

Prerequisites:
Applicants must be at least eighteen years of age and have a high school diploma or equivalent.

Tuition:
In 1997 the average tuition was $15,750 ($250 per credit).

Financial Assistance:
The Tuition Assistance Program (TAP) is available to eligible New York State residents attending postsecondary institutions in the State of New York. The school also participates in all the standard federal loan programs.

Application Deadline:
Contact the school for a current calendar of classes and financial aid deadlines.

Other Programs:
New Center offers several other programs, including a master's degree in acupuncture (see chapter 2) and a certificate program in holistic nursing (see chapter 14).

New Mexico Academy of Healing Arts (NMAHA)
501 Franklin Street
Santa Fe, NM 87501
(505) 982-6271

Program:
NMAHA offers three massage certification programs ranging from 650 hours to 1200 hours of course work. The six-month program (650 hours) trains students in Swedish and therapeutic massage and introduces them to Feldenkrais movement therapy, t'ai chi ch'uan, and yoga. Students may also choose to take this as an evening program (twelve months).

The 1,000-hour and 1,200-hour programs take nine and eleven months respectively. The school recommends the 1,000-hour program to students who are comfortable with strong academic demands in a short period of time. Both courses offer additional training in aromatherapy, energetic nutrition, medical massage, meditation, Ortho-Bionomy, and polarity therapy, as well as allowing for bodywork electives. Students in the two longer programs are advised not to work while they are attending school.

Prerequisites:
Students must have a high school diploma or equivalent, and be at least eighteen years of age.

Tuition:
In 1997 the average cost for full-time students ranged from $6,000 to $9,500, depending on the length of the program.

Financial Assistance:
NMAHA offers payment plans.

Application Deadline:
Applications are accepted throughout the year. Call for starting dates for individual programs.

Other Programs:
NMAHA also offers certification for polarity practitioners and a dual certification for polarity/massage (see chapter 12).

New Mexico School of Natural Therapeutics (NMSNT)
117 Richmond NE, Suite A
Albuquerque, NM 87106
(505) 268-6870 or (800)654-1675 (toll-free)
http://www.nmsnt.org/nathealth

For more than twenty years, NMSNT has offered a course based in polarity therapy and massage.

Program:
The curriculum includes classes in shiatsu, homeopathic medicine, herbology, hydrotherapy, Chinese Five Element, Bach Flower Remedies, reflexology, integrated neuromuscular techniques, and the theory of nature cure. The program is designed to meet or exceed the requirements for licensure as a massage therapist in most states. Day and evening programs are available.

Prerequisites:
Applicants must be at least eighteen years of age and have a high school diploma or equivalent. Students may need to take an anatomy and physiology class before entering.

Tuition:
In 1996/97 tuition averaged $4,800 plus books and supplies.

Financial Assistance:
Installment plans are available through the school.

Application Deadline:
Applications should be received at least two months before the starting date of the desired program. NMSNT has offered a preparatory class each May and November in the past.

Other Programs:
The school sponsors continuing education seminars in areas such as sports massage, Ayurveda, pregnancy massage, and the various movement modalities.

Pennsylvania School of Muscle Therapy, Ltd. (PSMT)
994 Old Eagle School Road, Suite 1005
Wayne, PA 19087
(610) 687-0888
http://www.psmt.com

PSMT is recognized by the International Association of Pfrimmer Deep Muscle Therapists, and also has accreditation through the Associated Bodywork and Massage Professionals (ABMP) for its full massage therapy program. PSMT is an approved provider for the National Athletic Trainers Association Board of Certification, so athletes may receive credit for PSMT programs.

Program:
The nine-month professional massage therapist program is designed for a beginner or intermediate massage therapist who wants a foundation in Pfrimmer Deep Muscle Therapy and other advanced work. The curriculum covers the basic education needed by students wishing to specialize later in certification programs such as Pfrimmer Deep Muscle Therapy, sports massage, neuromuscular therapy, and evaluation certification offered by PSMT.

Prerequisites:
Applicants must be at least eighteen years of age and have a high school diploma or equivalent to enter the professional massage therapist program. Certificate programs may require additional training or qualifications.

Tuition:
In 1996/97 tuition and fees for the nine-month program averaged $4,850 plus books and supplies.

Financial Assistance:
Payment plans are offered.

Application Deadline:
Applications are accepted throughout the year.

Other Programs:
The Swedish/shiatsu extended massage program has been approved by the New York State Department of Education to qualify for licensing board exams in the state of New York. The school also offers continuing education courses for neuromuscular therapy.

Phoenix Therapeutic Massage College
2225 North 16th Street
Phoenix, AZ 85006
(602) 254-7002 or (800) 390-1885 (toll-free)

Program:
Students may choose between a therapeutic massage program (735 hours) or a professional certification program (1,110 hours). The latter includes deep tissue massage, traditional Chinese massage, lymphatic/immune system massage, pregnancy massage, geriatric/hospice massage, and advanced sports massage.

Prerequisites:
Students must have a high school diploma or equivalent, and be eighteen years of age before program completion.

Tuition:
In 1997/98 average tuition for the therapeutic massage program was $5,645 and $8,455 for the professional certification program. The school recommends budgeting $6,500 to $9,200 for the program to cover costs of books, table, and other supplies.

Financial Assistance:
The school participates in federal loan programs and Pell Grants.

Application Deadline:
Applications are accepted throughout the year.

Other Programs:
The school has continuing education certificate courses for graduates and LMTs.

Potomac Massage Training Institute
4000 Albemarle Street NW
Washington, DC 20016-1857
(202) 686-7046

The school's motto in 1997 was "celebrating 21 years of *hand made* health."

Program:
The program emphasizes client-centered massage, consideration of the specific needs and physical structure of the individual. Study of Swedish massage theory and techniques includes effleurage, petrissage, friction, tapotement, and vibration, as well as identifying the benefits, contraindications, and limitations of this therapy. Students take 515 in-class supervised hours and 663 out-of-class assignments, including fieldwork, massage practice, and written assignments. Fieldwork emphasizes community service, such as working with the residents of nursing homes. The program takes eighteen months to complete, with students meeting twice a week. No full-time program is offered.

Prerequisites:
Students must have a high school diploma or equivalent.

Tuition:
In 1997 tuition for the full program (three semesters) was $5,250.

Financial Assistance:
No financial assistance was offered at the time of publication.

Application Deadline:
Applications are due by January 15 or July 15. Classes begin in March and September.

Other Programs:
The school offers public education and professional continuing education and is approved as a National Certification Board for Therapeutic Massage and Bodywork (NCBTMB) Category A continuing education provider.

Sarasota School of Massage Therapy
1970 Main Street, 3rd floor
Sarasota, FL 34236
(941) 957-0577
e-mail: massage@gte.net

The school has accreditation from the Council on Occupational Education (formerly SACS/COEI).

Program:
The 540-hour program focuses on the musculoskeletal system and its integration with a psycho/somatic approach. Students may also meet New York state requirements by taking an additional 105 hours of Oriental bodywork.

Prerequisites:
The school requires applicants to be at least eighteen years of age and have a high school diploma or equivalent.

Tuition:
In 1997 the average cost for the 540-hour program was $3,600.

Financial Assistance:
The school provides payment plans.

Application Deadline:
Applications should be received no later than two weeks before classes begin. Contact the school for exact dates.

Other Programs:
The school offers continuing education programs in advanced massage techniques, Thai massage, and other modalities.

Seattle Massage School (SMS)
7120 Woodlawn Avenue NE
Seattle, WA 98115
(206) 527-0807

Alternate address:
2721 Wetmore Avenue
Everett, WA 98201
(425) 339-2678

Alternate Address:
5005 Pacific Highway East #20
Fife, WA 98424
(253) 926-1435

SMS, founded in 1974, is the largest massage school operating in Washington. Students may take classes in Seattle, Fife (Tacoma), or Everett, Washington.

Program:
The 906-hour comprehensive program lasts twelve months. Students may choose between a day or evening track. The core curriculum includes anatomy and physiology; kinesiology; massage theory and practice; seated massage; pregnancy massage; massage for chronic pain; and sports massage. Students gain clinical experience through the SMS student clinic or hospital internships.

Prerequisites:
Applicants should be at least eighteen years of age and have a high school diploma or equivalent. SMS asks that applicants schedule an information interview before making a formal application and meet with an admissions representative at the campus nearest to them.

Tuition:
Tuition for the comprehensive program was $8,990 in 1998.

Financial Assistance:
SMS offers federal financial aid programs, including the Pell Grant, Stafford Loan, and Parent/PLUS Loan to students who qualify. Payment plans were also available.

Application Deadline:
Applications are accepted throughout the year (see informational interview under prerequisites).

Other Programs:
SMS offers continuing education classes for licensed massage practitioners.

Scherer Institute of Natural Healing
935 Alto Street
Santa Fe, NM 87501
(505) 982-8398

Alternate Address:
PO Box 2118
1337-H Gusdorf Road
Taos, NM 87571
(505) 751-3143

Program:
The 700-hour curriculum, three terms or approximately one year, takes a holistic approach to bodywork with courses in therapeutic massage, connective tissue bodywork, shiatsu, herbology, hydrotherapy, reflexology, nonspecific stretches, basic homeopathic theory, and movement therapy.

During massage classes, Scherer maintains a high teacher/ assistant to student ratio. The institute emphasizes that a maximum of thirty students per class are accepted at the Santa Fe facility and twenty-six students per class at Taos. Students stay together as a group as they work through the program.

Prerequisites:
Applicants must be twenty years of age and have a high school diploma or equivalent.

Tuition:
In 1997 the average tuition was $6,000 for the full three terms.

Financial Assistance:
Scherer has several work-study positions and some partial scholarships available in each program.

Application Deadline:
Allow three to four weeks for the processing of applications and the arrangement of a personal or phone interview. Applicants interested in receiving financial assistance should contact the school as early as possible. The program begins in September or March at Santa Fe and October or April in Taos.

Other Programs:
The school offers a variety of continuing education programs throughout the year for beginning and advanced students. Past courses included nutrition for the childbearing year; trigger point therapy; somatic treatment of trauma; and Watsu.

Seminar Network International, Inc.
School of Massage and Allied Therapies
518 N. Federal Highway
Lake Worth, FL 33460
(561) 582-5349 or (800) 882-0903 (toll-free)

Program:
The 600-hour massage therapy program can be completed in six months or one year. The emphasis is on practical massage training.

Prerequisites:
Applicants must have a high school diploma, GED, or ATB.

Tuition:
In 1997 the average tuition was $5,000. The school suggests budgeting an additional $200 for books and lab fees.

Financial Assistance:
Assistance is available; contact the school for current information.

Application Deadline:
Applications are accepted throughout the year. Classes start in December, March, June, and September.

Other Programs:
The school offers a 100-hour certificate program in colon therapy as well as NCBTMB continuing education courses.

Somerset School of Massage Therapy
7 Cedar Grove Lane
Somerset, NJ 08873
(732) 356-0787
Fax: (732) 469-3494
http://www.massagecareer.com

The school is approved by the New Jersey Department of Vocational Education.

Program:
The 512-hour program includes massage therapy theory and practice, anatomy, physiology, myofascial and deep tissue techniques, neuromuscular therapy, reflexology, prenatal massage, sports massage, clinic practicum, business management, CPR, hydrotherapy, and electives. Graduates are eligible to sit for national certification, Florida, Iowa, and other licensing exams.

Prerequisites:
Applicants must be at least eighteen years of age and have a high school diploma or equivalent.

Tuition:
Average 1996/97 tuition was approximately $4,800 plus supplies, fees, and books.

Application Deadline:
The twelve-month winter class begins in January. A six-month spring class begins in March.

Other Programs:
Somerset has continuing education accreditation from the NCBTMB.

Suncoast Center for Natural Health, Inc.
4910 W. Cypress Street,
Tampa, FL 33607
(813) 287-1099

The school is approved and licensed by the Florida Department of Education Board for Vocational Schools.

Program:
The basic massage and hydrotherapy program covers 500 hours. The massage therapies taught in this program include Swedish, Esalen, sports massage, and myofascial release. Students are also introduced to allied modalities such as aromatherapy, kinesiology, seated massage, and others.

The basic massage and hydrotherapy program with specialization (600 hours) covers the same material as the basic program, but also allows the student to chose more intensive training in Oriental modalities, sports massage, or Coremassage. Both programs take six months to complete. The school also provides 75 hours of instruction in myology (the muscular system of the body) and 105 hours of Oriental modalities required for the New York state license.

Prerequisites:
Applicants must be eighteen years of age and hold a high school diploma or equivalent.

Tuition:
In 1997/98 average tuition was $4,200 for the 500-hour program, and $5,200 for the 600-hour program.

Financial Assistance:
The school participates in federal student loan programs. The 600-hour specialization program qualifies for Pell Grant assistance.

Application Deadline:
Classes start in February, May, August, and November. Students needing financial aid should allow four to eight weeks to complete that process before starting class.

Other Programs:
Suncoast sponsors community and professional workshops, seminars, and lectures.

Utah College of Massage Therapy, Inc.(UCMT)
25 South 300 East
Salt Lake City, UT 84111
(801) 521-3330 or (800) 617-3302 (toll-free)
http://www.ucmt.com

UCMT opened a new campus in Lindon, Utah, in May of 1997 to serve the Utah County region, which includes Provo and Orem.

UCMT also opened a new facility in Layton in 1997 to serve the northern Utah region. Call or check the school's web site for schedules at the branch campuses.

Program:
The standard massage program ranges from 712 to 780 hours, depending on the course of study chosen. Classes include massage therapy, therapeutic touch, shiatsu, acupressure, Touch for Health, trigger-point therapy, reflexology, sports massage, injury massage, and other therapeutic techniques including movement therapy. Basic academic courses such as anatomy and physiology are also required.

The Utah College of Massage Therapy has developed a team of experienced students to assist athletes at events across the state of Utah and neighboring states in swimming, running, rock climbing, cross country skiing, downhill skiing, bobsledding, bicycling events, and sporting activities such as the Utah Summer/Winter Games and the Special Olympics.

Prerequisites:
Applicants should have a high school diploma or equivalent.

Tuition:
In 1996/97 tuition ranged from $5,200 to $5,600, depending on the program and number of hours.

Financial Assistance:
Federal loans and grants are available to eligible students.

Application Deadline:
The school accepts applications throughout the year.

Other Programs:
Call the school or check the web site for events and classes at the various campuses.

Virginia School of Massage (VSOM)
2008 Morton Drive
Charlottesville, VA 22903
(904) 293-4031 or (888) 599-2001 (toll-free)
http://www.vasaom.com

Established in 1988, VSOM is connected with the Baltimore School of Massage.

Program:
The 500-hour professional massage training program emphasizes the transformational approach to bodywork. Students attend part-time, and the course takes approximately eighteen months to complete.

Prerequisites:
Applicants must have a high school diploma or equivalent.

Tuition:
In 1997 the cost for the entire program was approximately $4,350.

Financial Assistance:
Check with the school at time of application. It has been approved for the training of veterans.

Application Deadline:
The school accepts applications throughout the year.

Other Programs:
VSOM also offers a 100-hour vocational program in massage and has been approved by the NCBTMB as a Category A continuing education provider.

Wellness & Massage Training Institute
618 Executive Drive
Willowbrook, IL 60521
(630) 325-3773
http://www.wmti.com

Program:
The massage therapy curriculum lasts for 700 hours. Clinical experience and outreach programs are designed to help students become familiar with specific client populations, such as the elderly or athletes. Electives include seated massage techniques, sports massage, positional release, active assisted stretching, Esalen, structural massage, and pressure sensitivity techniques. Other courses offered include Touch for Health (Thie's system), Ortho-Bionomy, Jin Shin Do (acupressure), shiatsu, and cranialsacral. Most students take two to three years to complete this program. Students may take up to five years or fifteen trimesters.

Prerequisites:
Applicants must be at least eighteen years old and have a high school diploma or equivalent. They must also receive a one-hour full-body Swedish style professional massage before their acceptance into the program (a verification form must be signed by therapist and submitted with application).

Tuition:
In 1997 the full program was approximately $7,000.

Financial Assistance:
The school offers installment payment plans.

Application Deadline:
Applications are accepted on an ongoing basis.

Other Programs:
The school offers an Oriental bodywork program (750 hours), an Ortho-Bionomy program, and continuing education classes.

Canadian Schools

West Coast College of Massage Therapy (WCCMT)
Box 12110
555 West Hastings Street
Vancouver, British Columbia V6B 4N6
(604) 689-3854
e-mail: wccmt@wccmt.edu

Founded in 1983, WCCMT is registered with the Private Post-Secondary Education Commission. WCCMT is accredited by the British Columbia Ministry of Health and the College of Massage Therapists of British Columbia.

Program:
The 3,000-hour program has the most academic hours of any diploma program of massage therapy training in North America. The academic area of study covers physiology, kinesiology, and pathology. The clinical education area introduces students to a variety of soft tissue

modalities that form the treatment system of massage therapy, including hydrotherapy, movement therapy, and joint mobilization.

Students intern for 600 hours of instruction in college's professional clinic. Additional clinical experience comes through the school's Community Outreach Service Program. There students practice in retirement and nursing homes, performance athletes training centers, and long- and short-term care facilities in hospital settings.

Prerequisites:
Applicants must have a minimum of high school graduation with grade twelve chemistry and first-year college- or university-level biology. WCCMT offers approved, equivalent prerequisite biology and chemistry courses in the evenings.

Tuition:
In 1997/98 tuition was $24,900 CDN for the entire program.

Financial Assistance:
Students are eligible for both federal and provincial student loans.

Application Deadline:
Classes enter in September and January. Contact the college for financial aid deadlines as well as information on the fulfillment of prerequisite classes.

Other Programs:
WCCMT offers approved, equivalent prerequisite biology and chemistry courses in the evenings for students who need to fulfill educational requirements before entering the massage program.

Sutherland-Chan School and Teaching Clinic
300 Dupont Street, 4th Floor
Toronto, Ontario M5R 1V9
(416) 924-1107

The massage therapy programs are accredited or recognized by the College of Massage Therapists of Ontario, the Ministry of Education, and the British Columbia Massage Practitioners' Organization. The school has also earned approval from the AMTA.

Program:
The two-year diploma program covers anatomy, massage techniques, massage treatments, pathology, physiology, remedial exercise, and

other therapeutic techniques. Students gain clinical experience through clinical practicums and outreach programs at hospitals, clinics, and senior citizen residences.

Prerequisites:
Applicants must have a high school diploma or equivalent. Prerequisite class work needed includes an introduction to massage course, college-level biology, and a standard first aid/CPR class.

Tuition:
In 1996/97 the average tuition was $14,600 CDN.

Financial Assistance:
Qualified students may receive provincial or national student loans. Payment plans are available.

Application Deadline:
Applicants need to arrange with the school to take the introduction to massage class before enrollment and check the financial assistance deadlines.

Other Programs:
In addition to the introduction to massage class, the school also offers a preadmission science course to help prospective students who have an inadequate science background.

✨PROFESSIONAL ORGANIZATIONS AND OTHER EDUCATIONAL RESOURCES

There are at least four national organizations for massage therapists in the United States and one national organization in Canada. Contact them for lists of schools affiliated with their organization as well as information on the educational and professional resources offered by their organizations.

UNITED STATES

American Massage Therapy Association (AMTA)
820 Davis Street, Suite 100
Evanston, IL 60201
(847) 864-0123
http://www.amtamassage.org

Started in 1943, AMTA is the largest and oldest organization for massage therapists in the United States, with member chapters in all fifty states. AMTA is actively involved in legislative matters pertaining to the uniform licensing of massage therapists and accreditation of schools. The Commission on Massage Training Accreditation/ Approval (COMTAA), an independent body funded by AMTA, acts as the primary accreditation agency for massage schools. Contact AMTA for a current list of approved and accredited schools as well as a current list of legal regulations pertaining to massage therapy in the United States.

American Oriental Bodywork Therapy Association (AOBTA)
AOBTA National Headquarters
Glendale Executive Campus
1000 White Horse Road, Suite 510
Voorhees, NJ 08043
(609) 782-1616

AOBTA was formed in 1989 by the joining of several associations that represented individual disciplines of Oriental bodywork therapy. For membership, AOBTA requires documentation of training of a minimum of 500 hours of AOBTA-approved training for the designation of certified practitioner and a minimum of 150 hours for an associate. To find AOBTA certified teachers and training programs, contact the association.

Associated Bodywork and Massage Professionals (ABMP)
28677 Buffalo Park Road
Evergreen, CO 80439-7347
(303) 674-8478
http://www.abmp.com

ABMP concentrates on promoting ethical practices, protecting the rights of practitioners, and educating the public as to the benefits of massage, bodywork, and somatic therapies. Contact the association for a list of affiliated schools.

International Massage Association (IMA)
3000 Connecticut Avenue, NW., Suite 308
Washington, D.C., 20008
(202) 387-6555
http://www.internationalmassage.com

IMA is a grassroots massage association formed in 1994. The association sells video courses on various bodywork techniques, which may be combined with two- or three-day professional seminars taught in Washington, D.C. The costs for professional courses ranged from $1,300 to $3,000 in 1997. Contact the association for a list of affiliated schools or check their web site.

National Association of Nurse Massage Therapists (NANMT)
PO Box 1150
Abita Springs, LA 70420
(888) 462-6686 (toll-free)

Founded in 1987, the 700-member association began holding annual conferences in 1996. NANMT provides a network of nurses who use massage therapy as well as sponsoring bodywork-related educational programs. It is currently working on national certification for nurse massage therapists.

CANADA

Canadian Massage Therapist Alliance (CMTA)
365 Bloor Street East, Suite 1807
Toronto, Ontario M4W 3L4P
(416) 968-2149

The Canadian Massage Therapist Alliance is a nationwide organization composed of provincial professional associations. For information about massage therapy schools, CMTA suggests contacting the appropriate provincial member association (see Appendix B: Professional Organizations, Useful Resources, and Internet Sites).

❧CONTINUING EDUCATION

Many of the bodywork and movement therapies listed in part 3 also qualify as continuing education credits for massage therapists.

International Association of Infant Massage
1720 Willow Creek #516
Eugene, OR 97402
(800) 248-5432

The four-day instructor training is offered at various sites through the country. Teachers are independent contractors and cost varies depending on location. Courses meet NCBTMB continuing education requirements and may qualify for nursing continuing education units in some areas.

International Association of Infant Massage
Canadian Chapter
1309 Parc du Village Street
Orleans, Ontario K1C 7B2
(613) 830-6690

The International Association of Infant Massage is a nonprofit organization whose mission is to promote nurturing touch and communication through training, education, and research. Classes and educational materials are offered through the organization.

✒Recommended Reading

Mitchell, Stewart. *Massage: A Practical Introduction.* Rockport MA: Element Books, 1992.

> Mitchell gives a very straightforward explanation of the basics of massage along with some ideas on how it can be combined with other therapies, such as aromatherapy. This title was originally published in Britain, so resources are more focused on European practice.

Massage Magazine. 1315 W. Mallon Avenue, Spokane, WA 99201. (800) 533-4263.

> *Massage Magazine* publishes in-depth articles on bodywork therapies, updates on legislative issues, and carries many advertisements for schools and continuing education programs. Use it as a resource for finding a school in your region or for finding more specialized bodywork programs.

5

Licensed Midwife (LM) and Certified Nurse-Midwife (CNM)

In Europe, midwives attend approximately 75 percent of all births. In the United States, midwives are involved in less than 10 percent of all births. Although midwives have practiced in North America since colonial days, their legal status has often been challenged or denied.

Traditionally, midwives gained their education through apprenticeships with older, experienced women and then practiced in rural or poor urban areas where women had little access to obstetricians and allopathic care. Today, midwives still provide necessary care for medically underserved populations, as well as offering their services to women interested in natural childbirth. Since the 1970s, several research studies have been published to support the use of midwives in low-risk births as a cost-effective alternative to obstetricians.

The overwhelming majority of students and practitioners in midwifery are women. Some come into the profession after working as childbirth educators or labor assistants, while others are inspired by their own experiences with midwives. One midwifery school noted that more than half their students were mothers who had experienced natural childbirth.

Women interested in entering this profession can follow two distinct educational tracks: by training at an independent midwifery school including a formal apprenticeship with a working midwife or by training as a nurse-midwife in a conventional nursing school.

At the independent schools, students take classes covering gynecology, fetus development, obstetrical complications, nutritional assessment, counseling, community health, family planning, and other issues surrounding pregnancy and natural childbirth. Delayed Entry Midwives (DEMs) also study natural therapies. As part of their clinical training as a DEM, students work under the supervision of a midwife giving prenatal, newborn, and postpartum exams as well as participating in delivery. Deliveries take place in homes, birthing centers, or other out-of-hospital settings. This clinical training varies depending on the state's licensure requirements and the structure of the school's program. The accrediting agency for independent schools requires that the minimum clinical training include active participation in twenty births; functioning as a primary midwife under supervision at twenty additional births (ten in homes or out-of-hospital settings); seventy-four prenatal exams; twenty newborn exams; and forty postpartum exams. Many schools require their students to do more than these minimums.

In the states that license midwives, students sit for a licensing exam after completing their education and take the professional title of licensed midwife (LM).

The licensed midwife generally works in an independent practice. She monitors the health of the mother and fetus, delivers the baby, and does follow-up care. Depending on the practice, the LM may deliver babies in the home or at a licensed birthing center. Some LMs choose to work in clinics or hospital settings, although this is less typical.

Licensed midwives may use natural therapies, such as herbs and massage, to help ease the discomforts of pregnancy. Nutritional assessment and counseling is an important part of their practice.

The focus of the LM's practice is on well-woman care. Typically, the LM provides care to the mother from conception through six weeks postpartum and refers families to additional social and medical services as needed. An LM may also diagnose certain conditions that may require the mother to be under a physician's care.

The North American Registry of Midwives (NARM) provides a national examination for direct-entry midwives. This examination is based on the core competencies and standards of practice established by Midwives' Alliance of North America (MANA). The NARM certification process leads to the credential of certified professional midwife (CPM). In states that do not license midwives but do allow their practice, women may choose to use the CPM designation. Certification by NARM may not be necessary for licensure.

Certified nurse-midwives (CNM) are trained and regulated as part of the nursing profession. Many have established independent practices, but CNMs can also be found working in HMOs, hospitals, private clinics, and birth centers. Like direct-entry midwives, CNMs focus their practice on healthy women and healthy babies. The CNM provides prenatal care, labor and delivery management, well-woman gynecology, normal newborn care, and family planning.

A CNM must be a registered nurse before beginning her training as a midwife, or must earn her nursing degree during midwifery training. Although the CNM's practice emphasizes well-woman care and natural childbirth, academic training includes courses on the use of prescription drugs and has a stronger allopathic emphasis than the independent midwifery schools. CNMs can issue prescriptions within the scope of their license.

Some universities are now offering a combined nursing/ certified nurse midwife (RN/CNM) program for those who do not have an RN. Applicants will need to have a bachelor's degree and will probably need to have taken a year of biology, anatomy, and physiology in their undergraduate studies. Some schools may allow conditional entry based on completion of the necessary science courses concurrently with the degree.

In areas that legally prohibit direct-entry midwives, this approach can still allow a student to enter midwifery practice without having to earn two separate degrees. The combined RN/CNM program is approximately four years, about one year less than earning an RN degree and then entering a separate CNM program.

Some CNM programs will allow advance standing for students who already have a physician's assistant (PA) degree. Contact the American College of Nurse-Midwifery to find a university program suited to your needs.

Income varies greatly, depending on the type of practice. Midwives may qualify for third-party reimbursement (insurance) or they may bill clients directly. In Washington state licensed direct-entry midwives are providers for the state Medicaid program as well as preferred providers in many private health plans. Many midwives choose to work in low-income areas.

COST OF EDUCATION

Cost of education varies depending on the institution. It ranges from $5,000 to $20,000 for a full program.

At the time of publication, financial assistance for direct-entry midwifery students was extremely limited. None of the independent schools in the United States participated in the federal loan programs. Some states, like Washington, offer financial assistance to midwifery students who are willing to work in rural or under-served communities after qualification as a direct-entry midwife.

A few schools offer scholarships (usually one per year). Most schools are willing to work out a payment plan for students.

LENGTH OF TRAINING

Direct-entry midwifery students spend approximately one to two years in an academic setting. The rest of their training takes place in internships with practicing midwives.

For the second half of their training, the emphasis is on the number of births attended, the number of patients seen, and so on. The amount of time needed to fulfill these clinical requirements can vary greatly. The average length of training, including academic courses, is four years; but students can take as few as three years or as many as seven years to complete all requirements.

ADMISSIONS PROCESS

Midwifery schools follow an admissions process similar to the other colleges listed in part 2. Applicants are required to submit transcripts, essays or letters of interest, recommendations, and proof of the ability to pay tuition.

Most schools admit students only once a year, and usually receive more applications than spaces available. Usually applicants need to begin the admissions process a year or more before they plan to attend school.

The schools place a strong emphasis on the applicant's personal ability to meet the demands of the profession rather than their educational background (see prerequisites below), and generally require personal interviews prior to admittance.

UNDERGRADUATE PREREQUISITES

Some schools require that applicants have completed a bachelor's degree. Others want applicants to have completed certain science courses prior to entry.

The applicant's life experience and readiness to enter this field may count for far more than academic background in securing admission. The schools are looking for personal experience, such as work as a childbirth educator or labor assistant; related medical training; membership in a midwifery or parenting organization; or other evidence of commitment to midwifery.

Several schools recommend that applicants undergo training as a labor assistant or childbirth educator before starting midwifery school. Some schools require this training as an educational prerequisite.

✎LICENSING OF MIDWIVES AND ACCREDITATION OF SCHOOLS

UNITED STATES

Licensed midwives (LMs) may practice independently in certain states. In 1997 the following states licensed midwives: Alaska, Arizona, Arkansas, Colorado, Florida, Louisiana, Montana, New Hampshire, New Mexico, Oregon, Texas, and Washington.

In some states, the practice of non-nurse midwives is specifically prohibited. In others, their practice is tolerated but not regulated. Check with MANA for the current status of direct-entry midwives in your state.

Registered nurses who have completed graduate-level programs in midwifery and have been certified by the American College of Nurse-Midwives (ACNM) can legally practice as certified nurse-midwives (CNMs) in all fifty states and the District of Columbia. Restrictions to the scope of their practice varies from state to state. The ACNM is the only accrediting body for nurse-midwifery programs recognized by the Department of Education.

The Midwifery Education Accreditation Council (MEAC) functions as the independent accreditation body for the schools affiliated with MANA, and their educational standards meet the NARM standards. Graduates of MEAC-accredited programs are considered qualified to take the NARM Certified Professional Midwife (CPM) exam.

Midwifery Education Accreditation Council
Mary Ann Baul, President
318 W. Birch #5
Flagstaff, AZ 86001

CANADA

Midwives were integrated into Ontario's provincial health-care system with the passage of Bill 56 in December 1993. In 1997 Alberta, British Columbia, and Manitoba also considered the integration of midwifery into their provincial health-care systems. Check with provincial authorities for the current status of midwives.

US Schools

In 1997 the following independent schools had been accredited or were undergoing accreditation with MEAC.

Birthingway Midwifery Center
5731 North Williams Avenue
Portland, OR 97217
(503) 283-4996

Birthingway meets or exceeds the educational standards set by the Oregon Midwifery Council and the Oregon State Board of Direct-Entry Midwifery. In 1997 the school applied for accreditation by the Washington State Department of Health.

Program:
The school's program trains practitioners in the traditional midwifery model of care. The first year focuses on the normal aspects of pregnancy, birth, and postpartum, including normal variations, as well as some basic deviations and complications as they relate to identifying and managing a normal pregnancy.

The second year expands on the themes of the first year, including the management of normal variations as well as emergency care for complications occurring during pregnancy and delivery. The third year covers more professional topics as well as physical exams and cultural issues.

Clinical training takes place in private midwifery practices or in the student clinic scheduled to open in 1998. Depending on where and how a student completes the clinical training, the program may take more than three years.

Prerequisites:
Applicants must be twenty years or older, already have a high school diploma or the equivalent, and have successfully completed a college-level course in anatomy and physiology (grade point average or

GPA of 3.0). Applicants may be asked to demonstrate their knowledge and commitment to the midwifery model of care through previous work experience as a birth educator or in a related field; academic training in areas related to midwifery; or involvement in midwifery organizations and classes.

Tuition:
Tuition varies based on the year of the program. In 1997 first-year students paid approximately $5,000, second-year students paid $4,000, and third-year students paid $3,000. Books for the first year cost approximately $400, and students are also responsible for purchasing their own medical equipment, such as stethoscopes.

Financial Assistance:
The school has a work-study program.

Application Deadline:
Applications are due no later than December 1, but the small class size may cause admissions to close early. Classes begin in March.

Other Programs:
Birthingway offers an anatomy and physiology course that satisfies its educational prerequisites, as well as continuing education credits for local midwives.

Birthwise Midwifery Training
66 S High Street
Bridgton, ME 04009
(207) 647-5968

Birthwise was founded in 1994 in response to a growing interest in midwifery and a lack of formal learning opportunities for aspiring midwives.

Program:
Students earn a certificate of graduation that qualifies them to sit for certification through NARM. The program includes three semesters of academic classes and six to twelve months of clinical preceptorship. Academic classes include anatomy and physiology; physical assessment; normal prenatal; normal labor and birth, postpartum; newborn; prenatal complications; the art of traditional midwifery; complications of labor and birth; mind/body connection; counseling

techniques; well-woman care; lab work; hospital birth; homeopathy; and the business of midwifery.

During clinical training, students are expected attend twenty births as an active participant, and to attend twenty births as a primary midwife.

Prerequisites:
Applicants must have a high school education or equivalent; a strong interest in women's health issues and birth at home; and a strong motivation to learn.

Tuition:
In 1997 tuition was $4,200 plus $500 for the clinical component.

Financial Assistance:
The school has a payment plan.

Application Deadline:
Applications for entry in February are due no later than November. Birthwise accepts a very small number of students each year (fifteen for 1997/98) and early application is strongly recommended.

Other Programs:
The school offers doula training (see page 152) as well as continuing education for midwives.

Maternidad La Luz
1308 Magoffin
El Paso, TX 79901
(915) 532-5895

Founded in 1987, Maternidad La Luz serves a diverse population on the Texas, New Mexico, and Mexico border areas. Approximately 85 percent of the women giving birth at the school's birthing center are Spanish-speaking only. One of the first schools to earn MEAC accreditation, Maternidad La Luz is also an approved educational program in Texas.

Program:
The school offers a variety of programs ranging from four quarters (one year) to nine quarters. First-year students attend approximately twenty-five to thirty-five births a quarter in addition to academic

classes. By the end of the fourth quarter, students have acted as a primary at approximately twenty-five to thirty births, and double primary at fifteen births. During the first quarter, students are required to work a rotating schedule of three twenty-four-hour shifts weekly, plus one twenty-four-hour on-call day.

The first four quarters concentrate on the basic and advanced clinical skills. The fifth through ninth quarters are designed to enhance clinical and academic skills while increasing birth attendance numbers. Students who require a three-year program for licensing must successfully complete all nine quarters. During this time students attend birth talks, peer review, and weekly intern meetings, and participate in community outreach. Students have on-call clients and two twenty-four-hour shifts per week.

Prerequisites:
Applicants must have a high school diploma or equivalent and be eighteen years of age or older. A thorough understanding of English is required, and a basic understanding of Spanish is recommended. Advanced placement may be available for health professionals who have already satisfied some of the academic requirements.

Tuition:
In 1997, under a "combined fee" program, the first four quarters cost $4,500. Otherwise, tuition was $1,450 per quarter. Cost for the full nine quarters ranged between $11,750 to $13,050. Students are also required to have a working car and valid driver's license to accompany clients.

Financial Assistance:
The school sponsors one full-tuition scholarship to assist women of color. There are also some work-study scholarships available for the fifth through ninth quarters.

Application Deadline:
Applications are due six months before the starting date and space is limited. Students can begin the first quarter in March or September.

Other Programs:
When openings are available, the school allows short-term placements for those investigating a career in midwifery, experienced midwives who want to participate in a birth center setting, or others interested in studying at Maternidad La Luz.

Midwifery Institute of California
3739 Balboa #179
San Francisco, CA 94121
(415) 248-1671

Program:
The three-year program prepares students for certification through NARM and for midwifery licensure in the State of California. Part-time students are accepted.

Prerequisites:
Applicants must have a high school diploma or equivalent.

Tuition:
Total cost for a full-time student for the three-year program was $7,100.

Financial Assistance:
No financial assistance was offered at the time of publication.

Application Deadline:
The school has an open admissions policy. Contact the admission office for more information.

Other Programs:
No other programs were offered at the time of publication.

Oregon School of Midwifery (OSM)
342 East 12th Avenue
Eugene, OR 97401
(541) 338-9778
http://www.efn.org/~osm

Mailing address:
PO Box 40591
Eugene, OR 97404

The school meets the educational standards of the Oregon State Health Division Board of Direct-entry Midwifery, which may also satisfy the requirements of other state midwifery organizations.

Program:
Students at the Oregon School take two years of academic classes plus one or more years of clinical training. Only full-time students were accepted into the program at the time of publication.

First-year students focus on normal antepartum, intrapartum, postpartum, and newborn care. Classes include reproductive anatomy and physiology; embryology and fetal development; principles and applications of nutrition; and the use of herbs and homeopathics. Second-year students focus on variations of normal birth, including complications and abnormalities as well as advanced midwifery skills. The third year is primarily clinical training or apprenticeship. The school provides structured objectives, skill check-off lists, and an evaluation mechanism for both the student and the preceptor.

Independent research projects, optional workshops, special courses, and retreats are also part of the educational process.

Prerequisites:
Applicants must have a high school diploma or GED, and have successfully completed a college-level human anatomy and physiology course. The following factors are also considered: previous study or training in midwifery or doula; work experience in childbirth education or related fields; related academic, medical, or technical training; membership in midwifery, breast-feeding, or parenting organizations; and evidence of commitment to midwifery as shown by reference letters and application essays.

Tuition:
In 1997 students paid approximately $4,875 plus fees, equipment, and books for the first two years. The school suggests budgeting approximately $750 per year for books. Third-year fees vary depending upon the clinical site chosen.

Financial Assistance:
A limited number of work-study jobs are available. The school also maintains a small scholarship fund for women of color or native Spanish speakers who plan to work in communities with low-income populations.

Application Deadline:
Applications are due by May 1 for entrance in the following fall term.

Other Programs:
The school holds open courses for doula training, herbs, nutrition, first aid, and general health issues. OSM offers an anatomy and physiology course each summer as a separate preparation class for those applicants unable to take this course at their local community college.

Seattle Midwifery School (SMS)
2524 16th Avenue South
Room 300
Seattle, WA 98144
(206) 322-8834

Program:
Full-time students can complete the three-year program in twenty-seven consecutive months. Four quarters of classes are taught at the Seattle location and deal with the biological sciences and basic knowledge needed for professional practice. These courses include embryology and fetal development; genetics; gynecology and women's health; perinatal nutrition; perinatal statistics and epidemiology; and pharmacological and alternative treatments.

Clinical courses (five quarters) are completed in a variety of practices in the United States and abroad. Students experience one-on-one mentoring from experienced midwives in settings ranging from home-birth practices to hospital maternity wards.

SMS emphasizes small class sizes (the school accepted fourteen new students in 1997) and personal attention to students.

Prerequisites:
Applicants must be twenty-one years of age. They must have a high school diploma or equivalent; two years of college or relevant women's health-care experience; and show successful completion of a labor support or doula course approved by the Doulas of North America (DONA). Education prerequisites include the completion of the following college-level courses within the past seven years with a 3.0 or better GPA: basic English (3 credits), human anatomy and physiology (5 to 8 credits), math (3 credits or two years of high school math), microbiology (5 credits), nutrition (3 credits), social sciences (5 or more credits), and biology (3 to 5 credits or one year of high school biology).

Tuition:
In 1997/98 full-time tuition was $187 per credit. The standard-track students take 123 credits over the three years for an average tuition cost of $23,000.

Financial Assistance:
SMS does not participate in any federal loan programs. The Washington State Health Professional Loan Repayment and Scholarship Program will help eligible applicants with tuition costs in return for a commitment to work in underserved areas of Washington state following graduation. The school recommends Canadian students check with their provincial representatives for information concerning eligibility for the Canadian Student Loan Program.

Application Deadline:
Applications are due by February 1 for enrollment in September. SMS enters only one class per year, and the class is generally filled in February. Late applications may be placed on a waiting list.

Other Programs:
The SMS Extension Education Program can be used to fulfill the labor support and nutrition prerequisites. Contact the school for more information.

Canadian Schools

Ryerson Polytechnic University
350 Victoria Street
Toronto, Ontario, M5B 2K3
(416) 979-5000
http://www.ryerson.ca

Ryerson offers a baccalaureate program in midwifery in association with McMaster and Laurentian Universities.

Program:
The courses cover basic science, social and health sciences, and women's studies. Classes may be taken on a part-time basis, but students will be attending full-time when they move into clinical placements. First-year courses include introduction to midwifery, social and cultural dimensions of health care, topics in biological science, women's studies, and midwifery care 1.

The clinical placements allow the students to work with an established midwife for an extended period of time. Students may need to relocate for clinical placements.

The suggested time to complete the program is between three to five years (the maximum allowed is seven years).

Prerequisites:
All applicants for admission must have the Ontario Secondary School Diploma (OSSD) with a minimum average of 60 percent in six Ontario Academic Courses (OACs) or equivalent. Ryerson places a strong emphasis on the applicants' personal qualities, relevant experience, and the ability to cope with the stresses of a new and demanding profession.

Tuition:
In 1997 average full-time tuition and fees ranged between $3,500 CDN and $4,000 CDN. Some midwifery courses may be subject to additional departmental fees and charges.

Financial Assistance:
Call the school for information and current deadlines.

Application Deadline:
Applications are due by February 2, but Ryerson predicts that entry into the midwifery program will be highly competitive and suggests starting the applications process early.

Other Programs:
Ryerson offers a number of bachelor's degrees in other fields.

OTHER CAREER OPPORTUNITIES

Childbirth Educator

Childbirth educators and labor assistants provide pregnant women with information about the birth process, available technology, and alternatives. The childbirth educator generally teaches prenatal classes to help women and their families experience a safe, healthy birth. These classes may focus on a specific childbirth technique, such as Lamaze, or deal with the more general aspects of pregnancy and birth.

Labor Assistant (Doula)

The labor assistant is also called a doula, monitrice, labor companion, or birth assistant. The labor assistant works one-on-one to help the pregnant woman avoid unnecessary interventions or Cesarean birth through education, knowledge of alternatives, and by facilitating a smooth, unimpeded labor. Labor assistants might teach expectant mothers and their partners to use natural therapies such as massage to help cope with pain during labor; how to take advantage of variations in position; and what other labor support techniques are available. The labor assistant may also act as an advocate for the birthing woman when dealing with other health professionals on the birth team.

The labor assistant also works with the expectant mother and other family members to ensure that they understand the benefits, risks, and alternatives for all tests and procedures. The goal is to achieve an unmedicated, nontechnical, woman-centered childbirth as long as it is the safest possible choice for mother and baby. When technology or medication are indicated, the labor assistant supports the family in their choices, helping them to achieve the optimal outcome.

Labor assistants provide continuous, uninterrupted care for the laboring woman and her partner, and help them participate fully in their experience by offering physical and emotional support. They may meet with the woman or couple during the pregnancy, go to their home in early labor, and accompany them throughout labor and delivery in the setting of their choice. Many labor assistants also do follow-up visits during the early postpartum period.

According to the Association of Labor Assistants and Childbirth Educators, labor assistants typically earn $150 to $500 per patient and are employed by families, physicians, midwives, or clinics. This type of training works well as the first step for individuals considering midwifery as a career or nurses seeking to expand their practices.

❧ PROFESSIONAL ORGANIZATIONS AND OTHER EDUCATIONAL RESOURCES

American College of Nurse-Midwives (ACNM)
1522 K Street, Suite 1000
Washington, DC 20005

This organization certifies nurse-midwives, and has set the standards for the profession since 1955. Contact the ACNM for current listings of accredited nurse-midwifery programs, both certificate and master's degrees, offered through both state and private universities. Approximately thirty such programs were available through the United States in 1997 (see Appendix C).

American Society of Psychoprophylaxis in Obstetrics
(Lamaze International)
1200 19th Street, NW Suite 300
Washington, D.C. 20036
(800) 368-4404

The society offers both classes and certification of childbirth educators using the Lamaze method.

Association of Labor Assistants and Childbirth Educators
(ALACE)
PO Box 382724
Cambridge, MA 02238
(617) 441-2500
http://www.alace.org

ALACE certifies labor assistants who act as professional care providers trained to help pregnant women and their families identify what is important to them during labor and birth, and to work cooperatively within the birth team of health professionals to help realize these goals. Contact ALACE for current educational and professional requirements for certification. ALACE also provides a childbirth educator training program. Based on classes first developed in the 1970s, it is designed to help childbirth educators build a better curriculum for the classes that they offer. In 1997 the cost was approximately $695.

The Bradley Method
PO Box 5224
Sherman Oaks, CA 91413-5224
(800) 4-A-Birth
http://www.bradleybirth.com

This group provides workshops and certification for childbirth educators using the Bradley Method. A free packet of information is provided upon request.

Canadian Childbirth Education
2043 Ferndale Street
Vancouver, British Columbia V5L 1Y2

Contact this organization for information about childbirth education courses in British Columbia (national information may also be available).

Doulas of North America (DONA)
Connie Sultana, Certification Chair
1106 Hamilton Way
Columbia, MO 65203
http://www.dona.com

This international association of doulas was founded in 1992. DONA-approved labor support (doula) training courses include fourteen or more hours of training that covers the emotional and psychological process of labor and birth; the anatomy and physiology or reproduction, labor and birth; comfort measures and non-pharmacological pain management techniques; appropriate topics for prenatal and postpartum discussion with clients; discussion of ethics and standards of practice for the doula; referral sources for client needs beyond the scope of the doula; and communication skills and values clarification.

To become a certified doula through DONA, applicants need to complete a certification packet, take an approved course, and submit to review by appropriate health professionals. Contact the association for information about the certification process. The web site includes a calendar of current workshops and seminars approved by DONA (prices vary depending on instructor, length, and location).

Midwives Alliance of North America (MANA)
PO Box 175
Newton, KS 67114
http://www.mana.org

This professional alliance of direct-entry midwives holds annual conferences, works on legislative issues pertaining to direct-entry midwives, and helps set standards for midwifery education.

North American Registry of Midwives (NARM)
PO Box 15
Linn, WV 26384

NARM tests midwives for the credential-certified professional midwife (CPM) credential. CPM certification indicates that the recipient has achieved the entry-level knowledge, skills, and experience necessary for a midwifery practice. Applicants for NARM certification may have gained their knowledge through apprenticeship, private midwifery schools, college- and university-based midwifery programs, private practice, or nurse-midwifery practice. To maintain NARM certification, midwives must take a certain number of continuing education classes over a set time period.

✌Recommended Reading

Gaskin, Ina May. *Spiritual Midwifery.* Summerton, TN: The Book Publishing Co., 1977.

> Gaskin is often called the mother of the modern midwifery movement. Her practice, centered around a vegetarian community named The Farm, is seen as a model of the ideal midwife-assisted birth. The book itself took the view of pregnancy, childbirth, and breast-feeding as a natural and spiritual event, rather than a medical problem.

Getting an Education: A Book for Aspiring Midwives. Eugene, OR: Midwifery Today Inc., 1995.

> These reprints of articles originally ran in *Midwifery Today* magazine. They cover a multitude of topics, including the difference between the direct-entry midwife and the CNM, legal issues, and educational programs. The magazine continues to update midwives on issues relating to their practice. For more information, write to Midwifery Today, Inc., PO Box 2672-350, Eugene, OR 97402.

6

Naturopathic Doctor (ND)

Licensed naturopathic doctors (NDs) in the United States and Canada work as primary-care physicians. NDs treats illnesses through a variety of natural techniques, including botanical medicine, homeopathy, nutrition, physical manipulation, and hydrotherapy. In 1993 the American Association of Naturopathic Physicians (AANP) estimated that more than 1 million American citizens used NDs as their primary-care provider.

Most students choose to become NDs because they want to work with people in a preventative medicine setting using natural therapies. The schools described in this chapter operate graduate-level programs intended to qualify their students to practice as licensed naturopathic doctors according to the standards of the Council on Natural Medicine Education (CNME).

The oldest operating naturopathic college was established in 1956, and the newest one accepted its first class in 1997. Several of the colleges have recycled their classroom facilities from buildings meant for other purposes, and the effect can be more alternative than Ivy League. However, their clinics occupy much more upscale settings, similar to a highly prosperous family medical practice. All the schools report high demand and patient traffic at their clinics.

Students are expected to study the life sciences and many forms of standard medical procedure as well as the natural therapies. By the third year, students move into a clinical setting, generally a clinic run by the school. There they diagnosis and treat patients while working under the supervision of an experienced naturopathic physician.

Most of the colleges also offer extensive training in acupuncture and traditional Chinese medicine. Often an ND will choose to specialize in one area, such as homeopathy, following the basic training. At least one school offers a combined ND/midwife training in a five-year program.

On graduation from a naturopathic college, students earn a doctor of naturopathy degree. After graduation, students must sit a series of standardized national exams called the Naturopathic Physicians Licensing Exams (NPLEX). This series of tests lasts several days and serves the same purposes as board exams do for medical doctors, to demonstrate the student's grasp of the basic skills of a physician. These exams cover physical and clinical diagnosis; laboratory diagnosis and diagnostic imaging; emergency medicine, public health, and basic skills; *materia medica* and toxicology; principles and practices of nutrition; psychology and lifestyle counseling; physical medicine; minor surgery; and homeopathy. Depending on the state licensing requirements, students may be required to take additional exams in such areas as acupuncture.

A newly licensed naturopathic doctor must find a job in somebody else's clinic or pay to establish a private practice. The cost of establishing a private practice varies greatly from area to area. The AANP web site also advertises established practices for sale. All of the schools listed in this chapter provide some career and business counseling for their students. At least one public health project begun in 1996 integrated naturopathic physicians into a more conventional medical setting.

The average income of naturopathic doctors tends to fall in the low to mid-range of family practice doctors, according to a survey done by the AANP. A National College graduate advertising for a partner in his Connecticut practice estimated that an ND in his area could earn $90,000 or more a year.

Although naturopathic doctors often rely on their patients to pay all fees, third-party reimbursement is becoming more common. As more insurance companies recognize the profession, the income potential will probably rise. Again, most students go into this profession for the personal satisfaction rather than the financial rewards.

Over the past few years, NDs have also branched out into such careers as consultants for natural foods or natural medicine manufacturers, authors, and college teachers. A small but growing pool of research grants has become available to NDs interested in studying the effectiveness of natural therapies. Like most research work, these jobs tend to be located within the academic institutions of natural medicine.

Given the length of time and financial cost of this type of education, medical professionals may not find an ND program the most cost-effective way to move into natural therapies. However, for college students or others interested in becoming primary-care providers, the ND programs allow them to learn a multitude of natural therapies to help their patients.

Sixty to 70 percent of naturopathic students are women. The average age of naturopathic students tends to be in the mid-thirties, although that has been steadily dropping as more students are electing to go straight from undergraduate programs into a graduate ND program.

✂ COST OF EDUCATION

Tuition at the naturopathic colleges runs approximately $14,000 a year. The schools suggest budgeting another $600 to $1,600 a year for books and supplies. For a four-year program, students can expect to pay at least $55,000; and this figure is more likely to go up than down. Although this is far less than the educational costs of the average medical doctor, prospective students must consider the pros and cons of this financial commitment. Financial aid varies from institution to institution, so be sure to ask before you get too far into the admissions process.

Naturopathic students, like medical students, usually rely on a mix of financial resources, such as savings, family support, loans, and working during the summer break. Some students work while going to school, but the intensive structure of these programs rules out most full-time jobs. Even part-time work requires some flexibility to allow for finals, clinic work, and the normal class load of a graduate program.

If you plan to go directly into private practice following graduation, be sure to budget the costs of establishing a medical office into your overall plan. Cost varies dramatically, depending on where you plan to practice. The school may be able to put you in touch with graduates practicing in a similar area so that you can discuss business issues as well as their thoughts about their educational experiences.

All the colleges listed in this chapter require students to attend classes at the school. Bastyr University and the University of Bridgeport College of Naturopathic Medicine (UBCNM) provide housing on campus, and all the schools provide some assistance in locating housing in their area. Like most colleges, groups of students living off-campus often share housing and commuting costs.

LENGTH OF TRAINING

Most ND academic programs are structured to last four years, although the Southwest College of Naturopathic Medicine and Health Sciences has a three-year program that allows students to take classes all year-round. Southwest and UBCNM allow students to enter twice a year, rather than having only one class per year starting in September. At the other schools, the schedule follows a typical academic schedule. Classes start in September, with short breaks in the winter and spring followed by a long break in the summer.

If you already have a medical degree, you might qualify for advanced standing. Be sure to ask during the admissions process.

ADMISSIONS PROCESS

Over the past few years, the naturopathic colleges have been in the advantageous position of having more applicants than openings, almost three to one in some cases. As the colleges move to larger campuses with more classroom space, and with UBCNM now open on the East Coast, some of this pressure may ease. Nonetheless, applicants should continue to pay close attention to the admission deadlines and start the application process approximately one year in advance of the desired starting date.

All of the schools follow a similar application process. Prospective students complete an application form and pay a small fee. Letters of reference are generally required with the initial application. If you know a naturopathic doctor, you may want to ask the ND to write one of the letters of recommendation to demonstrate your knowledge and interest in the field. The schools also ask applicants to write a personal essay explaining their motivation for becoming a naturopathic doctor.

After the applications are accepted, applicants go through a round of interviews with an admissions team or admissions officer. The goal of these interviews is to determine how well-prepared the applicant is to enter the program.

Prior to beginning the whole admissions process, the colleges allow prospective students to tour the facilities. Ask if you can monitor a class or talk with a faculty member and a student member. Visit the clinics.

❦UNDERGRADUATE PREREQUISITES

In general, the naturopathic colleges are seeking applicants who have a premed bachelor's degree or the equivalent education. If you have a bachelor's degree but lack the science courses, or you have been out of college for more than ten years, you may need to go back to college to complete or update your science courses.

Work experience can sometimes be substituted for educational requirements, but this must be approved by the school. Avoid delays or the refusal of your application by checking first.

Prerequisites shown for the schools date from 1997. These should be regarded as the bare minimum needed, and you should also check with the institution to make sure that these requirements have not changed.

❦LICENSING AND ACCREDITATION

UNITED STATES

In 1997 eleven states licensed naturopathic doctors graduating from CNME-recognized colleges. Applicants must also pass the NPLEX. The exact requirements of the license may vary from state to state, so check with the licensing body of the state where you want to practice to confirm requirements. The colleges also keep this information on file. In 1997 the following states licensed NDs: Alaska, Arizona, Connecticut, Hawaii, Maine, Montana, New Hampshire, Oregon, Utah, Vermont, and Washington. In 1997 Florida recognized NDs practicing in the state before their licensing laws changed, but did not issue any new licenses.

The CNME has been recognized by the US Department of Education as the accreditation agency for naturopathic medical schools in the United States.

Council on Naturopathic Medical Education (CNME)
PO Box 11426
Eugene, OR 97440
(402) 391-6714

CANADA

In 1997 naturopathic doctors were licensed in Alberta, British Columbia, Manitoba, Ontario, Quebec, and Saskatchewan. The Canadian Naturopathic Association (listed at the end of the chapter) can provide current information on required education and legal status.

US Schools

The following schools are currently accredited by the CNME or follow the standards of naturopathic medical education as set by CNME.

Bastyr University
14500 Juanita Drive NE
Bothell, WA 98011
(425) 823-1300
http://www.bastyr.edu

Bastyr University is located approximately forty-five minutes north of Seattle. In 1996 the university moved to its present location, a former Catholic seminary located in wooded acreage on the shores of Lake Washington. The university has received accreditation from the CNME and the regional accrediting body, the Northwest Assocation of Schools and Colleges.

Program:
The ND degree at Bastyr is a four-year program, although many students elect to stretch it out to five years. Students enter each year in September, and the program follows a standard academic year including a long summer break.

During the first two years, students spend most of their class time in lectures and labs. These classes cover the basic medical sciences and clinical diagnostic skills. The core naturopathic curriculum, which is integrated throughout all four years of study, includes instruction in nutritional sciences, counseling, botanical medicine, homeopathy, Oriental medicine, childbirth, physiotherapy, naturopathic manipulation, and other medical procedures. ND students may also elect to take advanced training in midwifery, traditional Chinese herbal medicine, and homeopathy.

By the third year of study, students begin clinical training through supervised practice at Bastyr's outpatient clinic in Seattle or externships in the offices of practicing physicians.

Bastyr's active research program has received major grants to examine naturopathic therapies in AIDS/HIV treatment as well as smaller studies in such areas as the effectiveness of echinacea to treat frequent respiratory infections. In 1996 Bastyr participated in the establishment the King County Medical Clinic in Kent, a city located approximately one hour south of the campus. Funded by a mix of federal and state funds, this public health clinic was established as a model for integrating standard medical treatments with natural therapies such as acupuncture, naturopathy, and chiropractic care. Qualified students also worked as naturopathic interns at this clinic along with medical doctors and other professionals from different disciplines.

Prerequisites:
Overall requirements include a bachelor's degree with a minimum grade point average (GPA) of 2.5. Transcripts must show that the applicant has completed the following with a grade of "C" or better: one class of college-level algebra or precalculus, including polynomial functions, exponential functions, logarithmic functions; one statistics class including basic, inferential, and probability; two general chemistry classes with labs designed for science majors; two organic chemistry classes with labs designed for science majors; one academic year of general biology or combination of lab courses for science majors which includes cell and molecular biology, genetics, botany, and taxonomy; one physics class (no lab required); two classes of psychology (one introductory, one developmental); two English classes, such as composition and literature; and two classes in the humanities, such as public speaking, foreign language, music, art, philosophy, or religion.

Applicants without a bachelor's degree must show the completion of at least 135/90 quarter/semester credits (45/30 of which must be upper-division). They must also demonstrate significant life experience, such as relevant work experience, that could be substituted for course work.

Tuition:
In 1997 average tuition for full-time students was $13,700 per year. Students should budget at least $1,300 per year for books and supplies.

Financial Aid:
Stafford Loans, work-study, and other programs are available through the financial aid office.

Application Deadline:
Applications are accepted starting September 1 for the following academic year. Early acceptance deadline closes on the subsequent February 1.

Other Programs:
Bastyr also offers a BS degree as well as master degrees in acupuncture and nutrition. The students who elect to take the additional midwifery training may also satisfy the requirements for licensed midwives and work as an ND/LM.

National College of Naturopathic Medicine (NCNM)
1049 SW Porter Street
Portland, OR 97201
(503) 499-4343
http://www.ncnm.edu

Founded in 1956, National College of Naturopathic Medicine is the oldest accredited school of natural medicine in the United States. In 1997 NCNM moved to a new facility.

Program:
The intensive four-year graduate medical program is structured to prepare students for the general practice of naturopathic medicine and meet the standards of licensure. The first two years focus on the standard medical sciences as well as the history and philosophy of naturopathic medicine. During the third and fourth years, students receive clinical training in diagnosis and naturopathic therapeutics, including working at the NCNM clinic under the supervision of naturopathic physicians. By graduation, students will have completed a minimum of 4,500 clock hours of classroom and clinical work.

Prerequisites:
Students must have a bachelor's degree and, according to the college's web site, demonstrate "outstanding moral character, maturity, academic aptitude, and commitment to naturopathic medicine." Prospective students are also advised to choose those undergraduate courses that are recommended for premedical students.
    The standard medical prerequisite classes (20 semester/30 quarter credits) must be met with grades of "C" or better prior to admission. These classes must include lab classes in chemistry and organic chemistry; one course in physics; a minimum of 6 semester/9 quarter

hours in the social sciences, including at least one course in psychology; and 6 semester/9 quarter credits in the humanities.

Tuition:
In 1997 average tuition for a full-time student was $13,800 per year.

Financial Aid:
Only Stafford subsidized and unsubsidized loans were listed in the literature. Contact the financial aid office during the application process for further information.

Application Deadline:
NCNM starts accepting applications on September 1 for the next academic year. Applications close February 1 for the academic year beginning in September.

Other Programs:
NCNM sponsors continuing education classes and workshops.

The Southwest College of Naturopathic Medicine
    and Health Sciences
2140 East Broadway Road
Tempe, AZ 85282
(602) 858-9100
http://www.scnm.edu

Southwest originally opened its doors in Scottsdale in 1993, and moved to a larger facility in Tempe, Arizona, in 1997. The campus, located in a former athletic club, has been remodeled to house a large auditorium, laboratories, library, and classrooms, while keeping such features as the saunas, steam rooms, Jacuzzi, tennis and basketball courts, and a swimming pool.

Program:
Southwest enters new classes twice a year, in March and September. Students may elect to complete the naturopathic program in three or four calendar years. The three-year program requires students to remain in school throughout the year without the summer break found in the more traditional four-year program.

At the beginning of each term, nationally recognized experts in the field of natural medicine are invited to give intensive seminars to the students. The curriculum emphasizes the practice of preventive care that establishes a continuity between the traditions of natural therapies and the latest scientific discoveries in epidemiology and risk assessment.

Clinical training takes place in established naturopathic physicians' offices in the area as well as at the college's Southwest Naturopathic Medical Center. Students are expected to work with a broad range of patients under the supervision of naturopathic physicians, and Southwest calls its entire curriculum "very practice oriented."

The Southwest College Research Institute offers students opportunities to participate in a wide variety of research projects.

Prerequisites:

Candidates for admission must demonstrate "the motivation, intelligence, perseverance and character essential for physicians," according to the school's web page. Applicants must have completed a BA or BS degree at an accredited or candidate college or university. Any applicant whose science classes are more than ten years old must demonstrate competency through documented work in the field or must retake those classes at an accredited institution. Candidates need to earn a grade of "C" or better in the required prerequisite courses: English classes, including composition; humanities courses, including philosophy, religious studies, fine arts, history, foreign languages, women's studies, or performing arts; medical terminology; psychology, with credits in development psychology recommended; biology, including general biology for science majors; anatomy and physiology with lab; a botany class with a lab course preferred; and chemistry courses, including general chemistry classes designed for science majors and an organic chemistry class with a lab.

Depending on whether the undergraduate school followed a quarter or semester system, the number of class hours required varies. Check Southwest's web page or admissions packet for further details.

The following courses may not be required for admission but are highly recommended: biochemistry; genetics; public speaking; college algebra; counseling; statistics; philosophy of science; microbiology; nutrition; biomedical ethics; computer skills; and additional courses in psychology beyond the required hours in areas of child, adolescent, abnormal, personality theory, and psychology of adjustment.

Tuition:

Tuition expense per year varies depending on whether students are in the four-year or three-year program. In 1997 tuition per quarter was approximately $3,100 to $3,800 depending on the program.

Financial Aid:
Standard financial aid packages available.

Application Deadline:
Deadlines vary depending on which program the student wishes to attend. Contact the admissions office for current deadlines.

Other Programs:
An optional acupuncture program allows students to achieve certification in states that recognize licensed acupuncturists.

The University of Bridgeport College of Naturopathic Medicine (UBCNM)
221 University Avenue
Bridgeport, CT 06601
(203) 576-4109
http://www.bridgeport.edu

UBCNM began accepting students in the fall of 1997 for a four-year graduate program. Because the college is a part of the older, accredited University of Bridgeport, it can offer financial aid, on-campus housing, and other services through the university's offices. The administrators of the program intend to follow the standards set by the CNME. At the time of publication, this college was too new to have achieved accreditation status with CNME, but the program was licensed by the state of Connecticut in December 1996.

Program:
The intensive four-year program concentrates on the basic sciences in the first two years, and the clinical skills and natural therapeutics in the last two years. During the final two years, students will receive clinical training under the supervision of licensed naturopathic physicians in the college's teaching facilities. In addition to the traditional didactic and clinical training, students must submit a thesis before graduation.

At the time of publication, students could elect to enter the program in the fall or spring. Fall semester runs from August through December, and spring semester runs January through May. The entire program runs four academic years, or eight semesters, and students must attend full-time.

Prerequisites:
Admission requirements include a bachelor's degree with a minimum grade point average (GPA) of 2.5, although a minimum GPA of

3.0 in the sciences courses is preferred. The prerequisite courses required are: 6 hours of communication/language skills; 3 hours of psychology; 3 hours of social sciences; 3 hours of humanities; 9 hours of electives in social sciences and/or humanities; 6 hours of general biology, zoology, or anatomy and physiology; 6 hours of general chemistry; 6 hours of organic chemistry; and 6 hours of physics. Each science course must include a laboratory portion and have been designed for science majors.

Tuition:
In 1997 full-time tuition was projected to be $12,800 per year. Students should also budget $1,200 per semester for textbooks, equipment, and fees.

Financial Aid:
Subsidized and unsubsidized Stafford Loans, alternative loans from non-federal sources, and Federal Work-Study are the most common sources of aid available.

Application Deadline:
In 1997/1998 the college accepted applications for entry in both the fall and in the spring semester. Contact the admissions department for current deadlines.

Other Programs:
The University of Bridgeport is a private, nonsectarian university offering a variety of degrees and programs, including a college of chiropractic medicine.

Canadian Schools

At the time of publication, the following Canadian college was under review for accreditation by the CNME.

Canadian College of Naturopathic Medicine (CCNM)
60 Berl Ave
Toronto, Ontario M8Y 3C7
(416) 251-5261
http://www.ccnm.edu

Located approximately ten minutes north of Lake Ontario in a wooded four-acre tract of land, CCNM is connected by bus to the

Toronto subway system. The college was established in the 1970s to meet the training requirements for naturopathic doctors established in the Canadian licensure laws. Because the school is also conforming to CNME standards, students may qualify for licensure in the United States as well.

Program:

CCNM's four-year, full-time program in naturopathic medicine centers around seven major disciplines: acupuncture and Oriental medicine, botanical medicine, clinical nutrition, homeopathic medicine, hydrotherapy, naturopathic manipulative therapy, and prevention and lifestyle counseling. Each discipline is taught in a manner that includes both diagnostic principles and clinical practice, as well as therapeutic skills and techniques.

The other major areas of study are the basic medical sciences and clinical disciplines. These classes emphasize developing problem-solving skills through lectures, case discussions, tutorial groups, and clinical simulations. Science courses include a laboratory component. The clinical disciplines include physical and clinical diagnosis, differential and laboratory diagnosis, radiology, naturopathic assessment, and orthopedics. At the completion of their four-year course, students have received more than 4,000 hours of classroom and clinical training.

Prerequisites:

Applicants must have completed a minimum of three years (90 semester hours, 30 semester credits, 130 quarter credits, or 15 full-year credits) at a university in Canada or its equivalent. While three years is the basic requirement, the admissions department recommends a bachelor of science degree.

All prerequisite courses must be completed by June 30 of the year of application. No credit is given for the completion of prerequisites unless the grade earned is a C (minimum of 60 percent) or better. Required courses include general biology, biochemistry, general chemistry, organic chemistry, and psychology. The biology requirement may be fulfilled by either a one-year general biology course or by one semester of cell biology and one semester of anatomy, botany, genetics, microbiology, physiology, or zoology. A laboratory component is required with these courses.

Applicants should also consider taking courses in some or all of the following areas in order to prepare for the college's curriculum: anatomy, environmental science, genetics, human physiology, microbiology, physics, sociology, and statistics.

Tuition:
In 1996 the average full-time tuition was $9,500 CDN per year.

Financial Aid:
The Ontario student assistance plan is available, as are other provincial assistance plans for out-of-province students. Canadian federal loans and child-care bursaries are available for Canadian students.

Application Deadline:
Applications close at the end of February for the academic year beginning in September. Admissions interviews are conducted in Toronto, although the school arranged for out-of-province interviews in Vancouver, BC; Edmonton, AB; Winnipeg, MB; and Berwick, NS, in 1996.

Other Programs:
The ND was the only degree offered at the time of publication.

PROFESSIONAL ORGANIZATIONS AND OTHER EDUCATIONAL RESOURCES

The schools listed above provide continuing education classes for NDs. Local organizations affliated with the national associations listed below often hold workshops or conferences for their members.

American Association of Naturopathic Physicians (AANP)
601 Valley #105
Seattle, WA 98109
(206) 298-0126
http://www.infinite.org/naturopathic.physician

This national association for licensed naturopathic physicians meets once a year in an annual convention. It maintains an extensive web site about naturopathic medicine, including a "classified" service for NDs (see below). Call or check the web site for addresses of state chapters.

Canadian Naturopathic Association
PO Box 4520, Station C
Calgary, Alberta T2T 5N3
(403) 244-4487

This is the national association for naturopathic physicians practicing in Canada. Call for a list of provincial chapters.

Homeopathic Academy of Naturopathic Physicians (HANP)
12132 SE Foster Place
Portland, OR 97266
(503) 761-3298
e-mail: hanp@igc.apc.org

HANP is a specialty society affiliated with the American Association of Naturopathic Physicians. Its purpose is to encourage the development and improvement of the homeopathic curriculum at naturopathic colleges; and set educational standards of practice in homeopathy through board certification and the education of naturopathic physicians. The society publishes the quarterly professional homeopathic journal *Simillimum,* and hosts the HANP Annual Case Conference each fall. This conference features naturopathic physicians as well as other classical homeopaths from all over the world presenting case studies from their practices.

CAREER OPPORTUNITIES ADVERTISED ON THE WEB

At the time of publication, the AANP provided classified job listings for their members on their web site. Several of the naturopathic colleges were also discussing providing similar services through their alumni offices at the time of publication. Check the web sites listed for the schools for this information.

If you are a medical professional interested in working in a naturopathic clinic, but not in becoming an ND, there are new opportunities opening up for integrated clinics. Check the AANP web site for NDs seeking to open integrated clinics.

Recommended Reading

Boice, Judith, ND. *Pocket Guide to Naturopathic Medicine.* Freedom, CA: Crossing Press, 1996.

Written by a graduate of NCNM, the book contains a basic overview of naturopathic principles, some self-help hints, and an interesting appendix comparing classroom and clinical hours of two naturopathic colleges with four medical colleges.

Pizzorno, Joseph and Michael Murray, ND. *The Encyclopedia of Natural Medicine*, Revised 2nd Edition. Rocklin, CA: Prima, 1998.

Written by the president of Bastyr University and a renowned member of its faculty, the second edition of this popular encyclopedia gives a good idea of a naturopathic physician's approach to the treatment of disease and current scientific research in naturopathic medicine.

7

Osteopathic Doctor (DO)

Osteopathic medicine began as a holistic system of health care based on the ideas of Andrew Taylor Still, MD (1828–1917). Unhappy with the results of the allopathic medicine of his day, Still developed a system that emphasized preventative care. Therapeutic techniques, such as manipulation, addressed the relationship of the body's structure to its function. Still used manipulative techniques and also counseled patients on exercise and proper diet to promote general good health.

In 1892 Still founded the first school of osteopathic medicine, the American School of Osteopathy, in Kirksville, Missouri. By 1996 there were eighteen osteopathic medical colleges in the United States.

Today, osteopathic physicians receive training very similar to allopathic physicians. The most visible difference between the two professions is the use of osteopathic manipulative treatment (OMT) by osteopaths, who combine this technique with allopathic medicine. For example, an osteopathic physician may surgically remove a gall bladder and then use OMT as a postoperative technique for pain reduction to lessen the need for painkillers and reduce the chances of drug side effects. Osteopathic physicians do prescribe drugs and use the methods of allopathic medicine as standard treatment in their practices.

Osteopathic medical students spend the first two years studying the basic medical sciences. Their clinical training occurs in the last two years of their program, and includes rotations in college clinics, community health centers, or affiliated hospitals. Several colleges emphasize working with the medically indigent, those who cannot afford to participate in the standard medical system in the United States.

After completing their education, graduates must pass the licensing examinations as well as completing their internship and residency requirements. In many states, the osteopathic doctors (DOs) sit the same general medical boards as medical doctors (MDs). Graduates may also choose to take three- to seven-year residency programs in specialties such as anesthesiology or nuclear medicine.

More than half of the DOs in the United States work as general practitioners. Their practices tend to emphasize preventative health care, family medicine, and pediatrics. Many work in small towns or country settings; and several schools emphasize rural health care as part of their DO programs.

In Michigan DOs make up nearly one-fifth of the state's practicing physicians. Approximately 64 percent of all DOs were in primary care in the 1990s, and many practiced in towns with populations of 10,000 or less, according to the American Osteopathic Association (AOA).

DOs earn approximately the same salaries as MDs. Income varies depending on the type of practice. The mean average for physicians in family practice was approximately $110,000 in 1993, according to the American Medical Association.

While many DOs choose to establish their own practices, their medical licenses allow them to work in clinics, hospitals, and HMOs. They can also chose to become board certified in any medical specialty. DOs are well entrenched in the medical mainstream in the United States, having served in almost every capacity including Surgeon General of the United States Army (General Ronald Blanck, DO).

Although the majority of DOs are men, women were welcome in osteopathic colleges long before they gained general acceptance in the medical colleges. In September 1996 women made up 44 percent of the entering class at the Michigan State University College of Osteopathic Medicine.

✒ COST OF EDUCATION

Tuition alone costs more than $20,000 a year at the private colleges. Osteopathic colleges connected with a state university tend to cost much less for residents of that state. Students must also budget for lab fees, books, and medical supplies. One college estimated such expenses could add an additional $2,000 in a year.

Like the other medical programs, financial aid comes primarily in the form of student loans. A few scholarship programs aimed specifically at osteopathic students are sponsored by the profession. Check with your local osteopathic association to see if they sponsor scholarships for your state or province. Contact the national associations listed at the end of this chapter for the addresses of local chapters.

The financial aid office at each college will provide additional material on loan, grant, and scholarship programs available through a specific institution. Like medical students, osteopathic students usually find working during their training difficult. Most rely on savings or family support.

✺LENGTH OF TRAINING

The standard osteopathic program lasts four academic years. Graduates also need to complete a residency program in a hospital after graduation. Some residency programs can last up to seven years if the residents wish to become specialists in a particular area of medicine.

In most osteopathic colleges, students receive training in osteopathic philosophy and technique throughout their four years. During the first two years, they also take classes in anatomy, histology, biochemistry, physiology, microbiology, and pharmacology. Osteopathic college courses also place a strong emphasis on preventative medicine and the importance of primary care.

Clinical training generally begins in the third year and includes rotations in college or community clinics and hospitals in such areas as ambulatory care, family medicine, surgery, pediatrics, obstetrics and gynecology, psychiatry, radiology, pathology, and emergency care.

✺ADMISSIONS PROCESS

Unlike the other schools listed in this book, the osteopathic colleges participate in a centralized applications process.

The American Association of Colleges of Osteopathic Medicine Application Service (AACOMAS) collates the materials, such as undergraduate transcripts, received from the applicant and then transmits the standardized information to their selected osteopathic colleges. As an applicant, you would also receive a copy of this information mailed back to you at the same time.

AACOMAS takes no part in the evaluation, selection, or rejection of applicants, which is done by the admissions department of the osteopathic college. After the receipt of the AACOMAS material, the college may request additional material from an applicant such as a non-refundable application fee, letters of recommendation or other academic materials. The admissions office will usually schedule a personal interview during this process. Candidates are expected to be familiar with the philosophy and practice of osteopathic medicine prior to an interview.

AACOMAS applications close each February 1 for admissions into the osteopathic colleges in the following September. Admissions directors recommend mailing your materials to AACOMAS well before the February 1 deadline, as many schools start processing applications much earlier. Many osteopathic colleges are receiving ten applications for every space available, and schools often close admission early.

Some schools offer an "early decision" application process where students may receive a place in the program by October if they apply exclusively to that school and meet the standards of early admissions. If you are interested in going to a particular school, be sure to ask if it has an early decision program. Generally, to qualify for early admissions, you must get all your material to the school a year or more ahead of your desired entrance date.

Colleges affiliated with a state university often give preference to state residents. Some colleges also have specific programs aimed at recruiting minorities into the medical profession. Others prefer applicants who are willing to commit to service in a particular regional area or serving an underserved population. Ask about these preferences if you think this applies to your situation.

The osteopathic colleges will send out information on AACO-MAS in their standard information packages, or you can write to the AACOMAS directly.

American Association of Colleges of Osteopathic
  Medicine Application Service (AACOMAS)
6110 Executive Boulevard, Suite 405
Rockville, Maryland 20852-3991

❧UNDERGRADUATE PREREQUISITES

Osteopathic colleges prefer applicants to have completed a BA or BS before entering their first year of osteopathic college. The undergraduate degree must include one full academic year or the equivalent (generally 8 semester or 12 quarter hours) in each of the following courses: English, biology, physics, inorganic chemistry, and organic chemistry. Science courses should include a laboratory portion, and science courses without labs may not be acceptable. Most osteopathic colleges also recommend that students take undergraduate courses in biochemistry and human anatomy. A standard premed undergraduate degree will probably satisfy the prerequisites of an osteopathic program. Some osteopathic colleges will consider students who have completed three years of undergraduate work with exceptional grades. Besides satisfying the standard educational prerequisites, applicants must also achieve a satisfactory score on the Medical College Admission Test (MCAT). This test is given each April and August.

Most osteopathic colleges recommend that applicants should take the MCAT at least one year before expected admission. If an applicant's MCAT scores are more than three years old, however, the college may require a prospective student to take the test again.

Prerequisites discussed here for the osteopathic colleges date from 1996/97 entrance requirements given by AACOMAS. These should be regarded as the bare minimum needed. Check with the institution to make sure that these requirements have not changed. Many of the colleges listed here raise the minimum grade point average needed on a regular basis.

❧LICENSING AND ACCREDITATION

UNITED STATES

An osteopathic physician (DO) is licensed for the full practice of medicine and surgery in all fifty states. In some states the same licensing exams are given to DOs and MDs; other states administer separate licensing exams. DOs can also become board certified in any medical specialty.

For more information on the practice of osteopathic medicine in the United States, contact the American Osteopathic Association. The AOA's Department of Education is the recognized accrediting body for osteopathic colleges in the United States. Most osteopathic colleges also have regional accreditation.

CANADA

Licensing of osteopathic doctors varies by province. Check with your provincial health authorities or the national association for the status of osteopathic doctors in your province.

OTHER COUNTRIES

In some parts of Europe and other areas outside of North America, osteopaths do not study allopathic medicine and have medical practices similar to chiropractic physicians.

US Schools

The following colleges of osteopathic medicine were accredited by the American College of Osteopathic Medicine in 1996.

Arizona College of Osteopathic Medicine
Midwestern University
19555 N. 59th Avenue
Glendale, AZ 85308
(602) 937-5643 or (800) 458-6253
   (toll-free—Midwestern University)

Arizona College, founded in 1995, is affiliated with the Chicago College of Osteopathic Medicine and is part of Midwestern University (MWU). MWU operates as a private institution of higher education in Illinois, under the authority of the Illinois Board of Higher Education, and in Arizona, under the authority of the Arizona State Board for Private Postsecondary Education. MWU has regional accreditation under the Commission on Institutions of Higher Education of the North Central Association of Colleges and Schools.

Program:
Arizona College emphasizes primary care but includes the traditional specialties and subspecialties in its program. Scholarly activities, including research, are encouraged for the faculty and student body.

Prerequisites:
Applicants must have completed three years of college including the minimal course work of 6 semester hours in English and 8 semester hours in the following sciences: biology, inorganic chemistry, organic chemistry, and physics. Classes in humanities, social sciences, and be-

havioral sciences are recommended. MWU admissions uses the mean grade point averages (GPA) and mean MCAT scores of the previous year's class to set a baseline for granting interviews. For the class entering in 1998, the mean GPAs and MCAT scores were projected to be science GPA 3.40 (mean), total GPA 3.40 (mean), and MCAT scores of 8 through 9 in all categories.

Tuition:
In 1996/97 the college estimated that full-time tuition and fees were $20,800 per year.

Financial Assistance:
The college participates in the standard federal loan programs.

Application Deadline:
Applications are due no later than February 1, but the college often awards all interview slots well before this date.

Other Programs:
See Chicago College of Osteopathic Medicine, below.

Chicago College of Osteopathic Medicine (CCOM)
Midwestern University
555 31st Street
Downers Grove, IL 60515
(708) 969-4400 or (800) 458-6253 (toll-free)

The first Chicago College opened in 1900. After merging with another osteopathic school, the college eventually expanded to the present Midwestern University (MWU). See Arizona College of Osteopathic Medicine (above) for more information on MWU.

Program:
CCOM's four-year curriculum educates students in the basic medical arts and sciences, as well as the biopsychosocial approach to patient care. Students spend their first two years both completing their basic science curriculum and preparing for their clinical studies. During their third and fourth years, students rotate through a variety of clinical departments, accruing 92 weeks of direct patient care experience.

Prerequisites:
Applicants must have completed a minimum of 90 semester hours from an accredited college with 6 semester hours in English and 8

semester hours each in biology, inorganic chemistry, organic chemistry, and physics. MWU admissions uses the mean grade point averages (GPA) and mean MCAT scores of the previous year's class to set a baseline for granting interviews. For the class entering in 1998, the mean GPAs and MCAT scores were projected to be science GPA 3.40 (mean), total GPA 3.40 (mean), and MCAT scores of 8 through 9 in all categories.

Tuition:
In 1996/97 tuition for Illinois residents was listed at $18,411, while out-of-state tuition was $22,374.

Financial Assistance:
The college participates in the standard federal loan programs. Check with the financial aid office for other aid packages available.

Application Deadline:
To be competitive within the rolling admissions process, students must apply early. MWU admissions recommends getting the applications packet to the college before January.

Other Programs:
MWU includes a College of Pharmacy and a College of Allied Health Professions in Illinois as well as the College of Osteopathic Medicine in Arizona.

Kirksville College of Osteopathic Medicine
800 West Jefferson
Kirksville, MO 63501
(816) 626-2237
http://www.kcom.edu

Formerly called the American College of Osteopathic Medicine, Kirksville College is the oldest osteopathic medical school in the United States. The college also houses the Still National Osteopathic Museum dedicated to the history of osteopathic medicine and its founder, Andrew Taylor Still. The log cabin where Dr. Still was born and the original school building can be found in the same complex.

Program:
The four-year program begins with basic sciences in the first and second years, although some clinical courses and training are mixed with

these classes. Third-year students begin clinical rotations, which last through the fourth year. Typical rotations are emergency medicine, general practice, internal medicine, surgery, obstetrics/gynecology, pediatrics, psychiatry, and radiology.

In the "Compute Now" program, students learn to use a Macintosh Powerbook notebook computer to tie into a medical education information network for interactive video and distance learning, collaboration, information access, and increased mobility.

Prerequisites:

Applicants must have achieved a minimum of 2.50 grade point average (GPA) overall, on a 4.0 scale, and a 2.50 science GPA as well as completed a minimum of 90 semester hours or three-fourths of the credits required for a degree at a college or university accredited by a regional educational association. Required courses include one full academic year (8 semester hours) or the equivalent in biology, physics, inorganic chemistry, organic chemistry, and English. Most accepted applicants do have a BA degree.

Tuition:

In 1996/97 estimated full-time tuition and fees were $21,900 per year.

Financial Assistance:

The college participates in the standard federal loan programs. Check with the financial aid office for other aid packages available.

Application Deadline:

The college uses a rolling admissions cycle. As candidates are interviewed, seats are filled, and starting the process early is recommended. Applications are accepted from June 1 through February 1 for the following September.

Other Programs:

Kirksville College offers master-level course work in physical therapy, occupational therapy, sports health care, and physician assistant studies at its Southwest Center site in Phoenix, Arizona.

Lake Erie College of Osteopathic Medicine
1858 West Grandview Boulevard
Erie, PA 16509
(814) 866-6641

Lake Erie College started accepting classes in 1992.

Program:
The four-year program is divided into three phases. Phase I introduces students to the basic medical sciences as well as osteopathic principles and practices. Phase II begins at the end of the first year and extends through the second. During this phase, course work emphasizes a systems approach where the basic and clinical sciences are incorporated into the study of the related organ system.

Phase III begins in the third year, when students move into rotations and gain clinical experience in such areas as internal medicine, pediatrics, obstetrics/gynecology, rural general practice, and so on.

Prerequisites:
A bachelor's degree is preferred, but the minimum requirement was listed as 96 credits including the basic premedical sciences. Applicants must have a minimum grade point average of 2.7 and show completion of the following, including laboratory work: biology (8 semester hours); inorganic chemistry (8 semester hours); organic chemistry (8 semester hours); physics (8 semester hours); English composition and literature (6 semester hours); and behavioral sciences (6 semester hours).

Tuition:
In 1996/97 full tuition was listed at $20,500 per year.

Financial Assistance:
Check with the college for current deadlines.

Application Deadline:
Decisions to award interviews are made as soon as all the required preliminary materials are submitted. Interviews are conducted November through April.

Notification of acceptance begins in December.

Other Programs:
No other programs were listed on the information received.

Michigan State University College of Osteopathic Medicine
   (MSUCOM)
East Fee Hall
East Lansing, MI 48824
(517) 353-7740

The College of Osteopathic Medicine was created as part of this Big Ten university in 1969 by an act of the Michigan Legislature.

Program:
MSUCOM offers a standard four-year osteopathic medical program.

During clinical training, the school provides many opportunities for students to work with populations typically underserved by standard allopathic medicine.

The department of pediatrics acts as the largest single provider of pediatric care to poor children in the Lansing area. MSUCOM personnel work at the Black Child and Family Institute, at the Ingham County Jail, and at clinics that serve the homeless, people with substance abuse problems, and the indigent. College students also provide medical services for the Special Olympics, and help the faculty maintain a special muscular dystrophy clinic.

MSUCOM's international programs for health have included malaria research and clinical care in Malawi; health-care consultation in the United Arab Emirates; establishment of a medical clinic in the Belize; studies of hypertension and HIV infection in Zimbabwe; and development of clinical clerkships abroad by the International Health Project, a student organization.

Prerequisites:
Students may be admitted to MSUCOM without bachelor's degrees but with 90 semester or 135 term credits of undergraduate work if space is available. Virtually all of these students elect to pursue a program leading to the bachelor of science degree as well as the osteopathic degree, according to the college's admission's department.

Tuition:
In 1996/97 in-state tuition for a full-time first year student was estimated at $14,556. Books and instruments were budgeted at $3,674 for the first year.

Financial Assistance:
The university offers all standard state and federal financial aid packages.

State residents pay a lower tuition than out-of-state residents.

Application Deadline:
The AACOMAS application, complete with all official transcripts, must be filed no later than December 15 of the year prior to the year of entrance. Interviews are conducted from November to late February.

MSUCOM offers an Early Decision Program (EDP) for applicants who have exceptional GPA and MCAT scores, and apply only to Michigan State University College of Osteopathic Medicine. The AACOMAS application must be received by MSUCOM on or before September 1, and the supplemental application must be received on or before October 1. Early Decision candidates receive a decision by October 31.

Other Programs:
The school also offers a joint DO/Ph.D. degree in medical scientist training.

New York College of Osteopathic Medicine (NYCOM)
New York Institute of Technology
Box 170
Old Westbury, NY 11568
(516) 626-6947
http://www.nyit/nycom

NYCOM was established in 1977 and has formed associations with affiliated and cooperative hospitals throughout the New York City area and in upstate New York. The college's Office of Minority Affairs sponsors a variety of outreach efforts to enhance the visibility of the osteopathic profession among minorities, and the college lists a higher than average minority enrollment.

Program:
NYCOM's curriculum emphasizes the incorporation of the osteopathic philosophy of medicine within the primary care system found in the United States. Osteopathic students learn patient education and counseling, preventive medicine, community and public health medicine, environmental and occupational impacts on health, and the economic factors affecting human health.

Family Practice Centers affiliated with the college provide opportunities for students to work with the medically indigent and underserved.

Prerequisites:
Applicants must have a bachelor's degree with a minimum science 2.75 GPA on a 4.0 scale and an overall 2.75 GPA on a 4.0 scale. Applicants must have completed one academic year including lab with no grade below 2.0 on a 4.0 scale in each of the following subjects: biology, general chemistry, organic chemistry, physics, and English.

Tuition:
In 1996/97 average full-time tuition was $21,000 per year not including books, lab fees, and miscellaneous expenses.

Financial Assistance:
NYCOM's financial aid department has information on numerous loan and scholarship programs.

Application Deadline:
NYCOM begins accepting applications June 1. Applications close February 1.

Other Programs:
A basic science summer program provides premedical education in critical topics for pre-matriculated minority students. An accelerated program for émigré physicians allows them to complete the osteopathic medical program in three years. The DO/MS in clinical nutrition and DO/MBA are concurrent degree programs offered by NYCOM and NYIT through its School of Allied Health and Life Sciences and School of Management.

Nova Southeastern University (Nova)
Health Professions Division
College of Osteopathic Medicine
1750 NE 167th Street
North Miami Beach, FL 33162
Osteopathic Admissions (800) 356-0026 ext. 1121 (toll-free)

Nova's osteopathic college is housed within the Health Professions Division, which has a new $40 million health professions complex.

Program:
The college's four-year curriculum focuses on the preparation of students for a generalist career in osteopathic medicine. Special attention is given to community medicine, geriatrics, rural medicine, and minority medicine.

Starting in the third year, students take clinical rotations in affiliated hospitals, clinics, health centers, and private offices. After twenty-two months of clinical training, students return to campus for a senior pre-internship seminar, consisting of basic and clinical science correlations and preparation for internship, residency, and

practice. The principles and practice of osteopathic medicine, emphasizing osteopathic manipulative techniques, are taught throughout
the four years.

Prerequisites:
A bachelor's degree from a regionally accredited college or university
is the minimum requirement. Nova encourages students to complete
additional courses in embryology, genetics, behavioral sciences, and
the humanities. Preference is given to students with a cumulative
grade point average of 3.0 or higher.

Tuition:
In 1996/97 full-time tuition and fees were approximately $18,500
per year.

Financial Assistance:
Various loans, scholarships, and grants are available to qualified students, according to the financial aid office.

Application Deadline:
Nova recommends the early completion of all applications material
due to limited space. In some years the college has received more
than 3,000 applications for 150 class spaces.

Other Programs:
Other colleges in this university system include pharmacy, optome-
try, allied health, and medical sciences. Osteopathic medical students
in good standing who are already enrolled in the college may apply
for the combined DO/master of public health program. The MPH
program has an emphasis on general public health.

Ohio University College of Osteopathic Medicine (OUCOM)
Grosvenor Hall
Athens, OH 45701
(800) 345-1560 (toll-free)
http://www.tcom.ohiou.edu/oucom

Nearly 60 percent of OUCOM's osteopathic graduates practice
primary care medicine, and students are encouraged to examine practice opportunities in underserved and economically disadvantaged
communities.

Program:
The four-year program emphasizes a holistic approach to practicing primary care. Students may choose to take a primary care continuum to provide more specific training in the areas of family medicine, internal medicine, and pediatrics.

The curriculum is taught through a combination of learning activities including case-based learning, computer-based programs, independent and group study, and early clinical contact as well as traditional lectures and laboratories.

Prerequisites:
A four-year baccalaureate degree from a regionally accredited college or university is preferred, although 90 semesters hours or equivalent of exceptional work at a regionally accredited college or university might be considered.

Applicants must have completed one academic year of the following: general chemistry, organic chemistry, biology, physics, behavioral sciences, and English. Additional courses in the biological sciences are highly recommended. As a state institution, preference is given to state residents.

Tuition:
In 1996/97 average tuition for state residents was $10,785 per year; nonresidents' tuition was $15,279.

Financial Assistance:
Contact the financial aid office for assistance with state and federal aid programs.

Application Deadline:
Admissions are based on a rolling admissions process. Applications filing closes by January 1, and interviews are conducted between September and April. The college recommends that applicants apply early.

Other Programs:
OUCOM was one of twenty-five medical schools nationwide selected as a Center of Excellence. The center is designed to recruit and support racial and ethnic minority students and faculty in an effort to increase the number of underrepresented health-care providers.

Oklahoma State University College of Osteopathic Medicine
1111 West 17th Street
Tulsa, OK 74107
(918) 582-1972 or (800) 677-1972 (toll-free)

Established in 1972, the College of Osteopathic Medicine merged with Oklahoma State University in 1988 and is now part of the state university system. The college's basic mission is to prepare primary care physicians for service in rural and medically underserved areas of Oklahoma.

Program:
The four-year curriculum is taught in a semester system with summers off, except for the final year and half of continuous clinical rotations. The first two years emphasize basic sciences and preliminary clinical concepts. During the junior and senior year, students work with patients under the supervision of faculty/physician supervision.

Clinical training can include work in a small rural hospital, a primary care clinic, a psychiatric facility, a community health facility, and private medical offices.

Prerequisites:
Applicants must have completed four years of college with a minimum 3.0 GPA and a 2.75 average or better in the science courses. Check with the college for required science courses. Strong preference is given to Oklahoma residents, applicants from nearby states, and applicants from those states having no medical school.

Tuition:
In 1996/97 tuition for Oklahoma residents was $7,550 per year; out-of-state tuition was $18,660 per year.

Financial Assistance:
Contact the financial aid office for assistance with state and federal aid programs.

Application Deadline:
Applicants are encouraged to apply before November 1, and all official transcripts must be received by AACOMAS by December 15. Interviews are conducted from September through February for classes beginning in August.

Other Programs:
The college is part of a larger state university system.

Philadelphia College of Osteopathic Medicine (PCOM)
4170 City Avenue
Philadelphia, PA 19131
(215) 871-6770 or (800) 999-6998 (toll-free)

Founded in 1898, PCOM is the largest osteopathic college in the United States and the fifth largest medical school in the country.

Program:
PCOM calls its program "Doctors from Day One." In addition to the standard osteopathic curriculum, students receive strong training in patient/physician interaction.

To increase communication skills, the college developed a Standardized Patient Clinical Learning Laboratory. In this setting, professional actors assume the roles of patients, with specific medical problems. The students are videotaped interviewing the "patient," developing a history and physical examination profile, and suggesting a diagnosis. At the end of the session, the student's performance is reviewed with a faculty member.

PCOM's Community Health Care Center provides health care to medically underserved communities. Students are given a two-month assignment at PCOM's rural center and a two-month assignment to an inner-city center to introduce them to the needs of patient care in underserved communities and the health concerns of people living in difficult circumstances.

Prerequisites:
A bachelor's degree is preferred. Applicants must have completed 8 semester hours each, including 2 semester hours of laboratory, of the following science courses: general chemistry, organic chemistry, biology, and physics. A course in biochemistry is also advised. Other undergraduate requirements include 6 semester hours of English composition and literature.

Tuition:
In 1996/97 average tuition was $21,000 per year for the DO program.

Financial Assistance:
Besides participating in the standard federal and state aid programs, PCOM also offers scholarships for minority women.

Application Deadline:
Interviews begin in October and continue through May, after all other applications materials are received and processed.

PCOM offers an early decision if the applicant applies exclusively to PCOM. Early decision applicants must have a minimum 3.10 grade point average and competitive scores in the MCAT. Credentials for early decision must be filed by mid-August, interviews take place in September and acceptances will be sent in October.

Other Programs:
PCOM offers two five-year programs leading to the DO/MBA or the DO/MPH (master of public health) degree. The MBA is held in conjunction with St. Joseph's University. The DO/MPH, in affiliation with Temple University, prepares graduates for service in community health, government, and occupational or environmental medicine. PCOM also has a two-year graduate program in biomedical sciences leading to a master of science degree in various clinical specialties.

San Francisco College of Osteopathic Medicine
Touro University
1210 Scott Street
San Francisco, CA 94115
(415) 567-7500

San Francisco College of Osteopathic Medicine is a division of Touro University, located in central San Francisco. This is one of the newest of the osteopathic colleges.

Program:
The focus of curriculum is on primary care, including the medical treatment and osteopathic management of patients in a broad range of social and economic settings. Courses emphasize how osteopathic philosophy, concepts, and techniques apply to the practice of primary care medicine. Most students remain in the San Francisco Bay region throughout their four-year program, including clinical training.

Prerequisites:
Applicants should have a BA and have achieved a minimum of 2.7 GPA overall, on a 4.0 scale, and a 2.7 science GPA. Applicants must have completed one full academic year or the equivalent in each of the following: biology (general or zoology); physics; inorganic chemistry; organic chemistry; and English. Science courses must include a lab portion.

Tuition:
In 1997 the average tuition was $22,500 per year.

Application Deadline:
The college operates on a rolling admission cycle, so candidates should apply before the AACOMAS deadline of February 1 to receive full consideration.

Other Programs:
The college is part of a larger university system.

The University of Health Sciences College of
    Osteopathic Medicine (UHS-COM)
1750 Independence Boulevard
Kansas City, Missouri 64106-1453
(816) 283-2000 or (800) 234-4UHS (toll-free)
http://worldmall.com/erf/uhscom.htm

UHS-COM was founded in 1916.

Program:
The four-year DO program requires students to spend the first two years in classroom and lab studies. The second two years are spent in clinical rotations in hospitals and clinics.

The first two years of study include gross anatomy, biochemistry, histology, physiology, neuroanatomy, immunology, radiology, physical diagnosis, medical ethics, sports medicine, medical jurisprudence, human sexuality, microbiology, pharmacology, pathology, psychiatry, obstetrics, gynecology, pediatrics, osteopathic diagnosis and treatment, family medicine, internal medicine, cardiovascular medicine, gerontology, neurology, oncology, emergency medicine, surgery, ophthalmology, otorhinolaryngology, anesthesiology, and a primary care practicum. The third and fourth years include twenty-two clinical rotations, three months of which are spent in an ambulatory care, rural clinic setting.

Prerequisites:
A baccalaureate degree is preferred. Applicants must also demonstrate satisfactory completion of the following college courses, including laboratory work when appropriate: English composition and literature (6 semester hours); general chemistry (8 semester hours); organic chemistry (aliphatic and aromatic compounds, 8 semester hours); biological sciences (12 semester hours); physics (8 semester hours). Applicants are also expected to have studied genetics, bacteriology, and mathematics; and they are encouraged to have taken

courses in comparative vertebrate anatomy, sociology, philosophy, and psychology.

Tuition:
In 1997/98 average annual tuition was $23,310. Books, instruments, and fees may cost an additional $2,550 in a year.

Financial Assistance:
The primary sources of student aid are the Subsidized Stafford, Unsubsidized Stafford, and HEAL loan programs. Other forms of financial assistance may be available, depending upon the students' needs and background.

Application Deadline:
Applicants are encouraged to complete applications before the AACOMAS February 1 deadline. Qualified applicants are awarded interviews until the class is filled.

Other Programs:
The college is part of a larger university that offers a variety of degrees in the standard health sciences/medical field.

University of Medicine and Dentistry of New Jersey
   School of Osteopathic Medicine (UMDNJ-SOM)
Academic Center
One Medical Center Drive
Stratford, NJ 08084
(609) 566-7050

The School of Osteopathic Medicine, one of the divisions of the University of Medicine and Dentistry of New Jersey, was established in 1976 by act of the Legislature of the State of New Jersey.

Program:
The curriculum emphasizes primary patient care, the principles of scientific medicine, and the interrelation between structure and function in explaining the disease process. Teaching affiliates include the Kennedy Memorial Hospitals-University Medical Center, with divisions at Stratford, Cherry Hill, and Washington Township; Atlantic City Medical Center; Christ Hospital; and Our Lady of Lourdes Hospital.

Prerequisites:
In-state applicants are expected to show a minimum achievement equivalent of at least a 3.0 GPA in both science and nonscience areas for consideration. Out-of-state residents are not encouraged to apply with less than a 3.0 overall and science average. Accepted applicants must have completed a baccalaureate degree from an accredited college or university at time of matriculation into the osteopathic program. Required academic work includes two years (16 semester hours) of biological laboratory courses; one year (8 semester hours) of physics with lab; one year each (8 semester hours each) of inorganic and organic chemistry, each with laboratories; one year (6 semester hours) of college level math; one year (6 semester hours) of English which must include one semester of English composition; and one year (6 semester hours) of behavioral sciences (psychology, sociology, or cultural anthropology). Additional recommended courses include: history, philosophy, the arts, and modern language.

Tuition:
In 1996/97 average tuition for New Jersey residents was $14,492 per year. Out-of-state tuition was $22,679.

Financial Assistance:
UMDNJ-SOM awards merit scholarships, providing half and full tuition to students with superior qualities. These scholarships are renewable for each of the four years of study, contingent on continued successful academic performance. Check with the financial aid office for more information on federal and state assistance.

Application Deadline:
Selected applicants are invited for interviews beginning in September. Students are admitted on a rolling admissions basis until the class is filled.

Other Programs:
The college is part of a larger allopathic medical/dental school system.

University of New England (UNE)
College of Osteopathic Medicine
11 Hills Beach Road
Biddeford, ME 04005
(800) 477-4863 (toll-free)

The University of New England is an independent, coeducational university on the southern coast of Maine. Founded in 1978 by the combination of the New England College of Osteopathic Medicine with St. Francis College, the university's 425-plus acre campus is set on the banks of the Saco river and shore of the Atlantic Ocean. About two-thirds of the recent DO graduates pursued careers in primary care.

Program:
Students are trained to care for the sick and work with their patients to promote health. The two-and-one-half-year on-campus portion of the program is primarily lab-and-lecture classes, including instruction in the core basic sciences. The second-year curriculum shifts to an integrated body-system approach, wherein the impact of the various disciplines is integrated with the clinical sciences into each body system. A consistent emphasis is placed on osteopathic principles and manipulative practice, human behavior, community health and health maintenance, and the humanities.

Beginning in the spring of their first year, all students observe and then experience clinical practice through part-time clinical preceptorships. In their third year, students begin seventeen months of full-time hospital-based clerkships and office-based preceptorships. For seven of the seventeen months, students have the option to select their own hospital sites and rotations, upon approval from the college. The college is affiliated with more than twenty college community hospitals and medical centers throughout the Northeast.

Prerequisites:
Applicants must have a minimum of 90 semester hours or 75 percent credit toward a baccalaureate degree from an accredited college or university. In addition to the basic educational prerequisites, students are encouraged to enroll in science courses such as: calculus, anatomy, physiology, biochemistry, genetics, microbiology, and physical and quantitative or analytical chemistry. The admissions committee prefers to see undergraduates who have received a broad-based education that includes the humanities and social sciences as well as the sciences.

Tuition:
Average tuition for the academic year ending in Spring 1997 was $21,150.

Financial Assistance:
The financial aid office will help students find the appropriate loan or scholarship programs. The Maine Osteopathic Association grants an award of $1,000 to a first-year student who is a Maine resident and presents proof of enrollment at an approved college of osteopathic medicine.

Application Deadline:
The college reviews and interviews students on a "rolling admissions" basis beginning in the fall. Applicants are urged to complete their applications through AACOMAS as soon as possible.

Other Programs:
UNE grants bachelor's, master's, or first professional degrees in several areas. Contact the university for more information.

University of North Texas (UNT)
Health Sciences Center at Fort Worth
Texas College of Osteopathic Medicine (TCOM)
3500 Camp Bowie Boulevard
Fort Worth, TX 76107-2970
(817) 735-2204
http://www.hsc.unt.edu

While many graduates choose primary care, TCOM also lists graduates who have entered every allopathic medical field from family medicine to psychiatry, aerospace medicine to pediatrics, sports medicine to heart transplant surgery. TCOM and the Graduate School of Biomedical Sciences make up the UNT Health Science Center at Fort Worth.

Program:
The first two semesters are devoted primarily to classroom and lab instruction in the basic sciences. At the same time, students are introduced to the clinical sciences through activities in the departments of family medicine and manipulative medicine. By the second year, more class time is devoted to the clinical sciences. During their last three semesters, students rotate through a series of preceptorships and clerkships in physicians' offices, college clinics, and teaching hospitals.

Prerequisites:
Students need a minimum of at least three years (90 semester hours or 135 quarter hours) of undergraduate credits toward the baccalaureate degree from a regionally accredited college or university. Recently, all selected applicants have earned a bachelor's degree by the time of matriculation. Minimum course requirements include one academic year of each of the following, including laboratory experiences: general or inorganic chemistry, organic chemistry, biological sciences, physics, and expository writing. The school also recommends that applicants pursue broad undergraduate study in the behavioral sciences and the humanities. By state law, 90 percent of the class must be Texas residents. To be competitive, nonresident applicants should have superior academic credentials.

Tuition:
In 1996/97 average in-state resident tuition was $6,550; while out-of-state tuition was $19,650.

Financial Assistance:
Check with TCOM for state and federal financial aid available.

Application Deadline:
The school recommends that applicants submit all material prior to October 1. TCOM has an early decision program for Texas residents so they can secure a place before October 1. Contact TCOM for the current early decision deadlines.

Other Programs:
TCOM also grants a Baccalaureate/DO, a DO/Ph.D., and a DO/MPH. Contact the Office of Medical Student Admissions for current programs and application requirements.

University of Osteopathic Medicine and Health Sciences
College of Osteopathic Medicine and Surgery
3200 Grand Avenue
Des Moines, IA 50312
(515) 271-1450

The University of Osteopathic Medicine and Health Sciences was founded in 1898 as the Dr. S. S. Still College of Osteopathy, but the institution has changed its name and location several times to accommodate an expanding enrollment and program of study. In 1972 the College moved to its present twenty-two-acre site on Grand Avenue, where it remains the second largest osteopathic medical college in the United States.

Program:

For the major part of the first year, students take core courses in the basic sciences, which is followed in the second year by the study of basic sciences and clinical medicine using an integrated organ system approach. The entire third and fourth year are devoted to preceptorships, clinical clerkships, and hospital clerkships in medicine, sugery, pediatrics, obstetrics, gynecology, and psychiatry. The principles, practices, and theory of osteopathic manipulative medicine are taught during the entire curriculum.

The college maintains and operates teaching clinics within a thirty-five-mile radius of Des Moines and has affiliations with several others located in Iowa and throughout the nation. Teaching programs have been established with twelve hospitals throughout the East and Midwest.

Prerequisites:

In recent years, all admitted students have had at least a bachelor's degree. The minimum cumulative GPA (all course work) must be a 2.5 and all science grades must be at least 2.5 on a 4.0 scale. One academic year of each of the following including lab is required: biology, inorganic chemistry, organic chemistry, and physics. Applicants must also have successfully completed 6 semester hours or equivalent in English.

Tuition:

In 1996/97 average tuition was $21,500 per year.

Financial Assistance:

Contact the college for help with financial aid.

Application Deadline:

Applications are due at AACOMAS no later than February 1.

Other Programs:

The university also has a College of Podiatric Medicine and Surgery and a College of Health Sciences. Among the degrees offered are the Doctor of Podiatric Medicine (DPM), the Physician Assistant Program Bachelor of Science (BS) degree, and the Physician Assistant Certificate program. The university also offers master of science degrees.

Candidates may apply to only one program at a time. Dual applications to the DPM and DO, or PA and DO programs, and so on, will not be considered.

Western University of Health Sciences College of Osteopathic
  Medicine of the Pacific (WESTERNU/COMP)
309 East College Plaza
Pomona, CA 91766-1889
(909) 623-6116

WESTERNU/COMP is an independent, nonprofit institution of higher education incorporated in the state of California and located in Pomona.

Program:
The four-year semester-based curriculum stresses the interdependence of the biological, clinical, behavioral, and social sciences. The first two years of classes are taught in the Health Sciences Center in Pomona, California, with clinical instruction and field experiences on campus and in the surrounding area.

Students spend the last two years in the clerkship program in osteopathic and mixed staff hospitals. Clinical facilities are available in California and other states. WESTERNU/COMP also operates a family practice outpatient clinic in Pomona.

Prerequisites:
Applicants must have a minimum grade point of 2.5 in the sciences and cumulatively on a 4.0 scale. The average has been a 3.2 GPA. Applicants must also have a minimum of 90 semester hours, or three-fourths of the credits required for a baccalaureate degree, from a regionally accredited college or university, including a full academic year in organic chemistry, inorganic chemistry, biology, physics, English, and behavioral sciences.

Tuition:
In 1996/97 average tuition was $21,300 per year.

Financial Assistance:
Call for current information on financial assistance available.

Application Deadline:
The college recommends that prospective students apply before December 15. Official transcripts must be received by AACOMAS by February 1.

Other Programs:
Contact the Office of Admissions for information.

West Virginia School of Osteopathic Medicine (WVSOM)
400 North Lee Street
Lewisburg, WV 24901
(301) 647-6251

Opened in 1974 as Greenbrier College of Osteopathic Medicine, WVSOM became a unit of the West Virginia State System of Higher Education early in 1976. Greenbrier County was chosen because of its strategic location in rural Appalachia.

Program:
The program covers the basic requirements of a DO degree, with a unique focus on the medical needs of the Appalachian region and rural primary care. Basic and clinical sciences, clinical training in hospital and family medicine settings, and extensive training in diagnostic skills are tied to osteopathic principles and holistic medicine. The curriculum is presented in three phases: fundamentals of the biomedical sciences and osteopathic principles; the presentation of organ systems, in which basic and clinical sciences are integrated in several courses that cover the major organ systems of the body and osteopathic principles; and clinical education.

Prerequisites:
A grade point average of at least 2.5 in sciences on a 4.0 scale is the minimum requirement, as well as completion of three-fourths of the credits needed for a baccalaureate degree from an accredited college or university. Minimum course requirements include one academic year in English, general biology or zoology, physics (algebra and trigonometry based), and inorganic or general chemistry, organic chemistry (including aliphatic and aromatic compounds). Labs are required for each individual science course section. Cardiopulmonary resuscitation (CPR) certification is required prior to matriculation. The following science courses are recommended but not required: biochemistry,

cell biology, cell physiology, microbiology, modern genetics, comparative anatomy, embryology, histology, human anatomy, and mammalian physiology. Preference is given to West Virginia residents.

Tuition:
In 1996/97 in-state tuition averaged $10,050 per year, and out-of-state was $25,900 per year (see financial assistance below).

Financial Assistance:
WVSOM participates in a contractual arrangement through the Southern Regional Education Board (SREB) in which WVSOM may award class seats to Georgia, Mississippi, and Alabama residents. Students selected under this program are subject to the same tuition and fees as in-state students. Applicants may contact the admissions office for more information on this program and other forms of financial aid.

Other Programs:
None listed on the information supplied by AACOMAS.

✿PROFESSIONAL ORGANIZATIONS AND OTHER EDUCATIONAL RESOURCES

American Osteopathic Association
142 East Ontario Street
Chicago, IL 60611
(800) 621-1773 (toll-free)
http://www.aacom.org

The national association of osteopathic doctors has chapters throughout the United States and sponsors conferences. The Office of Education can supply current information on osteopathic schools and related educational issues.

Canadian Osteopathic Association
575 Waterloo Street
London, Ontario N6B 2R2
(519) 439-5521

Contact the COA for more information on the status of osteopathic medicine in Canada.

Canadian Osteopathic Education Trust Fund
Suite 126
3545 Cote des Neiges Road
Montreal 25, Quebec

In the past, this fund provided some financial assistance to Canadian students studying osteopathic medicine.

✎CONTINUING EDUCATION

American Board of Homeotherapeutics
802 North Fairfax Street #306
Alexandria, VA 22314
(703) 548-7790

This organization certifies DOs who have taken a required number of hours of continuing education in homeopathy and have passed an oral and written exam. See chapter 15 for more information.

The Upledger Institute, Inc.
11211 Prosperity Farms Road, Suite D-325
Palm Beach Gardens, FL 334101
(561) 622-4334 or (800) 233-5880 (toll-free)
http://upledger.com

Founded in 1985 by John E. Upledger, DO, OMM, the Upledger Institute teaches craniosacral therapy, a gentle, noninvasive form of light touch therapy based on manipulation of the craniosacral region. The institute conducts over 400 workshops each year, teaching noninvasive therapies to osteopathic doctors and other health-care professionals. Workshops are conducted by a certified instructor, a practicing health-care professional who has completed a teaching apprenticeship program. Costs vary depending on length and location of workshop.

✎Recommended Reading

Digiovanna, E., editor. *An Osteopathic Approach to Diagnosis and Treatment.* Philadelphia: Lippincott-Raven, 1996.

The second edition of this medical textbook is recommended or required reading in many programs.

Fulford, D. *Touch of Life.* New York: Pocket Books, 1997.

Fulford, a ninety-year-old osteopathic doctor, won Andrew Weil's admiration for his use of manipulative medicine. Read it for one man's approach to an osteopathic career.

Gevitz, Norman. *The DOs: Osteopathic Medicine in America.* Baltimore: Johns Hopkins, 1991.

This fairly concise history of osteopathic medicine explores the range and depth of this career field.

PART 3

Continuing Education and Certification in Specific Therapies

8

Acupressure, Reflexology, Shiatsu, and Watsu

The therapies in this chapter are derived from Oriental medicine. All use pressure on specific points on the body to relieve pain, stimulate energy or *qi*, and achieve a therapeutic effect.

Most of the training programs listed here give graduates a certificate upon completion. Some programs may qualify as continuing education units (CEUs) for professions that require continuing education for the maintenance of their license, such as massage therapists. Check with the school to see if it is certified with the appropriate organizations to grant CEUs. Regulation of these therapies may fall under laws governing massage therapy. The schools and organizations listed here can help you determine legal requirements, if any, needed for practice.

ACUPRESSURE

In acupressure, a massage technique, the practitioner applies pressure to specific points on the body related to acupuncture points. Like trigger point or myotherapy, acupressure is often used to control chronic pain such as muscular pain, migraine headaches, or backaches.

According to traditional Chinese medicine (TCM), stimulating certain points by pressure or the insertion of a needle (acupuncture) encourages the flow of vital energy along certain pathways or meridians in the body. This puts the body back into balance and increases wellness. Because acupressure uses the same points as acupuncture, therapists using this technique are generally trained in the basics of traditional Chinese medicine, including *qi,* TCM organ systems, yin-yang, and other concepts.

Because acupressure does not use needles, it is generally classified as massage technique and can be added by any professional using bodywork in their practice. Some massage schools allow students to choose acupressure as a specialization.

Jin Shin Do is a service-marked style of acupressure. It combines deep finger pressure with a mental-focusing technique.

REFLEXOLOGY

Reflexology is based on the theory that certain points on the hands and feet reflect specific organs and other parts of the body, such as sinuses. The therapist massages these points on the bottom of the foot or hand to stimulate health in other parts of the body. Many people find a good foot massage relaxing. This is a fairly gentle technique, often used for patients who can't or won't tolerate full bodywork.

SHIATSU AND WATSU

Shiatsu is a Japanese massage technique. The practitioner uses thumbs, palms, and fingers to apply pressure on specific points (*shi* means finger and *atsu* means pressure in Japanese). The touch is generally more forceful than regular massage. Rather than using a massage table, shiatsu practitioners may have the patient rest on a pad on the floor. This allows practitioners to use their own body to brace the patient during certain stretches and other shiatsu techniques.

Harold Dull, who teaches at Harbin Hot Springs in Northern California, has developed Watsu, a water-based therapy that combines shiatsu techniques with floating in a pool. In Watsu the practitioner floats and rocks the patient in warm water. This technique has been extensively used by physical therapists for rehabilitation work with the physically disabled and handicapped.

Some shiatsu programs may be substituted for massage therapist programs and qualify practitioners for licensing or registration. Check with the school or your local authorities.

Schools

UNITED STATES

Career Training Academy
ExpoMart
105 Mall Boulevard, Suite 300 W
Monroeville, PA 15146-2230
(412) 372-3900 or (800) 491-3470 (toll-free)
http://www.careerta.com

The basic shiatsu program (300 hours) includes hands-on massage practice as well as the study of human anatomy, physiology, and kinesiology. The advanced shiatsu technician program (600 hours) further develops the techniques learned in the basic shiatsu program and explores additional techniques. See chapter 4, Licensed Massage Therapist, for more information on the school.

Desert Institute of the Healing Arts (DIHA)
639 N. 6th Avenue
Tucson, AZ 85705
(520) 882-0899 or (800) 733-8098 (toll-free)
http://www.fcinet.com/diha

The 650-hour zen shiatsu program integrates theory, techniques, traditional Eastern medicine, anatomy and physiology, practical experience, and business communications and practice. The student/ teacher ratio is limited to twenty-six students in the individual-instruction, hands-on classes. In 1997 tuition was $5,655 for the entire program.

Emperor's College of Traditional Oriental Medicine
1807-B Wilshire Boulevard
Santa Monica, CA 90403
(310) 453-8300
http://www.emperors.edu

The college offers an acupressure and massage certification program. See chapter 4, Licensed Massage Therapist, for more information.

International Institute of Reflexology
PO Box 12642
St. Petersburg, FL 33733

The institute offers a 200-hour certification program that includes 100 hours of classroom instruction and 100 hours of documented reflexology sessions. Write to the school for a free brochure, including current calendar of classes and costs.

Jin Shin Do Foundation for Bodymind Acupressure
366 California Avenue #16
Palo Alto, CA 94306
(415) 328-1811

Mailing address:
PO Box 1097
Felton, CA 95018

To become a registered Jin Shin Do practitioner, students must successfully complete three modules of instruction. In 1997 total cost was almost $3,000 ($8 to $12 per hour). Classes qualify for National Certification Board for Therapeutic Massage and Bodywork (NCBTMB) continuing education credits.

Mueller College of Holistic Studies
4607 Park Boulevard
San Diego, CA 92116-2630
(619) 291-9811 or (800) 245-1976 (toll-free)
http://www.fcinet.com/mueller

The American Oriental Bodywork Therapy Association (AOBTA) has approved the acupressurist curriculum. Students must first complete a 100-hour massage technician course prior to taking the 626-hour acupressurist certificate program. Mueller recommends allowing one year to complete the acupressurist program. In 1997 the acupressurist program cost $4,625, plus supplies. For more information on Mueller, see chapter 4, Licensed Massage Therapist.

Process Acupressure
Registration through:
International Alliance of Healthcare Educators
11211 Prosperity Farms Road
Palm Beach Gardens, FL 33410
(800) 311-9204 (toll-free)

Aminah Raheem, Ph.D., combines traditional acupressure with light touch techniques to open, strengthen, and balance the body's energy systems. The hands-on seminars cover energetically balancing the whole body and opening process; a model of whole person development as related to energy flow in the body; basic psycho-spiritual process skills; methods for working alone on oneself using Process Acupressure; processing the meaning of a symptom in the body; chakra t'ai chi; and soul work. Classes are presented as seminars throughout the United States and Canada. In 1997 US seminars cost approximately $500. Raheem is the author of *Soul Return: Integrating Body, Psyche and Spirit.*

School of Shiatsu and Massage at Harbin Hot Springs
PO Box 889
Middletown, CA 95461
(707) 987-3801

The school offers week-long fifty-hour intensive courses in shiatsu, Jin Shin Do, and Watsu. Some continuing education credits are available. In 1997 the cost was $600, including group lodging at the 1,300-acre Northern California retreat.

CANADA

Canadian Acupressure Institute
301 - 733 Johnson Street
Victoria, British Columbia V8W 3C7
(250) 388-7475

The institute offers programs in modern shiatsu or Jin Shin Do acupressure. Upon completion of either program, graduates receive a diploma of acupressure. Space is limited, so contact the school for current deadlines. In 1997 tuition ranged between $550 and $650 CDN, depending on the program selected, but the shiatsu program was expanding to 1,000 hours in 1998.

Shiatsu Institute of Canada
47 College Street
Toronto, Ontario, Canada, M6G-1A9
(416) 323-1818 or (800) 263-1703
   (toll-free in Canada and the United States)
http://www.shiatsucanada.com

The 2,200-hour shiatsu program begins in September and may be completed through the full-time study program (eighteen months) or the part-time study program (thirty months). Courses include Western human anatomy, physiology, pathology, nutrition, and public health; Eastern medical theory; shiatsu theory, practice, and treatment; business; communications; ethics and jurisprudence; self-care; and shiatsu clinic. The Shiatsu School of Canada also offers a postgraduate acupuncture program for shiatsu therapists who have completed a 2,200-hour diploma program, or its equivalent, and other health-care professionals such as chiropractors, massage therapists, physicians, and sports therapists.

✺PROFESSIONAL ORGANIZATIONS

American Reflexology Certification Board
PO Box 620607
Littleton, CO 80162
(303) 933-6921

This nonprofit corporation certifies reflexologists who have taken a minimum of 100 hours of advanced instruction and can demonstrate a minimum of 100 hours of documented practice. Contact the organization for current examination costs.

✄Recommended Reading

Dawes, Nigel. *Shiatsu for Beginners.* Rocklin, CA: Prima 1995.

> Dawes explains the basics of shiatsu. Photographs help make the floor work involved in shiatsu much clearer to a reader who has never practiced or experienced it.

Dull, Harold. *Watsu: Freeing the Body In Water.* Middletown, CA: Harbin Springs Publishing, 1993.

> Detailed photographic workbook shows Dull's technique both in and out of water.

Rude, Paul. *Souls to Sole: A Self-Help Exploration of Reflexology.* Twin Lakes, WI: Lotus Light, 1997.

> Although most people think Mildred Carter's works are the definitive guides to reflexology, this little volume introduces a lot of concepts in a fun, easy-to-remember way, including crosswords.

9

Ayurveda and Yoga

Both Ayurveda and yoga have their roots in the folk medicine, philosophies, and religious traditions of India. In yoga, instruction is often based on the teachings of a particular yogic master or guru.

❧AYURVEDA

Ayurveda literally means the science of life. Ayurvedic medicine, which has been practiced in India for thousands of years, combines herbal remedies, diet, meditation, and exercise (yoga). Like most natural therapies, Ayurveda emphasizes the treatment of the whole person rather than just the symptom. It has been popularized in the West in recent years by Deepak Chopra, a physician trained in both Western and Ayurvedic methods.

India has a number of Ayurvedic medical colleges, and many of the Ayurvedic doctors teaching in this country graduated from these institutions. At present, there are no Ayurvedic medical degree programs in the United States or Canada, nor is there a legal designation of an Ayurvedic physician. Nonetheless, many of these therapies are used by medical doctors, osteopathic doctors, naturopathic physicians, and practitioners of Oriental medicine.

✹YOGA

Yoga is a popular form of exercise for many Americans and Canadians. Relying on gentle movement and stretching, yoga has been called the baby boomers' preferred replacement for high impact aerobics. Yoga can also have therapeutic applications.

Some yoga teachers specialize in techniques meant to help relieve stress, improve circulation, or boost the immune system, and some massage therapists and other bodyworkers like to add yoga exercises to their patients' regimes as a way to maintain good musculoskeletal health. Some techniques focus on the needs of people dealing with the effects of chronic diseases, such as rheumatoid arthritis, Parkinson's disease, heart disease, stroke, and multiple sclerosis.

Although there has been some discussion, no standardized certification for yoga teachers exists at this time in the United States or Canada. Because they are generally regarded as exercise instructors, no specific health licensing is needed to teach yoga. Most teacher training programs require that students spend one to two years studying and practicing yoga before taking the teacher training classes. Class length and format for teacher training can vary, from evening classes to a series of weekend retreats. Often schools will let students choose which type of classes that they want to take, making this a very flexible form of training.

To gain general yoga experience, check your local gym or community center for classes. Most of the schools will also provide names of approved teachers.

Schools

The Ayurvedic Institute
11311 Menaul NE
Albuquerque, NM 87112
(505) 291-9698

The Ayurvedic Institute's founder, Dr. Vasant Lad, has written several popular books on Ayurveda and was professor of clinical medicine at the Pune University College of Ayurvedic Medicine in India. The Ayurvedic studies program (three trimesters) is a general overview of the science of Ayurveda. Applicants are accepted on a first-come, first-served basis, and spaces fill quickly. Some prior knowledge or study of Ayurveda, anatomy and physiology, Sanskrit, and other vedic traditions is recommended but not required. In 1997 tuition was $1,000 to $1,600 per trimester. The institute is registered with the State of New Mexico's Commission on Higher Education as a private postsecondary institution but does not offer a degree program.

California College of Ayurveda
135 Argall Way, Suite B
Nevada City, CA 95959
(916) 265-4300

The two-year certification program consists of fifteen three-day weekend classes held once per month on Fridays, Saturdays, and Sundays, along with a three- to six-month clinical internship. Students who are not already licensed health-care professionals are required to take anatomy, physiology, medical terminology, general Western diagnosis, and medical communication classes. Students who have taken college-level anatomy and physiology may waive this elective by providing a college transcript. Program cost was $4,950, not including books or other equipment. The school enters two classes a year in spring and fall.

The Expanding Light
14618 Tyler Foote Road
Nevada City, CA 95959
(800) 346-5350 (toll-free)
http://www.expandinglight.org

The Expanding Light center teaches the Ananda Yoga technique developed by Swami Kriyananda, a direct disciple of Paramhansa Yogananda. The Ananda Yoga teacher training program (twenty-six days) includes classes on safe, correct technique and proper alignment; human anatomy (taught by medical professionals who practice yoga); yogic view of diet, health, and healing; and how to modify the postures to fit students' needs and abilities, including special groups such as the elderly, children, and students with disabilities or injuries. Cost ranges from $1,506 to $2,538, depending on housing needs. Expanding Light also offers continuing education units authorized by the California Board of Registered Nursing.

Kripalu Center for Yoga and Health
Box 793
Lenox, MA 01240
(800) 741-7353 (toll-free)

Courses offered include Kripalu Yoga teacher training, Phoenix Rising yoga therapy, and Kripalu bodywork. In the last program, bodyworkers and other health professionals learn how to use yoga asanas (postures) as a foundation for bodywork. Depending on the type of program selected, the cost may range from $2,000 to $5,000. Contact the center for a current calendar.

Rocky Mountain Institute of Yoga and Ayurveda
PO Box 1091
Boulder, CO 80306
(303) 443-6923

The Rocky Mountain Institute offers certificate programs in yoga teaching and Ayurveda/yoga therapy. Classes are offered in different locations throughout the Boulder and Denver region. Cost ranges from $75 to $350, depending on the instructor and the length of the class (day, weekend, month, and so on).

Shambhava School of Yoga
2875 County Road #67
Boulder, CO 80303
(303) 494-3051

The hatha yoga teacher training program lasts six months. Students learn classical yoga, principles of anatomy, and various styles of yoga, including kundalini yoga. In 1997 cost was approximately $1,800, and some weekend retreats were available.

Yoga Centers
2255 140th Avenue NE #1
Bellevue, WA 98005
http://www.yogacenters.com
(206) 746-7476

In the past, Yoga Centers has offered more than forty classes per week including some teacher training courses on the therapeutic applications of poses. Costs vary considerably, depending on the length of the class. Call or check the web site for a current calendar.

Yoga College of India
8800 Wilshire Boulevard
Beverly Hills, CA 90211
(310) 854-5800

The 500-hour teacher training program includes Bikram's hatha yoga system, integration of medical and yogic systems, application of yoga therapy to disorders, and yogic physical systems. Students attend full-time for three months. In 1997 the cost was $3,500 for the entire program.

Yoga and Health Studios
7918 Bolling Drive
Alexandria, VA 22308

This is the US contact for the Yoga for Health Foundation, a British organization. The Yoga for Health Foundation has developed remedial yoga techniques for relieving the symptoms of many types of chronic ailments, as well as training yoga teachers in these techniques. These classes have been taught in Great Britain for more than thirty years. Write to the Yoga and Health Studios for more information on training in the United States.

Recommended Reading

Lad, Vasant. *Ayurveda: The Science of Self-Healing.* Twin Lakes, WI: Lotus Press, 1984.

This brief introduction to Ayurveda is written by a respected teacher who has had years of clinical experience.

Yoga Journal, PO Box 12008, Berkeley, CA 94712. (800)-436-YOGA.

Published by the California Yoga Teachers Association, this magazine covers issues of professional and personal interest to yoga students and teachers.

10

Biofeedback, Guided Imagery, and Hypnotherapy

The influence of the mind on health has been a hot topic since Bill Moyers made his PBS special, but many of the therapies that concentrate on using the conscious or unconscious mind to control the body's health are much older. Yogis (see chapter 9, Ayurveda and Yoga) have always used breathing and meditation as a tool for relaxation as well as healing, and most of the holistic approaches emphasize the importance of assessing the patient's mental and emotional state. The therapies in this chapter concentrate on using the patient's mind to control certain physical problems, such as stopping a migraine headache or lowering blood pressure.

❧ BIOFEEDBACK

The term "biofeedback" was first used in the late 1960s to describe laboratory procedures that trained research subjects to alter brain activity, blood pressure, heart rate, and other bodily functions that normally are not controlled voluntarily. Today biofeedback is used as a treatment technique to help people to improve their health by understanding signals from their own bodies and working consciously to affect change. Most commonly, biofeedback is suggested for coping with stress-induced pain, such as migraines or muscle spasms. Clinicians are trained to use biofeedback machines to gauge a person's internal bodily functions and help patients to "see" or "hear" activity inside their bodies. A biofeedback machine might pick up electrical signals in the muscles and translate the signals into a form that patients can detect. For example, tensing a muscle would trigger a flashing light or activate a beeper. The patient learns to relax tense muscles by developing methods that slow down the flashing or beeping.

Specialists who use biofeedback training range from psychiatrists and psychologists to dentists, internists, nurses, and physical therapists. Patients usually learn to identify the circumstances that trigger their symptoms, and are taught some form of relaxation exercise to help them alleviate the symptoms.

GUIDED IMAGERY

Guided imagery may also be called visualization, mental imagery, or creative imagery. Essentially, this technique concentrates on using images or symbols to train the mind to create a definite physiological effect. Most often, this technique is used to relieve stress and physical problems created by stress, such as tension headaches, although it has also been used in cancer treatment programs.

The effect of this technique is directly linked to the patient's willingness to participate in the treatment. Although there is no regulation of guided imagery, the Academy for Guided Imagery (see below) restricts admittance to licensed health-care professionals.

HYPNOTHERAPY

Modern hypnosis was first tried as a therapeutic technique by Franz Anton Mesmer (1734–1815), an Austrian physician, whose name is still with us as "mesmerism." Like many medical pioneers, he spent much of his time justifying his ideas to highly skeptical colleagues. Although to this day no one knows exactly how hypnotism works, it is currently used in a variety of medical situations, from helping people stop smoking to relieving the pain of burn victims. Some dentists use hypnotism instead of pain-killers.

A variety of techniques are used to induce everything from light to heavy hypnotic states. Training is offered regularly in almost every major city, often at weekend seminars or longer workshops. There is no regulation or licensing of hypnotherapy, although some hypnotherapists may be defined as counselors and fall under the regulations pertaining to that profession.

Schools

Academy for Guided Imagery
PO Box 2070
Mill Valley, CA 94942
(415) 389-9324 or (800) 726-2070

The Academy for Guided Imagery has been offering training for health professionals since 1989. The 150-hour certification program takes approximately twelve to eighteen months to complete, and is approved for continuing education credits by the American Psychological Association, the California Board of Registered Nurses, and the California Alcoholism and Drug Counselor's Education Program. In 1997 the cost was approximately $3,000.

Heartwood Institute
220 Harmony Lane
Garberville, CA 95542
(707) 923-5000
http://www.heartwoodinstitute.com

The somatic therapist program (nine months, 750 hours) trains students in a synthesis of bodywork, breath work, hypnotherapy, movement, energy work, and counseling skills. Courses include Neo-Reichian massage, polarity therapy, somatic practices, anatomy, breath work, hypnotherapy and hypnotic techniques for bodyworkers, and therapeutic applications of hypnotherapy. In 1997 the cost was $6,565. Contact Heartwood for current schedule and classes (see chapter 4, Licensed Massage Therapist, for more information on Heartwood).

✂PROFESSIONAL ORGANIZATIONS

The Association for Applied Psychophysiology and Biofeedback
  (AAPB)
10200 W. 44th Avenue
Suite 304
Wheat Ridge, CO 80033-2840
(303) 422-8436 or (800) 477-8892 (toll-free)

AAPB was founded in 1969 as the Biofeedback Research Society. In 1997 it had 2,200 members representing the fields of psychology, medicine, nursing, social work, counseling, physical therapy, education, and other health-care areas. More than forty state chapters were active in 1997. Members receive a subscription to *Applied Psychophysiology and Biofeedback* (formerly *Biofeedback and Self Regulation*), a quarterly peer-reviewed scientific journal, a subscription to *Biofeedback*, the quarterly newsmagazine, and discounts on registration fees for the annual meetings and continuing education programs. Contact the AAPB for more information about membership and continuing education in the field.

International Medical and Dental Hypnotherapy Association
   (IMDHA)
4110 Edgeland, #800
Royal Oak, MI 48073
(810) 549-5594

This association certifies hypnotherapists and provides professional referrals. To become certified, training must take place at an approved program and the therapist must agree to take a certain number of continuing education credits each year. Contact IMDHA for more information on programs and approved instructors.

✒Recommended Reading

Rossman, Martin MD. *Healing Yourself: A Step-by-Step Program for Better Health Through Imagery.* New York: Walker and Company, 1987.

> Written by one of the founders of the Academy of Guided Imagery, this is a good introduction to the basic concepts behind the technique.

11

Deep-Tissue Bodywork: Myofascial Release, Bonnie Prudden, Rolfing, and Hellerwork

In deep-tissue bodywork techniques, the bodyworker tends to "dig" into the client, going beyond gentle massage to work on the deeper muscle and connective tissues. Each method is different, depending on the philosophy of the original teacher of the practice or the school.

In myofascial release, for example, the bodyworker applies pressure to "trigger points" in muscles. Trigger points, unlike acupressure points, can be created when a muscle is damaged or suffers trauma, such as from a sports injury, accidents, occupational injury, or disease. The therapist erases spasm by pressing on the appropriate trigger points and then "reeducates" the affected muscle to assume resting relaxed condition. Reeducation often includes special exercises designed for each individual problem. The therapist teaches the client how to do these exercises to remain free of pain.

While deep-tissue work is a standard part of most massage therapists' education, practitioners of these techniques can be seen as bodywork specialists who have gone beyond the general massage therapy training to focus on specific technique. Their earnings in private practice tend to be a little higher than the average massage therapist in private practice.

Depending on the local laws, practitioners of these techniques may fall under the regulations governing massage therapy. Check local requirements to determine what, if any, licensing would be required in your community and if you will have to take extra schooling outside of the deep tissue training. In some areas this type of training may satisfy continuing education requirements for licensed massage therapists.

✺BONNIE PRUDDEN

In 1976 exercise teacher and fitness coach Bonnie Prudden began writing about myotherapy as an effective way to stop muscle pain. Three years later she established a school to teach her technique, which combines the application of pressure to trigger points and educating patients on ways to prevent recurrence of pain. Over the years, her school has expanded the subjects taught to the students to increase their understanding of the human body, so that training now includes classes like sculpture and life drawing.

Graduates are known as Bonnie Prudden Myotherapists after they have successfully completed the 1,400 hour, one-year course of study and passed a series of certification exams. To maintain their certification as Bonnie Prudden Myotherapists, practitioners must take 45 hours of continuing education every two years.

✺ROLFING

In 1970, Dr. Ida P. Rolf created a school to teach her holistic system of soft-tissue manipulation and movement education. Rolf had spent the last twenty years developing a system that concentrated on manipulating the body's myofascial system. Dr. Rolf called her technique "structural integration," but it is commonly known as "Rolfing."

Rolfing is often used to ease pain and chronic stress, improve athletic performance, or address other physical problems. The deep-tissue bodywork and movement education associated with Rolfing may help reduce the spinal curvature of people with lordosis (sway back) and enhance neurological functioning.

Rolfing used to be known as one of the more painful bodywork therapies, and it was once recommended that practitioners weigh 140 pounds or more to get proper leverage. Today, however, modification of the technique "lightens" the experience for the client (and the practitioner) while achieving the same results.

According to the Rolf Institute, there are more than 840 certified Rolfers in twenty-six different countries. The nonprofit organization's international headquarters are located in Boulder, Colorado. Rolfing is now a licensed service mark of the Rolf Institute, and only people trained and certified by the Rolf Institute may use the Rolfing service mark.

✒HELLERWORK

Joseph Heller, one of Ida Rolf's students, developed his own series of one-hour sessions of bodywork and movement education called Hellerwork. Unlike Rolfing, the practitioner also talks with the client during the session to make the client more aware of emotional stresses that may cause the physical tension. Deep connective tissue bodywork, movement education, and verbal dialogue between practitioner and client are the three main components of Hellerwork.

Like Rolfing, Hellerwork is often sought by clients with chronic muscle pain; but practitioners are taught that physical relief is only part of the goal of Hellerwork. Clients are supposed to move through eleven "sections" to achieve an optimal state of health. More than one section may be accomplished in a session, or a section may take more than one session, based on the client's needs.

Hellerwork is the licensed service mark of Hellerwork International. Only practitioners who meet their training and certification process are allowed to use the Hellerwork service mark. To maintain their certification through Hellerwork International, practitioners agree to participate in approved continuing education after completing their initial training; to maintain professional standards of practice; to adhere to a code of ethics as set forth in the Hellerwork International licensing agreement; and to renew their certification annually.

Schools

Bonnie Prudden School for Physical Fitness and Myotherapy
7800 East Speedway
Tucson, AZ 85710
(520) 529-3979
http://www.bpmyo.com

The one-year, 1,400-hour course includes three trimesters of myotherapy and exercise therapy; two trimesters of anatomy, communication, and business skills; and one trimester of life drawing and sculpture, modern dance, and other forms of therapeutic techniques.

In 1997 this course cost approximately $13,000 for tuition and supplies. The school also offers shorter, introductory courses and workshops. The full 1,400-hour course may also qualify graduates to practice as licensed massage therapists in some areas (check with your state or province board).

Central Ohio School of Massage (COSM)
1120 Morse Road, Suite 250
Columbus, OH 43229
(614) 841-1122
http://www.cosm.org

COSM's MyoFascial Therapy program (COSM's service-marked name for its program of deep tissue and trigger point therapies) is given once a year and is open only to licensed massage therapists, graduates of the Central Ohio School of Massage, graduates of other Ohio approved massage schools, and members of other branches of the medical profession. The course includes the continuing studies of the muscular system, expansion of the use of Swedish and other massage techniques in the treatment of specific disorders, and the presentation of MyoFascial Therapy. Tuition in 1996/97 was approximately $1,750. Contact the school for the current year's starting times and costs.

Hellerwork International, LLC
406 Berry Street
Mount Shasta, CA 96067
(916) 926-2500 or (800) 392-3900 (toll-free)
http://www.hellerwork.com

The Hellerwork practitioner training is a 1,250-hour certification program (approximately one year) offered internationally. Applicants must be at least twenty-one years of age; have a high school diploma or the equivalent; and have received the Hellerwork series of treatment. Other educational prerequisites may be required for certain courses. Costs vary depending on location, but prospective students should budget $12,000 to $15,000 for the entire program. Contact Hellerwork International for current list of locations and instructors.

Pennsylvania School of Muscle Therapy (PSMT)
994 Old Eagle School Road, Suite 1005
Wayne, PA 19087
(610) 687-0888
http://www.psmt.com

PSMT offers a Pfrimmer deep muscle therapy course for health-care professionals. The course is approved by the International Association of Therese C. Pfrimmer Deep Muscle Therapists (IAPDMT). Students must have a degree in the healing arts or must have completed a minimum of 500 hours of study in massage and related sciences. In 1997 tuition was $2,800 for the two-week course.

The Rolf Institute of Structural Integration
205 Canyon Boulevard
Boulder, CO 80302
(303) 449-5903 or (800) 530-8875 (toll-free)
http://www.rolf.org

The course of study at the Rolf Institute has a flexible timetable to allow students to complete the entire program in one or two years. The cost in 1997 was between $10,000 and $12,000. Rolfers can then choose to pursue specialization in Rolfing Movement Integration, and have other continuing education obligations.

✂Recommended Reading

Prudden, Bonnie. *Myotherapy: Bonnie Prudden's Guide*. New York: Ballantine Books, 1994.

> This is myotherapy as taught by Prudden, but it also serves as a good introduction to the concepts of trigger point therapy.

Rolf, Ida. *Rolfing: Reestablishing Natural Alignment*. Rochester, VT: Inner Traditions, 1995.

> Ida Rolf developed her technique to put people's bodies back into the "proper structure" or natural alignment. She was such a deep influence on so many styles of deep-tissue work that this is also a good introduction to some basic concepts.

12

Energy Work, Polarity Therapy, Reiki, and Zero Balancing

A variety of therapies seek to balance the body's energy. Some draw from the traditional Chinese medicine concepts of *qi*, or vital energy; others adopt the language of physics, and talk about an Einsteinian view of the life force. Many of these therapies are combined with some form of bodywork, and several of the programs in this chapter are geared toward massage therapists and other bodyworkers.

Like biofeedback, guided imagery, and hypnotherapy, the primary benefit of these therapies seems to be relaxation and stress reduction (which can profoundly affect a person's health). Many recipients of these therapies find them deeply comforting.

These therapies are not regulated and can be used by anyone. Because they involve light bodywork, they work well in practices like massage therapy or holistic nursing.

❧POLARITY THERAPY

Polarity therapy was developed by Randolph Stone, DC, DO, ND (1890–1982). Stone taught that four therapeutic techniques were related: bodywork, diet, exercise, and self-awareness. In the bodywork portion of this therapy, practitioners place their hands lightly on the body to redirect the client's energy. Cleansing diets and yoga-like exercises may be recommended to enhance the client's health. The American Polarity Therapy Association approves educational programs that conform to Stone's methods.

REIKI

Reiki developed in Japan, although its original teachers traced its roots back to Tibetan Buddhist practices. As in polarity therapy, practitioners make minimal contact with the client, usually just placing their hands lightly on the client's clothed body. Recipients report feeling heat or energy from the points of contact. Practitioners continue to change the position of their hands in a certain pattern throughout the session.

Level 1 reiki training is available through many different sources, such as massage schools and even some yoga centers. Unlike the other therapies, the higher levels of some reiki training involve a certain amount of secrecy, which makes a few students uncomfortable. Reiki masters move students from one level to the next through the teaching of secret symbols and sounds that are meant to increase the practitioner's reiki energy. Several forms of reiki are taught under slightly different names, such as Reiki Plus or Usui-Reiki.

ZERO BALANCING

Zero Balancing integrates a Western anatomical view of structure with Eastern concepts of energy. Creator Fritz Smith, MD, is a medical doctor and the author of *Inner Bridges: A Guide to Energy Movement and Body Structure*, which covers the topic of Eastern/Western integration of energy, science, and structure.

In a Zero Balancing session, the therapist moves through a set protocol, keeping a close watch on the client's energy level and emotional state. The sessions are meant to promote a clearer, stronger energy flow through the body and a good physical result. Zero Balancing can be adapted as a follow-up to stronger forms of bodywork, such as chiropractic manipulation or massage therapy.

Schools

New Mexico Academy of Healing Arts (NMAHA)
501 Franklin Street
Santa Fe, NM 87501
(505) 982-6271

NMAHA's certification program is based on the comprehensive health-care system created by Stone. The associate polarity practitioner (APP) program is designed for bodyworkers who wish to add to their practice, or for beginners seeking an understanding of polarity therapy. This course takes two months to complete. In 1997 it cost approximately $1,550. The registered polarity practitioner (RPP) program takes six months and covers the topics of bodywork, polarity yoga, nutrition, and counseling in depth. Students are advised not to work during the first five months of this program. Upon completion, graduates receive a diploma and are eligible to apply for membership in the American Polarity Therapy Association (APTA) as a registered polarity practitioner. The cost in 1997 was $5,000. NMAHA also offers dual certification in massage and polarity therapy, which also covers the educational requirements of a licensed massage therapist (see also chapter 4, Licensed Massage Therapist).

Reiki Plus Institute
130 Ridge Road
Celina, TN 38551
(615) 243-3712

Reiki Plus Institute was founded in 1987 by David G. Jarrell, a well-known reiki practitioner, and is a National Certification Board for Therapeutic Massage and Bodywork (NCBTMB) continuing education provider. The school offers a variety of seminars at approximately $200 to $300 each.

Polarity Institute
17 Spring Street
Watertown, MA 02172
(617) 924-9150

Polarity Institute provides training approved by the American Polarity Therapy Association. Students can become registered polarity practitioners by completing two levels of training (approximately 700 hours). As a part of their graduation requirements, students must give seventy documented polarity sessions and receive twenty sessions from registered polarity practitioners. In 1997 the cost was approximately $6,000. A shorter, less intensive program earns students the degree of associate polarity practitioner (APP).

✄PROFESSIONAL ORGANIZATIONS

American Polarity Therapy Association
2888 Bluff Street, #149
Boulder, CO 80301
(303) 545-2080 or (800) 545-2080 (toll-free)

This nonprofit organization provides a variety of services to its members, including a newsletter, certification following approved training, a list of approved schools or teachers, and conferences.

The International Society for the Study of Subtle Energies and
    Energy Medicine (ISSSEEM)
356 Goldco Circle
Golden, CO 80401
(303) 278-2228
e-mail: 74040.1273@compuserve.com
http://www.vitalenergy.com/issseem

ISSSEEM is concerned with the study of traditional wisdom and shamanic knowledge about subtle energies in the context of scientific theory. Designed as "a bridge between scientifically inclined intuitives and intuitively inclined scientists," ISSSEEM supports research of the phenomena associated with the practice of energy healing. ISSSEEM sponsors conferences; the quarterly magazine *Bridges;* and a peer-reviewed scientific journal, *Subtle Energies.*

The Zero Balancing Association (ZBA)
PO Box 1727
Capitola, CA 95010
http://www.zerobalancing.com

The name Zero Balancing is service marked. Training should be done by individuals who have been certified by the ZBA. Write or check the web site for classes and teacher training courses. Cost varies depending on location. In 1997 classes offered through the International Alliance of Healthcare Educators cost approximately $500 (see Appendix B).

Recommended Reading

Jarrell, David. *Reiki Plus: Natural Healing.* Celina, TN: Reiki Plus, nd.

Jarrell has also written a practitioner's manual explaining the first level of the Reiki Plus training.

Stone, Randolph. *Health Building: The Conscious Art of Living Well.* Sebastopol, CA: CRCS, 1995 (reprint).

Stone's writings deal with his basic philosophies of health and energy as well as polarity therapy. His interest in the traditions of other natural therapies of cultures is evident.

13

Herbalism and Aromatherapy

Herbal medicine, including herbalism and aromatherapy, is probably the oldest form of medicine. The study of plants as medicine was a standard part of medical training until the twentieth century.

In North America, herbalism or herbal medicine generally refers to a system of medicine that uses European or American plants. Traditional Chinese medicine (TCM) uses plants native to China or Asia, while Ayurvedic herbalism uses plants native to India. Modern herbalists often use plants from many different regions of the world. Herbalists do not restrict their practice only to those plants classified as herbs (a seed plant whose stem withers away annually). In herbal medicine an "herb" can be a root, a piece of tree bark, a mushroom, or anything else that grows naturally and falls into the plant kingdom.

Herbalism concentrates on using plants or parts of plants, like the flower. Aromatherapy uses "essential oils," which are concentrations of specific volatile compounds taken from plants.

✾HERBALISM

Although Great Britain has a standardized designation and training for Medical Herbalists, protected by laws dating back to King Henry VIII, no American state or Canadian province has legally defined a

231

herbalist. One school in the United States has adopted the standards of the British training, but a variety of other types of training exist. The schools listed in this chapter are meant to give prospective students an idea of the range of programs available. Some are well-suited to health practitioners interested in expanding their knowledge, while others are geared to helping people start independent careers in making and marketing herbal remedies.

Independent teachers offer a wide variety of courses and approaches. Some courses deal with herbal drugs in the same manner as any drug therapy (how much to prescribe and when); others teach botany, fieldwork, and the actual preparation of raw herbs. As one herbalist put it: "I expect my students to get their shoes muddy!" If you want classes that offer "muddy shoes," look for such terms as "wildcrafting" (identifying and picking herbs in the wild), or ask if the herbalist has a garden you will be using.

Herbalists are now offering courses through community colleges, private colleges, and professional organizations. Some are structured as continuing education for practitioners. If you belong to a profession that requires continuing education, check with your local professional organization to see if there are any botanical classes that satisfy this requirement, or try the Internet or magazine resources listed below.

The American Herbalists Guild (AHG) offers a professional membership and a student membership. The professional membership is granted upon peer-review by the admissions committee. Applicants must submit a personal and professional biography outlining their experience and training, have at least three to four years experience in herbal medicine, provide three letters of reference from other professional herbalists, complete an AHG questionnaire, and pay an application fee. Licensed practitioners are granted membership upon submitting proof of their training and license as well as a short personal and professional biography and curriculum vitae. AHG student memberships are granted based on the documentation of the type of herbal training program taken by the applicant. Contact the Guild for more information. See also Appendix C.

❧AROMATHERAPY

The term *aromatherapie* was coined by a French chemist, Rene Gattefosse, in the 1930s. Having used oil of lavender to treat severe burns on his hands, Gattefosse conceived the idea that his healing had been speeded by the scent as well as the other properties of the lavender oil absorbed into his skin.

Another French physician, Dr. Jean Valnet, used essential oils in his practice for more than thirty years. Valnet's research into the properties of essential oils and his writings on the subject are often claimed as the beginning of modern aromatherapy.

Derived from natural substances, usually medicinal herbs, the essential oils used in aromatherapy are meant to be applied directly to the skin, added to a bath or massage oil, or just sniffed. The health benefit comes from the aroma and/or the absorption of the oil through the skin.

Aromatherapy can be used to help a specific condition like sinus congestion or to create a psychological effect, such as a dentist using aromatherapy to ease a patient's tension.

At the time of publication, aromatherapists, like herbalists, are generally self-defined. "Certified aromatherapists" indicate those who had completed a specific course of study and received a certificate. In 1997 some national organizations were discussing the standardization of education and certification.

Aromatherapy is particularly popular among massage therapists, because massage oils are an excellent medium of delivery for essential oils. Nurses, midwives, dentists, doctors, and other health professionals also use aromatherapy in their practices.

A number of aromatherapy shops have opened around the country. These stores generally offer classes as do many community colleges and evening adult classes. Much of the instruction in this field is still single practitioners offering classes (see also chapter 19, Distance Learning).

Schools

UNITED STATES

Atlantic Institute of Aromatherapy
16018 Saddlestring Drive
Tampa, FL 33618
(813) 265-2222

Some classes qualify for continuing education credits for massage therapists. Class prices range from $150 to $600 depending on the length of the course. Call for a free brochure and current calendar.

Michael Scholes School for Aromatic Studies
117 Robertson Boulevard
Los Angeles, CA 90048
(800) 677-2368 (toll-free)

The school offers both seminars and home-study courses. The five-day certification course requires attendance of classes, although some home-study work may be used to satisfy prerequisites. Call for current schedule.

National College of Phytotherapy
120 Aliso SE
Albuquerque, NM 87108
(505) 265-0795

National College of Phytotherapy has created a bachelor's degree based upon the model of the British Medical Herbalist. Cost for the first year of study in 1996 was $3,900. The program was not accredited at the time of publication.

The New Center College for Wholistic Health Education
    and Research
6801 Jericho Turnpike
Syosset, NY 11791-4465(516) 364-0808
http://www.newcenter.edu

The Chinese herbal medicine program concentrates on the role of herbs in Oriental medicine. Students are not required to study or know acupuncture. The 2,700-clock-hour program can be completed as a three-year, full-time program or as a five-year, part-time program. According to the school literature, graduates receive a diploma in Chinese herbal medicine, which makes them eligible to sit for the NCCAOM certification exam in Chinese herbal medicine. The cost for the entire program in 1996/97 was $26,650.

The New England School of Acupuncture
30 Common Street
Watertown, MA 02172
(617) 926-1788

This is a seven-semester traditional Chinese herbal medicine program (a total of 480 hours) for students who have completed at least two years of acupuncture study. The program includes both didactic courses and a clinical internship. In 1996/97 cost was approximately $775.

Northeast School of Botanical Medicine
PO Box 6626
Ithaca, NY 14851
(607) 564-1023

Like his former teacher, Michael Moore, 7Song (sic) concentrates on teaching classes that include lots of fieldwork and botanical identification. The most popular course for practitioners has been the April through October course that meets one weekend every month. This course was $860. 7Song also offers a three-day-a-week course that lasts six months ($1450).

Southwest School of Botanical Medicine
PO Box 4565
Bisbee, AZ 85603
(520) 432-5855 or (800) 454-8324 (toll-free)
http://chili.rt66.com/hrbmoore/homepage

This class has been going for more than eighteen years. The annual 500-hour, twenty-week training course led by respected herbalist and author Michael Moore tends to close out early. By late August 1997, the January through June 1998 program was full. The program tuition was $2,500 for 1998, and students also needed to budget for some additional material expenses and travel costs. Moore spends a lot of time in the field, and much of the program is devoted to the identification of herbs in their natural settings.

The TAI Chinese Herb Program
Traditional Acupuncture Institute
American City Building
10227 Wincopin Circle, Suite 100
Columbia, MD 21044-3422

This 480-hour program is an introductory course extending over a two-and-half years. It is open only to practicing acupuncturists and TAI students in the Level III clinical portion of the program. Course work covers embodying the "sense of the patient's energetics" into an herbal formula; the political, economic, and legal contexts in which herbalism exists; hands-on work filling herbal prescriptions; and exploration of the energetic nature of individual herbs and herbal formulas. Tuition for the program running September 1997 through December 1999 was $4,500, including a $500 nonrefundable enrollment fee.

Western States Chiropractic College (WSCC)
2900 NE 132nd Avenue
Portland, OR 97230T
(503) 256-5723 or (800) 215-3716 (toll-free)
http://www.wschiro.edu

In 1997 the college announced its first thirty-six-hour certification program in botanical medicine, cosponsored by the University of Colorado Health Science Center-College of Pharmacy as part of its postgraduate education program. Instructors included such well-known authorities as James Duke, Ph.D., Mark Blumenthal, executive director of the American Botanical Council, and Don Brown, ND. Contact the college to see when it will be offered again.

CANADA

Wild Rose College of Natural Healing
1228 Kensington Road NW
Calgary, Alberta T2N 4P9
(403) 270-0936

Established in 1975, Wild Rose College offered workshops and seminars in Calgary and Vancouver. For some diploma programs, some classes can be taken through the distance learning program (see chapter 19). College founder and director Terry Willard has authored several textbooks on botanical medicine. Call for a current calendar of class offerings.

UNITED KINGDOM

The School of Phytotherapy
Bucksteep Manor
Bodle Street Green
Hailsham, East Sussex, BN27 4 RJ
(0)1323 833812
Fax : (0)1323 833869

This four-year course is designed to meet the requirements of a Medical Herbalist in the United Kingdom. Students are required to undertake 500 hours of clinical training spread over four years as well as completing course work at home. Overseas students can arrange to do clinical training with an approved herbalist in their country. However, overseas students must also attend yearly five-day seminars held in the United Kingdom. Cost seems to vary depending on where and how students complete the course. Contact the college for a current calendar and costs. The college also grants a B.Sc. honors degree in phytotherapy as a residential program.

✺PROFESSIONAL ORGANIZATIONS

UNITED STATES

American Alliance of Aromatherapy
PO Box 309
Depoe Bay, OR 97341
(800) 809-9850 (toll-free)

Members receive a quarterly newsletter, information about business and educational events, and a complimentary copy of the *International Journal of Aromatherapy* (which carries several advertisements from various courses). Membership costs range from $40 to $75, depending on whether it is an individual or business membership.

American Botanical Council (ABC)
PO Box 201660
Austin, TX 78720
(512) 331-8868

The American Botanical Council publishes *Herbalgram,* a glossy magazine that carries scientific articles on herbs as well as news of interest to the general public and herbal practitioner. For several years, ABC has been preparing the English translation of *Therapeutic Monographs on Medicinal Plants for Human Use* by Commission E, an expert committee of the Federal Health Agency of the Federal Republic of Germany. The Commission E was asked by the German government to assess both the safety and efficacy of herbs. ABC plans to publish the Commission E monographs in 1998.

American Herbalists Guild (AHG)
PO Box 746555
Arvada, CO 80006
(303) 423-8800
http://www.healthy.net/herbalists

This organization limits professional membership to herbalists who have met certain training standards (see above). The AHG also promotes research and publishes literature of interest to herbalists.

American Herbal Products Association
4733 Bethesda Avenue, Suite 345
Bethesda, Maryland 20814

This national trade association represents the companies and individuals who grow, import, process, market, and/or manufacture herbs and herbal products. Cost of membership varies depending on the revenue of the member's business. The association encourages international symposia, workshops, and public education seminars related to the safe manufacture, medical use, and public knowledge of herbal products.

National Association for Holistic Aromatherapy (NAHA)
PO Box 17622
Boulder, CO 80308
(415) 731-4634

NAHA is working with other groups to establish some educational standards in this field. Contact the organization to find members who are also teachers.

CANADA

Canadian Herbal Practitioners Newsletter
302-1220 Kensington Road NW
Calgary, Alberta T2N 3P5

This newsletter covers issues of interest to Canadian herbalists. Write to them for current subscription information.

Recommended Reading

American Herbalists Guild. *Directory of Herbal Education.* Box 746555, Arvada, CO 80006

The American Herbalists Guild's *Directory of Herbal Education* covers many programs in the United States, including the specific herb tradition taught, program cost, type of certificate awarded, and a review of the known instructors. Information is arranged by state. This is a good starting place for researching distance learning programs. Ordering information is available on AHG's web site: http://www.healthy.net/herbalists.

Griggs, Barbara. *Green Pharmacy.* Rochester, VT: Inner Traditions, 1997.

This updated and expanded version covers the history of herbal medicine from earliest times to the current debates over standardization and licensure. All herbalists really should read this book.

Valnet, Jean. *The Practice of Aromatherapy.* Rochester, VT: Healing Arts Press, 1990.

While there are literally dozens of good books on essential oils that are much easier to read, Valnet offers several fascinating case studies drawn from his long clinical use of essential oils.

14

Holistic Medicine/Nursing, Anthroposophical Medicine, Integrative Medicine, and Environmental Medicine

Students or practitioners in these fields go through standard training (MD or RN) and then add various modalities to their practices. Holistic, anthroposophical, and integrative medicine all take a strong mind/body approach to medicine. Environmental medicine concentrates on the impact of the environment on health. Training comes through taking independent courses in the other areas, such as nutritional studies, or by taking seminars and workshops offered by the professional associations.

HOLISTIC MEDICINE/NURSING

Holistic medicine refers to a philosophy of medical care that emphasizes the patient's personal responsibility and participation in health care. Practitioners use all safe modalities of diagnosis and treatment while emphasizing the treatment of the whole person, including physical, mental, emotional, and spiritual aspects.

In 1978 the American Holistic Medical Association (AHMA) was formed for physicians (MDs and DOs) who practice holistic medicine. Membership is also open to medical students in these fields as well as to health-care practitioners in other fields, such as naturopathic doctors. There is a separate association for nurses, the American Holistic Nursing Association, and for dentists, the Holistic Dental Association.

No medical school teaches holistic medicine at the present time, although approximately forty medical schools offered courses in holistic health or related topics in 1997. According to a student paper published by the AHMA, some of these courses allowed the integration of natural therapies into clinical rounds.

In 1997 the AHMA founded the American Board of Holistic Medicine (ABHM) to examine and acknowledge practitioners who have mastered skills in a number of areas of healing that are not taught in medical school. The organization also holds annual conferences with seminars of interest to holistic physicians.

✽ANTHROPOSOPHICAL MEDICINE

Anthroposophy was developed by Swiss philosopher Rudolf Steiner in 1913. Today Anthroposophy recognizes and uses modern medicine in the fields of anatomy, physiology, biochemistry, and diagnosis, but practitioners also use the "spiritual scientific methodology" developed by Steiner. Anthroposophical physicians undergo complete conventional medical training and licensure. They then take intensive postgraduate courses, held annually by the Physicians' Association for Anthroposophical Medicine.

The practice of anthroposophical medicine includes the use of the complementary therapies that have been developed or enriched through Anthroposophy. These include therapeutic eurythmy (movement therapy); sculpture, painting, music and speech therapy; physical therapies, including rhythmic massage, hydrotherapy, compresses, and external applications; and psychological counseling.

✽INTEGRATIVE MEDICINE

In 1996 the University of Arizona began an integrative medicine program developed by well-known medical doctor and natural therapies advocate Andrew Weil. The program was designed to offer continuing medical education and professional development activities to physicians and other primary-care practitioners, including week-long conferences, month-long residency rotations, and long-term study courses using a combination of on-site and distance-learning models.

Proposed core subjects in the integrative medicine program include philosophy of science; history of medicine; mind/body medicine; spirituality and medicine; nutritional medicine; botanical medicine; and energy medicine. Proposed modalities to be studied include interactive guided imagery; medical acupuncture (as developed by the American College of Medical Acupuncture); basic homeopathy; and osteopathic manipulative therapy.

Several other medical schools are currently experimenting with creating models for integrative approaches for care. Columbia's Rosenthal Center for Alternative and Complementary Medicine concentrates on alternative approaches to women's health and was partly funded by the National Institutes of Health's Office of Alternative Medicine (OAM).

At present no organization or association exists to identify these types of programs. If you are a prospective medical or nursing student, you might try contacting the organizations listed below for information on programs that may be sympathetic to an integrative approach.

✌ENVIRONMENTAL MEDICINE

Of all the approaches discussed here, environmental medicine remains the closest to standard allopathic training. The American Academy of Environmental Medicine (AAEM) concentrates on the relationship between patients' physical environment and their health.

AAEM's classes concentrate on environmental causes of chronic and recurrent diseases; diagnostic testing and immunotherapy for allergy-related problems; chemical toxicity and sensitivity; nutritional causes of problems and nutritional therapies; and indoor air-quality assessment and remediation. Classes on environmental medicine are also offered in many standard medical and osteopathic colleges.

Schools and Programs

American Academy of Environmental Medicine
Box CN 1001-2001
New Hope, PA 18938
(215) 862-4544

Member status is granted to currently practicing physicians with MD or DO degrees who have completed the AAEM instructional courses (two- or three-day classes). This takes approximately one year to complete. Fellows are members of two years or more with MD or DO degrees who have successfully completed an examination that demonstrates their expertise in environmental medicine. Student memberships are available to medical or osteopathic students of an approved school. Courses are approved by the Accreditation Council for Continuing Medical Education (ACCME). In 1997 the cost was $225 to $375 per course. Allied health professionals may be sponsored into courses by an MD or DO member.

AHNA Certificate Program in Holistic Nursing
PO Box 307
Shutesbury, MA 01072
(413) 253-044

AHNA Certificate Program consists of four sections, Phase I through IV, and covers the core concepts and emphasizes self-care and self responsibility; the nurse-person-environment interaction; a self-designed practicum; and the review of advanced concepts in holistic nursing. In 1997 the cost was $375 to $750 per phase. Call for current locations and seminar dates. The program is sponsored by the American Holistic Nursing Association.

School for Wholistic Nursing
The New Center College for Wholistic Health Education
    and Research
6801 Jericho Turnpike
Syosset, NY 11791-4465
(516) 364-0808
http://www.newcenter.edu

New Center College offers two holistic nursing programs. In 1997 the regular fee for the holistic nursing program was $8,040; the nurses certificate program with AMMA Therapy® cost between $225 to $425 per course. New Center offers discounts for AHNA members for the certificate program. (See chapter 2, Licensed Acupuncturist, and chapter 4, Licensed Massage Therapist, for more on the college).

The Physicians Association for Anthroposophical Medicine
    (PAAM)
7953 California Avenue
Fair Oaks, CA 95628
(916) 967-8250

PAAM unites physicians who practice anthroposophical medicine as defined by the work of Rudolf Steiner. Members must take the intensive postgraduate courses offered annually. The association also supports regional study groups, conferences, and activities, including individual preceptorships with an experienced anthroposophic physician. Contact PAAM for information on the current cost and location of seminars as well as concentrated training opportunities available in Europe. An annual course in English is held at the Lukas Klinik, an anthroposophical Swiss hospital. After meeting the certification criteria, physicians can take an exam to become a diplomate of the board of Anthroposophically-extended Medicine of North America.

Program in Integrative Medicine
University of Arizona
PO Box 245153
Tucson, AZ 85724
http://www.ahsc.arizona/integrative_medicin

Two-year fellowships may be available to qualified medical doctors (MDs) or osteopathic doctors (DOs). Write or check the web page for current activities.

✖PROFESSIONAL ORGANIZATIONS

American Holistic Nurses' Association (AHNA)
PO Box 2130
Flagstaff, AZ 86003-2130
http://www.ahna.org

Members of AHNA are expected to have a broad and eclectic academic background; maintain a sensitive balance between art and science; and develop both analytical and intuitive skills. They may use a variety of modalities to promote the harmonious balance of human energy systems.

American Holistic Medical Association (AHMA)
4101 Lake Boone Trail, Suite 201
Raleigh, NC 27607
(919) 787-5181
http://www.ahmaholistic.com

In 1996 AHMA created the American Board of Holistic Medicine to certify practitioners of holistic medicine. The board planned to start administering exams in 1998. The exam is expected to contain six core knowledge areas: nutrition, physical activity, environmental medicine, behavioral medicine, social health, and energy medicine. Secondary subjects include botanical medicine, homeopathy, ethnomedicine such as traditional Chinese medicine or Ayurveda, manual medicine, biomolecular therapies, and health promotion. AHMA also sponsors annual conferences. Contact AHMA for information on local chapters or possible student chapters in conventional medical schools.

Holistic Dental Association (HDA)
PO Box 5007
Durango, CO 81301
e-mail hda@frontier.net

The HDA's members use biocompatible materials and treatment methods that have the least impact on the health and wellness of the whole person. Members are encouraged to maintain an ongoing continuing education regimen to enable them to provide the best and most up-to-date treatment to their patients. Many use natural therapies, such as aromatherapy or acupuncture, in their practice.

Recommended Reading

Ivker, Robert. *Sinus Survival.* New York: G. P. Putnam's Sons, 1995.

Written by an osteopathic physician and past president of the AHMA, this book shows a holistic approach to a single common health problem: chronic sinus infection. Since holistic medicine is basically defined by its practitioners, this may give you some ideas on how various modalities may be used to deal with one chronic ailment.

Weil, Andrew. *8 Weeks to Optimum Health.* New York: Knopf, 1997.

Almost everybody getting into the natural medicine fields these days has read Andrew Weil. But just in case, this is a highly readable, integrative approach for getting your own body in shape.

15

Homeopathy, Bach Flower Remedies, and Flower Essences

Practitioners of homeopathy and its close cousin, Bach Flower Remedies, use "remedies" derived from natural substances. Unlike herbalism or vitamin therapy, these remedies are prepared in a manner that leaves only the most minute substance in the base of the remedy, which can be in a liquid or pill form. The concept of the "minimum dose" in homeopathy holds that the more a remedy is diluted and succussed (vigorously shaken), the more effective the remedy becomes. All the therapies discussed in this chapter derive directly or indirectly from the theories of Samuel Hahnemann (1755–1843) concerning the minimum dose.

At the end of the eighteenth century, Hahnemann, a German physician, formulated the hypothesis of "like cures like," or the law of similars, based on his experimentation with *cinchona* bark, a recently discovered cure for malaria. By matching the symptoms produced by a substance to symptoms produced by the disease, Hahnemann and his successors discovered that a minimum dose of a substance could stimulate a patient's body to heal itself. Once a remedy was found to create the same type of result in a number of people (case histories and detailed note taking have always been a part of homeopathic medicine), the remedy was added to a dictionary of homeopathic remedies called a *materia medica*. Homeopaths also use repertories, indexes of symptoms in which a description of a symptom is then linked to an effective remedy.

The root of all homeopathic treatment is the idea that each individual's symptoms are unique. Just as a common cold produces slightly different symptoms in each sufferer (John gets blocked ears, or Mary gets a runny nose), each remedy is unique. The trick is to match the right remedy to the individual's symptoms as well the disease, so practitioners tend to do very detailed questionings of patients. A typical first homeopathic consultation takes about ninety minutes. In classical homeopathy, the homeopath gives only one remedy at a time to gauge its effect on the patient. Some modern homeopathic formulas, like those sold over the counter in pharmacies, may mix several remedies, taking the scatter-shot approach that one remedy in the combination will hit the target.

✺HOMEOPATHY

Today, there is no legal definition of a homeopath in North America, although homeopathy has been adopted as an effective natural therapy by American and Canadian medical doctors, naturopathic physicians, osteopathic physicians, chiropractors, physician assistants, acupuncturists, dentists, nurse practitioners, veterinarians, and other health professionals.

Constantine Herring established the first American homeopathic medical school in 1836. By the end of the century, one in five physicians in the United States was a homeopathic doctor. More than twenty homeopathic colleges and 100 homeopathic hospitals did booming business.

Then, in 1910, the Flexner report came out. Albert Flexner was hired by the Carnegie Foundation to review medical colleges to see who would receive grants. He placed homeopathic medical colleges at the bottom of the list because they generally didn't have laboratory facilities and their graduates weren't trained in the scientific methods of allopathic medicine. Fair evaluation or not, the Flexner report and a new wave of "miracle" drugs like sulfa helped kill the homeopathic colleges and put the homeopathic physicians out of business.

By the 1950s, all the schools in the United States were gone and homeopathy virtually went underground. Yet it continued to be practiced in Europe and absolutely flourished in India, where it earned a new reputation as a cheap and effective alternative to expensive

Western drugs. Currently, formal homeopathic programs are usually independent programs, held as workshops or a series of seminars. This training is geared to health professionals who wish to add homeopathy to their practices.

The naturopathic colleges listed in chapter 6 offer training in homeopathy as part of their naturopathic doctor (ND) degree programs, and many ND students decide to specialize in homeopathy.

It is important to note that the use of homeopathy in the treatment of one person by another may constitute the practice of medicine, depending on the regulations of the state or province. Homeopathic medicines are classified as drugs by the Food and Drug Administration (FDA), and since the homeopathic methods of treatment include diagnosis and prescription, most practitioners of homeopathy in the United States typically hold some type of medical license. Medical doctors (MDs) and osteopathic doctors (DOs) should be able to use homeopathy wherever they practice. Other health-care providers, such as naturopathic doctors (NDs), nurse practitioners, physician assistants, dentists, veterinarians, chiropractors, licensed acupuncturists, nurse-midwives, and podiatrists may be allowed to use homeopathy within the scope of their licenses, depending on the laws of the state or province where they practice.

Professional certification of competency to practice homeopathy in the United States is available to MDs and DOs through the American Board of Homeotherapeutics (D.Ht.); to NDs through the Homeopathic Academy of Naturopathic Physicians (DHANP); and to all professionals through the Council for Homeopathic Certification (CCH).

The Council on Homeopathic Education (CHE) was formed in 1982 to monitor and approve the quality of courses offered for licensed professionals. Outside of the naturopathic colleges, the following had CHE approval at the time of publication: The National Center for Homeopathy; International Foundation for Homeopathy; the Hahnemann College of Homeopathy; and the Canadian Academy of Homeopathy in Toronto.

Based on continuing reports of its popularity in Europe, where the British royal family are known adherents of homeopathy, homeopathy has experienced a come-back in the United States. Two studies published in the early 1990s in *Pediatrics* and *The Lancet* concerning the effective use of homeopathy in specific cases marked homeopathy's return to conventional medical journals and further strengthened its image on this continent.

✌BACH FLOWER REMEDIES AND FLOWER ESSENCES

At the beginning of the twentieth century, an English homeopathic physician, Edward Bach, concluded that sickness and disease were primarily due to distress of the mind. He felt that stress, anxiety, fear, and impatience wore down the body and destroyed its natural resistance to disease.

Bach further decided that the vast *materia medica* of homeopathy was largely unnecessary. Rather than use dozens of remedies for specific diseases and symptoms, Bach relied on only a few remedies drawn from flowers and plants to treat the distress of the mind. Once that was cured, he felt, the rest would follow.

Bach limited himself to thirty-eight remedies, mostly drawn from plants native to England. Much of his writings center on the necessity of using only wild plants growing in a certain soil and climate conditions.

The Bach Centre holds that only Bach's original remedies, derived from the original sources, can be called Bach Flower Remedies. Flower remedies drawn from other sources are generally called Flower Essences. Like the Bach Flower Remedies, these essences are diluted from the original flowers in a manner similar to the making of homeopathic remedies. The Flower Essence Society of North America has added a number of spiritual effects as well as psychological ones to their classifications of remedies. Although sometimes classified with herbalism because their remedies are drawn from plants, the practice and prescribing of Flower Essences are closer to Bach and homeopathy.

Programs

UNITED STATES

Bach International Educational Program
(800) 334-0843 (toll-free)

See United Kingdom, Dr Edward Bach Centre, for information.

The Flower Essence Society (FES)
PO Box 459
Nevada City, CA 95959
(916)265-9163 or (800)736-9222 (toll-free in the United States
   and Canada)

This nonprofit educational and research organization promotes the development of flower essence therapy as a mind/body therapy. The FES was founded in 1979 by Richard Katz, and is codirected today by Patricia Kaminski and Richard Katz. The society conducts training and certification programs for active flower essence practitioners and offers public classes and seminars throughout the world. The cost of classes varies depending on the length and level of instruction ($200 to $800). Contact FES for a current catalog and calendar of events.

Hahnemann College of Homeopathy
828 San Pablo Avenue
Albany, CA 94706
(510) 524-3117

Admission is open to all licensed health-care professionals with a degree from accredited, residential schools. Applicants must submit a copy of their medical license prior to registration. The 864-hour comprehensive course in classical homeopathy meets in four-day sessions several times during the year. The course takes four years to complete. Participants study history, philosophy, *materia medica*, case analysis, case taking, and related topics. In 1997 tuition was $15,000 for the full program. Contact the school for a current schedule and costs.

The International Foundation for Homeopathy (IFH)
PO Box 7
Edmonds, WA 98020
(206) 776-4417

The intensive IFH professional course (240 hours) features instruction by experienced licensed medical practitioners. Class work is focused on clinical practicality and incorporates the latest advances in Indian and European teaching. Registration is open to licensed medical practitioners such as MDs, DOs, DDSs, DCs, NDs, acupuncturists, physician assistants, nurse practitioners, RNs, veterinarians, and others who may diagnose and prescribe. A photocopy of the new student's medical license is required with registration. Four-year college graduates or students currently attending college may be allowed to take the course if they have completed, or agree to complete, a course in anatomy and physiology. A photocopy of the student's degree and transcripts for anatomy and physiology are required with registration.

In 1997 the cost was approximately $2,000. A brochure received at the end of 1997 indicated that course structure was changing in 1998. Contact IFH for current calendar and information.

The National Center for Homeopathy (NCH)
801 North Fairfax Street, Suite 306
Alexandria, VA 22314
(703) 548-7790

NCH's summer school in homeopathy offers highly specialized classes on homeopathic prescribing for health-care professionals in various medical specialties, such as veterinarians, dentists, nurses, chiropractors, medical doctors, and other health practitioners. The center also sponsors offers weekend workshops for people interested in learning more about the homeopathy. The annual NCH conference, held in a different location each year, offers workshops and seminars for consumers as well as professionals. In 1997 workshops cost approximately $200; and the week-long professional courses cost between $400 and $600, depending on the class.

CANADA

Bach International Educational Program
(705) 749-1894

See United Kingdom, Dr Edward Bach Centre, for information.

Canadian Academy of Homeopathy
3044 Bloor Street West, Suite 203
Toronto, Ontario M8X 1C4
(416) 503-4003

The four-part homeopathic program covers 728 hours of instruction in homeopathic prescribing, therapeutics, practice techniques such as case taking, *materia medica*, and study of the repertory. The first three parts take approximately one year to complete (students meet in four-day sessions, with other work required at home). The fourth part consists of forty-eight hours of continuing education spread over two years. Applicants must be primary contact health-care professionals, such as NDs, MDs, DCs, DOs, DDS's, nurse practitioners, and so on. Students currently enrolled in an academic program for these professions are also accepted. In 1997 tuition was $440 CDN per class. Contact the school for a current calendar.

Centre de Techniques Homeopathiques Inc.
910 Boulanger
Montreal, Quebec H2S 3P4
(514) 277-1007

The Centre de Techniques Homeopathiques organized the first International Homeopathic Congress in Montreal in September 1995. The professional program includes 1,000 hours in homeopathy and 500 hours in complementary courses. The training in classical homeopathy includes 250 hours of clinical training done through the presentation of actual homeopathic consultations with homeopaths working in Quebec. Applicants must have a college diploma in health sciences or the equivalent, or successfully pass all the homeopathy entrance exams required by the school. In 1997 the cost was $4,050 CDN for the full program. Contact the school for a current schedule of classes and application packet. The program is recognized by the Syndicate du Professionnel des Homeopathes du Quebec.

UNITED KINGDOM

The Dr Edward Bach Centre
Mount Vernon, Bakers Lane
Sotwell, Wallinford
Oxon OX10 0PZ
http://www.bachcentre.com

The practitioner training course is limited to practicing therapists, such as aromatherapists, reflexologists, counselors, homeopaths, medical herbalists, doctors, and nurses. People who are not practicing but intend to set up a practice in the future may also be accepted. Familiarity with Bach Flower Remedies is required. The school reserves the right to refuse applications from people who do not have the required level of competence, and may suggest alternative courses of study.

Study is divided into two parts. The first part consists of four study days, with intensive review of the practical use of the remedies in depth. Students must pass an exam and complete essays and class work at home in order to advance to the second part. The second part consists three months fieldwork practice in the student's practice or working environment. During this time students are required to prepare a number of in-depth case studies for presentation, as well as complete an extended essay.

The course takes approximately six months to complete. Upon successful completion, a student is registered as an approved practitioner of Bach Flower Remedies.

Outside the United Kingdom, the course is run through the Bach International Education Program. Completion of these programs leads to the same offer of registration with the Dr Edward Bach Foundation. Even if you live outside the United Kingdom, you can choose to take the UK course, but you are responsible to traveling to the Bach Centre in England for part one and the completion of part two. Cost varies, depending on the location of the course.

PROFESSIONAL ORGANIZATIONS AND OTHER EDUCATIONAL RESOURCES

American Board of Homeotherapeutics (ABH)
802 North Fairfax Street #306
Alexandria, VA 22314
(703) 548-7790

The ABH only certifies DOs or MDs who hold a current license in the United States, meet the minimum educational requirements in homeopathy, and pass written and oral exams. Successful candidates are awarded the designation of diplomate in homeopathy (D.Ht.)

Council for Homeopathic Certification (CCH)
1709 North Seabright Avenue
Santa Cruz, CA 95062
(408) 421-0565

CCH examinations are open to any qualified individual with at least 500 hours of formal training in homeopathy. After passing a written examination and an oral exam, candidates earn the designation of certified in classical homeopathy (CCH).

Council on Homeopathic Education
801 North Fairfax #306
Alexandria, VA 22314

Write for a list of currently approved educational programs.

Homeopathic Academy of Naturopathic Physicians (HANP)
12132 SE Foster Place
Portland, OR 97266
(503) 761-3298
e-mail: hanp@igc.apc.org

See listing in chapter 6, Naturopathic Doctor, for more information.

North American Society of Homeopaths
10700 Old County Road 15 #350
Plymouth, MN 55441
(612) 595-0459

The society publishes *American Homeopath*, a quarterly journal devoted to the practice in North America, and maintains a register of members.

✿Recommended Reading

Castro, Miranda. *The Complete Homeopathy Handbook*. New York: St. Martin's Press, 1991.

> Written by an English homeopath, the book takes a classical, European approach to homeopathy. It includes a brief, highly informative history of the changes in homeopathy through the late 1980s. Castro was working on the expansion of Bastyr University's homeopathic curriculum in 1997.

Coulter, Harris L. *Divided Legacy: A History of the Schism in Medical Thought.* Berkeley CA: North Atlantic, 1981.

> The four-volume set compares and contrasts the history of homeopathic and allopathic medicine. Volume 3 is available in softcover and recounts the battle between homeopathy and the American Medical Association. Recommended for those who want to know the homeopath's view of medical history.

Kaminiski, P. and R. Katz. *Flower Essence Repertory.* Nevada City, CA: Flower Essence Society, 1995.

> Updated regularly, this repertory lists flower essences as used by FES and its members.

Ullman, Robert and Judyth Reichenberg-Ullman, ND, MSW. *The Patient's Guide to Homeopathic Medicine.* Edmonds, WA: Picnic Point Press, 1995.

> The authors, both experienced homeopathic physicians, give a clear and concise description of standard treatment from the patient's point of view, including many frequently asked questions. Both authors taught IFH courses in the 1990s.

Weeks, Nora and Victor Bullen. *The Bach Flower Remedies: Illustrations and Preparations.* Saffron Waldon, England: C. W. Daniel Co., 1990.

> This classical work on the flowers used in the Bach Flower Remedies was originally written by two of Bach's students and was updated in 1990 by the Dr Edward Bach Centre.

16

Movement Education: Alexander, Aston-Patterning, Feldenkrais, and Tragerwork

In several movement therapies—including Alexander, Aston-Patterning, Feldenkrais, and Tragerwork—practitioners "reeducate" their clients into better posture, movement, and coordination. The practitioner may or may not use physical contact with the client as part of this therapy.

Because many physical problems, like lower back pain, stem from poor posture and movement habits, these techniques work well in many types of health-care practices. Some of the courses listed here may satisfy continuing education requirements for massage therapy and similar professions. Many of the massage schools listed in chapter 4 will host workshops in these techniques or offer movement therapy as an elective course.

Because practitioners of these techniques are often seen as teachers rather than therapists, they may not need separate licensing other than standard business licensing to teach classes or private clients. As always, it is advisable to check with your local authorities.

ALEXANDER TECHNIQUE

In Alexander Technique the practitioner leads clients through a series of lessons to improve postural habits, increase freedom of movement in the body, and reduce physical tension.

The Alexander Technique is named for Frederick Mathias Alexander (1869–1955), who developed his therapy to overcome vocal problems created by a stage career. Through experimentation and observation, Alexander decided that he had created a pattern of tension that was interfering with the correct relationship between his head, neck, and back. By retraining his body to eliminate this tension, Alexander cured himself. Later, he taught his technique to others, continuing to teach until his death at the age of eighty-six.

In health care this movement therapy may help those seeking relief from certain types of muscle and joint pain, vocal loss created by muscle tension, or other health problems created by poor posture. The Alexander Technique is often taught at theater or dance schools because it addresses so many of the physical problems experienced by actors and dancers. Athletes, musicians, and others whose careers demand complex physical coordination may use the Alexander Technique to improve their performance. Teachers of the Alexander Technique may choose to offer private lessons or group sessions. Some teach at private institutions, like drama schools.

ASTON-PATTERNING

Judith Aston began as a dance teacher and then worked for Ida Rolf designing a movement maintenance program meant to reinforce the effects of Rolfing. Eventually, Aston left Rolf to found her own training center and teach her own philosophy of movement and body-work therapy.

Aston-Patterning combines movement education, soft tissue bodywork, and consultations to help clients unlearn "patterns" that inhibit the body's natural grace, resilience, and movement. Teachers identify problems areas through observation and palpation of the soft tissues. The technique can be applied to a wide variety of physical problems, including sports injuries, back pain, neck pain, or other problems resulting from postural dysfunction.

FELDENKRAIS METHOD

The Feldenkrais Method was named after its originator, Dr. Moshe Feldenkrais, D.Sc. (1904–1984), a Russian-born physicist. Like other movement education therapies, instructors use gentle movement and directed attention to improve movement and physical functioning of the body. Feldenkrais has been reported as beneficial for those experiencing chronic or acute pain of the back, neck, shoulder, hip, legs, or knee; the method concentrates less on the head/neck/shoulders relationship than the Alexander Technique. In clinical or hospital settings, Feldenkrais teachers may work with individuals seeking to reduce the impact of such central nervous system conditions such as multiple sclerosis, cerebral palsy, and stroke.

✋TRAGERWORK

Developed by Milton Trager, MD, this technique seeks to unblock neuromuscular patterns that inhibit the body's natural, free-flowing motion. Clients begin by lying on a table while the practitioner uses a light, nonintrusive technique such as rhythmic rocking to loosen the limbs and torso. Clients are also taught exercises to repeat the effect of Tragerwork at home. Practitioners work in a meditative state to "hook-up" with the client and induce deep relaxation.

Schools and Programs

Aston Therapeutics I
Registration through:
International Alliance of Healthcare Educators
11211 Prosperity Farms Road
Palm Beach Gardens, FL 33410
(800) 311-9204 (toll-free)

Participants learn comprehensive visual assessment skills; a quick system of notation for easy record keeping; how to make sense out of complex body patterns; an understanding of asymmetry as a part of biomechanics; techniques to sustain their own physical stamina; and ways to reduce the risks of occupational injuries. Seminars take place in various locations. In 1997 average cost was $500 per seminar.

Trager Institute
21 Locust
Mill Valley, CA 94941
(415) 388-2688

The Trager Institute is approved by the National Certification Board for Therapeutic Massage and Bodywork (NCBTMB) and the California Board of Registered Nursing to provide continuing education units. Professional certification requires completion of classes and documented experience with Tragerwork (both giving and receiving sessions). Trainings are held throughout the country. Contact the institute for a current calendar and costs.

❧PROFESSIONAL ORGANIZATIONS

The Feldenkrais Guild
PO Box 489
Albany, OR 97321
(503) 926-0981 or (800) 775-2118 (toll-free)
e-mail: feldngld@peak.org

The three- to four-year Feldenkrais professional training program leads to professional certification as a Feldenkrais Practitioner. Costs varied depending on location and institution. Contact the guild for a current listing of schools and instructors offering the Feldenkrais training program (see also Appendix C).

North American Society of Teachers of the Alexander Technique (NASTAT)
3010 Hennepin Avenue South, Suite 10
Minneapolis, MN 55408
(612) 824-5066 or (800) 473-0620 (toll-free)

NASTAT was founded in 1987 to provide public education and standards for certification of teachers and teacher training courses. All NASTAT members must satisfactorily complete the society's requirements for teacher certification. NASTAT-approved teacher training courses require at least 1,600 hours of class instruction over a minimum of three years, and a five-to-one student/teacher ratio. Directors of teacher training courses must have a minimum of seven years of experience teaching Alexander Technique. NASTAT evaluates each teacher training program and reapproves programs every three years. Contact the NASTAT office for a list of approved teacher training courses.

✍Recommended Reading

Shafarman, Steven. *Awareness Heals: The Feldenkrais Method For Dynamic Health.* Reading, MA: Addison Wesley, 1997.

Shafarman is a certified Feldenkrais practitioner who worked with Dr. Feldenkrais. This book presents six basic lessons meant for use at home and serves as a good introduction to how movement therapies work.

17

Nutrition, Orthomolecular Medicine, and Macrobiotics

Almost every form of natural medicine incorporates good diet in some manner or other. In his famous lectures on homeopathy, Dr. J. T. Kent (1849–1916) stated that it didn't matter what remedy he gave a man if that man went home and ate lobster every night. Too much rich food, observed Kent, destroyed health faster than any disease.

Oriental medicine uses food as a medicine much as it does acupuncture or herbs. Naturopathic doctors study nutrition throughout their four years in college. Standard medical colleges and other schools mentioned in this book are adding more classes on diet and health based on their students' interest.

Many colleges and universities offer a master's program in nutrition. The schools listed here teach a specific "whole foods" approach to nutritional therapy or offer a joint degree intended to enhance a career in medicine. See also chapter 19, Distance Learning.

✿NUTRITION

In health care, nutrition usually refers to the effect of diet on the patient's health. Students study how certain dietary habits can cause health problems as well as how to use good nutrition to improve health. Many nutritionists have a master's degree, and maintain some type of registration or certification with the state or province in which they work. They usually do not have to go through formal licensing or examinations. They can work as community and outpatient clinic nutritionists, nutrition consultants to the food and fitness industries, and as nutrition counselors on a holistic health-care team. Nutritionists can also moonlight as cookbook authors, diet consultants, or teach classes to the public on healthy eating.

ORTHOMOLECULAR MEDICINE

The term "orthomolecular" was first coined by Linus Pauling, a nuclear physicist who became famous for his constant battle to get vitamin therapy accepted by allopathic medicine. This specialty within nutritional medicine holds that the biochemical pathways of the body have significant genetic variability and that diseases such as atherosclerosis, cancer, schizophrenia, or depression may be caused or aggravated by specific biochemical abnormalities. Orthomolecular practitioners may use vitamins, amino acids, trace elements, electrolytes, or fatty acids to help correct these biochemical abnormalities. Because of some success in the treatment of mental disease, such as schizophrenia or depression, orthomolecular medicine attracts many psychiatrists.

MACROBIOTICS

Of all the Oriental medicine food therapies, macrobiotics seems to be the best-known. As originally developed by George Ohsawa (1893–1966), macrobiotics was influenced by classical Japanese medicine as well as Western science. Ohsawa borrowed the name from a treatise by a nineteenth-century German physician who wrote about diet's effects on prolonging human life. However, the foods recommended came from Ohsawa's original treatments by a Japanese physician Ishizuka Sagen, as well as his later studies of Oriental medicine.

Macrobiotics was popularized in the United States by the writings of Michio Kushi, and has come to symbolize a diet based on cereal grains, beans, fresh local vegetables, and other natural foods. Foods are classified by a yin-yang system, and the diet is designed to provide maximum balance for the body. Macrobiotics emphasizes a mind/body approach to health in which mental and spiritual state may have as much influence as food.

The Kushi Institute, in association with the University of Minnesota, was awarded a grant from the National Institutes of Health to study the macrobiotic nutritional approach in cancer therapy.

Schools

UNITED STATES

Bastyr University
14500 Juanita Drive NE
Bothell, WA 98011
(425) 823-1300
http://www.bastyr.edu

Bastyr's master of science in nutrition takes a "whole foods" approach with an understanding of human behavior, human biochemistry, and nutrient metabolism. Classes include nutritional assessment, diet therapy, disease processes, the psychology of addiction, and principles of whole foods. To enter the program, applicants must have completed a bachelor's degree with an overall minimum GPA of 2.25 and undergraduate courses in general chemistry, general biology, general psychology, anatomy and physiology, organic chemistry, nutrition, foods, microbiology, biochemistry, and developmental psychology. The nutrition department also offers an academic track leading to qualification as a registered dietitian (RD). In 1997 tuition was approximately $7,000 per year, but it varies depending upon the track and total number of courses taken. See chapter 6, Naturopathic Doctor, for more information on Bastyr.

Kushi Institute
PO Box 7
Becket, MA 01223
(413) 623-5741

Since 1979, the Institute has provided a wide variety of seminars and workshops as well as a forty-two-week macrobiotic school of counseling program. Seminars take place in various locations throughout United States and Canada. Call the Kushi Institute for a current calendar and costs.

Natural Gourmet Cookery School
48 West 21st Street
New York, NY 10010
(212) 627-COOK

The school offers a four-month full-time or nine-month part-time program to train chefs in "health-supportive" cooking and theory with a vegetarian focus. The school also offers classes for the public. Call for catalog and current tuition.

New York College of Osteopathic Medicine
New York Institute of Technology
Box 170
Old Westbury, NY 11568
(516) 626-6947
http://www.nyit/nycom

New York College offers an MS in clinical nutrition, which may be taken concurrently with the doctor of osteopathy (DO) degree. See chapter 7, Osteopathic Doctor, for more information on the school.

University of Bridgeport
College of Chiropractic
75 Linden Avenue
Bridgeport, CT 06601
(203) 576-4352 or (888) UB-CHIRO (toll-free)
http://www.bridgeport.edu/ubpage/chiro

The University of Bridgeport offers a master of science degree in human nutrition, which may be taken concurrently with the doctor of chiropractic program. See chapter 3, Doctor of Chiropractic, for more information on the school. The college also offers some distance learning classes in nutrition for chiropractors.

CANADA

Canadian School of Natural Nutrition
10720 Yonge Street #220
Richmond Hill, Ontario NT L4C 3C9
(905) 737-0284 or (800) 569-9938 (toll-free)

The diploma in natural nutrition qualifies graduates to apply for membership in the Nutritional Consultants Organization of Canada and use of the designation registered nutritional consultant. Classes begin in January and September. In 1997 tuition was $3,950 for the one-year program (night students may take up to two years to complete). Some correspondence courses are also available.

✣PROFESSIONAL ORGANIZATIONS

International Society for Orthomolecular Medicine
16 Florence Avenue
Toronto, Ontario M2N 1E9 Canada
(416) 733-2117

The society publishes a journal on orthomolecular medicine. For subscription information, call the society. The annual conference includes presentations of interest to practitioners of orthomolecular medicine.

✣Recommended Reading

Haas, Elson. *Staying Healthy with Nutrition.* Berkeley, CA: Celestial Arts: 1992.

This is a big, big book on all aspects of nutritional therapy, including vitamin supplementation and diet modification. This text has been used as recommended or required reading at several of the naturopathic colleges.

Kushi, Michio and Alex Jack. *The Cancer Prevention Diet.* New York: St. Martins, 1993 (revised edition).

Taking a holistic approach to cancer prevention and treatment, this book combines the principles of the macrobiotic diet with a definite treatment protocol.

Pfieffer, Carl. *Nutrition and Mental Illness: An Orthomolecular Approach to Balancing Body Chemistry.* Rochester, VT: Inner Traditions, 1988.

This text is one of the most often cited popular books about orthomolecular medicine.

18

Veterinary Techniques

Although the primary focus of this book is on the treatment of human beings, there has been a movement over the past decade to apply some of these techniques to animal care. Holistic veterinarians, like holistic medical doctors, take standard veterinary training and then add to their skills through continuing education in particular areas.

❧ACUPUNCTURE

Acupuncture has drawn the biggest attention in the area of treating race and show horses because it allows veterinarians to treat inflammation and other problems without drugs that remain in the bloodstream and disqualify a healthy animal. For this reason acupuncture is seen by some trainers as having a definite advantage over allopathic treatments.

Acupuncture can be used on almost any animal. Some owners report that their dogs are so relaxed by the procedure that they fall asleep during treatment.

❧CHIROPRACTIC ANIMAL CARE

Chiropractic techniques have been used on all sorts of animals, from small pets to large horses. The certification course run by the American Veterinary Chiropractic Association (AVCA) is limited to veterinarians and chiropractors or students of either discipline in their last year of study. The professional regulation of animal chiropractic varies from state to state, and the AVCA recommends that chiropractors protect their licenses by working only on those animals referred to them by veterinarians. Both chiropractors and veterinarians interested in this type of work should contact their respective state regulation agency for more information concerning the practice of animal chiropractic.

Upon completion of the AVCA course, successful candidates receive a diploma that states they are "certified in animal chiropractic."

HORSE MASSAGE

Horses often love massage, and therapists working with them report that the animals come to greet them. Equine massage programs teach practitioners both general massage and specific approaches to problems experienced by show horses or race horses. Practitioners may be veterinarians, horse trainers, or massage therapists.

Training Programs and Professional Organizations

American Veterinary Chiropractic Association (AVCA)
Located at the Animal Chiropractic Center
(309) 523-3995

The basic certification course offered by AVCA consists of five modules, each with 30 hours of instruction. The first four modules can be taken in any order. Registration is restricted to chiropractors, veterinarians, or students in either discipline. The first module cost $495. Contact the AVCA for current seminar schedules and locations.

Equissage
PO Box 447
Round Hill, VA 22141
(800) 843-0224 (toll-free)

Equissage's certification program has trained students in equine sports massage therapy since 1991. In 1997 on-site training in Virginia cost $795. Call for a free brochure.

International Veterinary Acupuncture Society
PO Box 2074
Nederland, CO 80466
(303) 258-3767

Training takes place at locations throughout Canada and the United States. The veterinary acupuncture course qualifies as continuing education credits. Classes are open to licensed veterinarians. In 1997 the four-session acupuncture course cost approximately $2,700. A herbology course is available to graduates of the acupuncture course at approximately $350 to $400. Call for a current schedule.

✀Recommended Reading

Pitcairn, Richard and Susan Humble Pitcairn. *Dr. Pitcairn's Complete Guide to Natural Health for Dogs and Cats.* New York: Rodale Press, 1995.

> Pitcairn, a veterinarian, concentrates on nutritional care for dogs and cats.

Schwartz, Cheryl DVM. *Four Paws, Five Directions.* Berkeley, CA: Celestial Arts, 1996.

> Schwartz is a trained veterinarian who has used traditional Chinese medicine in her practice for more than fifteen years. She discusses acupressure, food, and herbal therapy for cats and dogs.

PART 4

Learning from Home

19

Distance Learning

Distance learning programs allow students to complete lessons by mail or e-mail at their own pace. Some may require students to attend a few local lectures, but generally people do not have to travel to fulfill the requirements and can study at home. Many programs have no prerequisites, and almost all allow students to start at any time during the year. Financial assistance is limited for these courses, traditionally the most inexpensive type of education.

A variety of people are attracted to distance learning. It suits those who can set their own deadlines and do not need or want a more traditional degree. Health-care professionals sometimes use these courses to supplement their knowledge. People involved in the retail side of natural medicine, such as owners of natural foods stores, often take distance learning classes to improve their own knowledge about products.

Other students use distance learning to train as consultants about natural health methods. CANI, a professional organization for consultants in the natural products industry, helps members network with manufacturers and others who might use their services. Graduates of the School of Natural Healing, one of the oldest distance learning programs in natural therapies, have become shop owners, authors, developers of their own herbal product lines, and teachers.

The credits, certificates, or diplomas earned through distance learning may not be recognized by other educational institutions. If you intend to use distance learning classes to fulfill requirements for some other program, make sure ahead of time that the credits will be accepted. Such courses normally do not satisfy the requirements for the professional licenses discussed in the chapters 2 through 7. If it is necessary for you to obtain a license, check with the appropriate state or provincial authorities to find out if they will accept distance learning credits.

If you are already licensed or working in a health-care profession and are more interested in researching a certain topic rather than taking formal classes, a variety of resources exist that can be used to find out more about specific protocols, outcomes, and natural therapies. A few of these are listed below and more can be found in Appendix B.

Distance Learning Programs

UNITED STATES

American Academy of Nutrition
1200 Kenesaw
Knoxville, TN 37919-7736
(800) 290-4226 (toll-free)
e-mail: aantn@aol.com

The American Academy of Nutrition is accredited by the Accrediting Commission of the Distance Education and Training Council, which is recognized by the US Department of Education. The school offers several nutritional programs, from a comprehensive nutrition program to an associate of science degree. In 1997 cost ranged from $1,500 to $5,140, depending on the program and number of courses taken. Some credits may be transferable.

Bastyr University
14500 Juanita Drive NE
Bothell, WA 98011
(425) 823-1300

Bastyr offers undergraduate courses in nutrition, Oriental medicine, and homeopathy in its distance learning program. These courses do not replace the Bastyr degree programs (see parts 2 and 3), and Bastyr does not offer any degrees through this program. In 1997/98, the tuition cost was $170 per credit plus materials. Call the university for a free brochure about current classes available.

Institute of Chinese Herbology
3871 Piedmont Avenue #363
Oakland, CA 94611
(510) 428-2061

The institute has offered several home-study courses in traditional Chinese herbology since 1983. The complete program, divided into three sections, covered basic Chinese herbology (categories, formulas, and preparations); diagnosis and therapeutic applications; and clinical case studies. Materials provided include audiotapes, printed notes, study guides, exercises, and herb samples. The last course of the third section covers information on the legal status of herbal prescribing and some career development advice. In 1998 the cost per section ranged from $315 to $563. Canadians and foreign students are charged slightly higher shipping fees ($5 to $20).

The School of Natural Healing
PO Box 412
Springville, UT 84663
(800) 372-8255 (toll-free)

The School of Natural Healing was founded by John Christopher, ND, in 1953. Many American herbalists credit Christopher's courses in keeping alive the traditions of the Thomasians and other early pioneers of the "vitalist" school of natural medicine. Course prices include audiotapes, videotapes, and textbooks as supporting material. The son of the founder, David Christopher, answers student questions by telephone during the week. In 1998 program costs ranged from $445 (vitalist program) to $995 (herbalist program) to $1785 (advanced herbalist program). Depending on the number of courses in a program, students normally take twelve to eighteen months to finish. The school also offers classes on iridology, weekly lectures at its facility in Utah, and will help students set up their own herbal teaching programs in their town.

The National Institute of Nutritional Education (NINE)
1010 South Joliet #107
Aurora, CO 80012
(800) 530-8079 (toll-free)

The Certified Nutritionist program teaches fasting, detoxification, herbs, nutritional supplements, and other aspects of nutritional science. The school has been teaching this program since 1983, and has registered the term "Certified Nutritionist" as a service mark with the United States Patent and Trademark Office reserved to those who successfully complete the NINE program. In 1997 fees for the six-course Certified Nutritionist program were $467 per course plus a one-time registration fee of $150.

Pacific Institute of Aromatherapy
PO Box 6723
San Rafael, CA 94903
(415) 479-9121

A six-part correspondence course on aromatherapy includes treatment of disease and toxicology. In 1997 the cost was approximately $350. Materials include essential oil samples, and the school has a recommended deadline for completing the course.

CANADA

Canadian School of Natural Nutrition
10720 Yonge Street, Suite 220
Richmond Hill, Ontario L4C 3C9
(905) 852-9660 or (800) 328-0743 (toll-free)

The school allows students to earn an RNC designation (see chapter 17, Nutrition, Orthomolecular Medicine, and Macrobiotics) through correspondence courses. In 1996/97 the cost was approximately $1,700 CDN. US and foreign students may be subject to additional fees.

Wild Rose College of Natural Healing
1228 Kensington Road NW #400
Calgary, Alberta, T2N 4P9
(403) 270-0936 or (888) WLD-ROSE (toll-free)
http://www.wrc.net

This school offers a variety of correspondence programs that take from two to three years to complete. Students are also responsible for completing some "option" courses that require hands-on work. Evening classes and weekend workshops may also be taken at the college. The correspondence programs offered in 1998 included the master herbalist program ($1,420 CDN or US funds) and holistic therapist diploma program ($1,810 CDN or US funds). Tuition costs did not include textbooks. These programs are open to Canadian or US students. See also chapter 13.

SELF-STUDY AND RESEARCH ASSISTANCE PROGRAMS

Herb Research Foundation
1007 Pearl Street, #200
Boulder, CO 80302
(303) 449-2265 or (800) 748-2617

Since 1983, the Herb Research Foundation has supplied scientific documentation on botanical medicine to doctors, health professionals, government agencies, scientists, herbalists, and members of the public. Members may request literature to be sent to them or do on-line literature searches. Cost of membership and literature searches varies depending on the services requested.

International Alliance of Healthcare Educators (IAHE)
11211 Prosperity Farms Road, D-325
Palm Beach Gardens, FL 33410
(800) 311-9204 (toll-free)

IAHE offers seminars in a wide variety of service marked manual therapies (see part 3). Instructional videos and support material for these therapies may also be available. Call IAHE for a current catalog.

Office of Alternative Medicine (OAM)
National Institutes of Health
PO Box 8218
Silver Spring, MD 20907
(888) 644-6226 (toll-free)

Created by congressional mandate in 1993, the Office of Alternative Medicine was the first serious effort by the federal government to channel research money into the study of alternative therapies. Interested professionals or members of the public can request free literature from the OAM on grants available; research protocols; alternative therapies as treatment for various diseases, such as cancer; and professional conferences.

PROFESSIONAL ORGANIZATIONS

CANI
1300 26th Avenue, Suite 605
San Francisco, CA 94122

CANI is a professional networking association for consultants working in the natural products industry. According to the organization, its membership directory is used by editors of trade magazines seeking experts, the NNFA (National Nutritional Foods Association) to set panels for association trade shows, and members of the natural products industry looking for consultants. To be considered for membership, consultants must have been in business for at least six months; have one current consulting client; and provide two references. Write to them for current information on membership dues and benefits.

Recommended Reading

Bear, John and Mariah Bear. *College Degrees by Mail.* Berkeley, CA: Ten Speed Press, 1995.

Bear has spent more than twenty years surveying distance learning programs. He has written several books on the topic, both self-published and through Ten Speed. Check for the latest edition for more information on distance learning programs and related issues.

APPENDIX A

Schools and Programs By State and Province

S chools listed in this appendix are more fully described in the chapters in parts 2 and 3.

UNITED STATES

Arizona

Massage

Desert Institute of the Healing Arts (DIHA)
639 N. 6th Avenue
Tucson, AZ 85705
520-882-0899 or (800) 733-8098 (toll-free)
http://www.fcinet.com/diha

Phoenix Therapeutic Massage College
2225 North 16th Street
Phoenix, AZ 85006
(602) 254-7002 or (800) 390-1885 (toll-free)

Naturopathic Doctor

Southwest College of Naturopathic Medicine and Health Sciences
2140 East Broadway Road
Tempe, AZ 85282
(602) 858-9100
http://www.scnm.edu

Osteopathic Doctor

Arizona College of Osteopathic Medicine
Midwestern University
19555 N. 59th Avenue
Glendale, AZ 85308
(602) 937-5643

Deep Tissue Bodywork

Bonnie Prudden School
7800 East Speedway
Tucson, AZ 85710
(520) 529-3979
http://www.bpmyo.com

Herbalism

Southwest School of Botanical Medicine
PO Box 4565
Bisbee, Arizona 85603
(520) 432-5855 or (800) 454-8324 (toll-free)
http://chili.rt66.com/hrbmoore/HOMEPAGE

Holistic and Integrative Medicine

Program in Integrative Medicine
University of Arizona
PO Box 245153
Tucson, AZ 85724
http://www.ahsc.arizona/integrative_medicine

California

Acupuncture

Academy of Chinese Culture and Health Sciences
1601 Clay Street
Oakland, CA 94612

(510) 763-7787
http://www.acchs.edu

American College of Traditional Chinese Medicine
455 Arkansas Street
San Francisco, CA 94107
(415) 282-7600
http://www.actcm.edu

Dongguk-Royal University of America
1125 West 6th Street
Los Angeles, CA 90017
(213) 482-6646

Emperor's College of Traditional Oriental Medicine
1807-B Wilshire Boulevard
Santa Monica, CA 90403
(310) 453-8300
http://www.emperors.edu

Five Branches Institute: College of Traditional Chinese Medicine
200 7th Avenue
Santa Cruz, CA 95062
(408) 476-9424
http://www.fivebranches.com

Kyung San University
8322 Garden Grove Boulevard
Garden Grove, CA 92644
(714) 636-0337

Meiji College of Oriental Medicine
426 Fillmore Street, Suite 3
San Francisco, CA 94115
(415) 771-1019

Pacific College of Oriental Medicine
7445 Mission Valley Road, Suites 103–106
San Diego, CA 92108
(619) 574-6909
http://www.ormed.edu

Samra University of Oriental Medicine
600 St. Paul Avenue
Los Angeles, CA 90017
(213) 482-8448
http://www.samra.edu

Santa Barbara College of Oriental Medicine
1919 State Street, Suite 204
Santa Barbara, CA 93101
(805) 898-1180

South Baylo University (Keimyung Baylo)
1126 N. Brookhurst Street
Anaheim, CA 92801
(714) 533-1495
http://www.kbu.com

Yo San University of Traditional Chinese Medicine
1314 Second Street, Suite 200
Santa Monica, CA 90401
(310) 917-2202
http://www.yosan.edu

Chiropractic Doctor

Cleveland College of Chiropractic
590 North Vermont Avenue
Los Angeles, CA 90004
(213) 660-6166 or (800) 466-CCLA (toll-free)

Life Chiropractic College West
2005 Via Barrett
San Lorenzo, CA 94580
(510) 276-9013 or (800) 788-4476 (toll-free)
http://www.lifewest.edu

Los Angeles College of Chiropractic (LACC)
16200 East Amber Valley Drive
PO Box 1166
Whittier, CA 90609-1166
(310) 947-8755 or (800) 221-5222 (toll-free)

Palmer College of Chiropractic West
90 East Tasman Drive
San Jose, California 95134

(408) 944-6024 or (800) 442-4476 (toll-free)
http://www.palmer.edu

Massage

American Institute of Massage Therapy, Inc.
2156 Newport Boulevard
Costa Mesa, CA 92627
(714) 642-0735

International Professional School of Bodywork
1366 Hornblend Street
San Diego, CA 92109
(619) 272-4142 or (800) 748-6497 (toll-free)
http://www.webcom.com/ipsb

National Holistic Institute
5900 Hollis Street, Suite J
Emeryville, CA 94608-2008
(510) 547-6442
Fax: (510) 547-6621
http://www.nhimassage.com

Massage and Shiatsu

Heartwood Institute
220 Harmony Lane
Garberville, CA 95542
(707) 923-5000
http://www.heartwoodinstitute.com

Mueller College of Holistic Studies
4607 Park Boulevard
San Diego, CA 92116-2630
(619) 291-9811 or (800) 245-1976 (toll-free)
http://www.fcinet.com/mueller

Midwifery

Midwifery Institute of California
3739 Balboa #179
San Francisco, CA 94121
(415) 248-1671

Osteopathic Doctor

San Francisco College of Osteopathic Medicine
Touro University
1210 Scott Street
San Francisco, CA 94115
(415) 567-7500

Western University of Health Sciences
College of Osteopathic Medicine of the Pacific
309 East College Plaza
Pomona, CA 91766-1889
(909) 623-6116

Acupressure and Shiatsu

Jin Shin Do Foundation for Bodymind Acupressure
366 California Avenue #16
Palo Alto, CA 94306
(415) 328-1811

School of Shiatsu and Massage at Harbin Hot Springs
PO Box 889
Middletown, CA 95461
(707) 987-3801

Ayurveda and Yoga

California College of Ayurveda
135 Argall Way, Suite B
Nevada City, CA 95959
(916) 265-4300

The Expanding Light
14618 Tyler Foote Road
Nevada City, CA 95959
(800) 346-5350 (toll-free)
http://www.expandinglight.org

Yoga College of India
8800 Wilshire Boulevard
Beverly Hills, CA 90211
(310) 854-5800

Guided Imagery

Academy for Guided Imagery
PO Box 2070
Mill Valley, CA 94942
(415) 389-9324 or (800) 726-2070 (toll-free)

Herbalism and Aromatherapy

Michael Scholes School for Aromatic Studies
117 Robertson Boulevard
Los Angeles, CA 90048
(800) 677-2368 (toll-free)

Homeopathy

Hahnemann College of Homeopathy
828 San Pablo Avenue
Albany, CA 94706
(510) 524-3117

Colorado

Massage Therapy

Boulder School of Massage Therapy
6255 Longbow Drive
Boulder, CO 80301
(303) 443-5131 or (800) 442-5131 (toll-free)

Colorado Institute of Massage Therapy
2601 E. St. Vrain
Colorado Springs, CO 80909
(719) 634-7347 or (888) 634-7347 (toll-free)
http://www.coimt.com

Ayurveda and Yoga

Rocky Mountain Institute of Yoga and Ayurveda
PO Box 1091
Boulder, CO 80306
(303) 443-6923

Shambhava School of Yoga
2875 County Road #67
Boulder CO 80303
(303) 494-3051

Deep Tissue Bodywork

The Rolf Institute of Structural Integration
205 Canyon Boulevard
Boulder, CO 80302
(303) 449-5903 or (800) 530-8875 (toll-free)
http://www.rolf.org

Connecticut

Chiropractic and Naturopathic Doctor

University of Bridgeport
75 Linden Avenue
Bridgeport, CT 06601
(203) 576-4352
http://www.bridgeport.edu

District of Columbia

Massage

Potomac Massage Training Institute
4000 Albemarle Street NW
Washington, DC 20016-1857
(202) 686-7046

Florida

Massage

Core Institute
223 W. Carolina Street
Tallahassee, FL 32301
(850) 222-8673

Florida College of Natural Health
2001 W. Sample Road, Suite 100
Pompano Beach, FL 33064
(954) 975-6400 or (800) 541-9299 (toll-free)
http://www.nhtc.com

Florida School of Massage
6421 SW 13th Street
Gainesville, FL 32608
(352) 378-7891

Sarasota School of Massage Therapy
1970 Main Street, 3rd floor
Sarasota, FL 34236
(941) 957-0577
e-mail: massage@gte.net

Seminar Network International, Inc.
School of Massage and Allied Therapies
518 N. Federal Highway
Lake Worth, FL 33460
(561) 582-5349 or (800) 882-0903 (toll-free)

Suncoast Center for Natural Health, Inc.
4910 W. Cypress Street
Tampa, FL 33607
(813) 287-1099

Osteopathic Doctor

Nova Southeastern University
Health Professions Division
College of Osteopathic Medicine
1750 N. E. 167th Street
North Miami Beach, FL 33162
Osteopathic Admissions (800) 356-0026 ext. 1121 (toll-free)

Herbalism and Aromatherapy

Atlantic Institute of Aromatherapy
16018 Saddlestring Drive
Tampa, FL 33618
(813) 265-2222

Georgia

Chiropractic Doctor

Life College
1269 Barclay Circle
Marietta, GA 30060
(770) 426-2884 or (800) 543-3202 (toll-free)

Massage

Atlanta School of Massage
2300 Peachford Road, Suite 3200
Atlanta, GA 30338
(770) 454-7167

Hawaii

Acupuncture and Herbal Medicine

Tai Hsuan Foundation
Acupuncture and Herbal Medicine College
2600 S. King Street #206
Honolulu, HI 96726
(808) 949-1050 or (800) 942-4788 (toll-free)

Mailing address:
PO Box 11130
Honolulu, HI 96728-0130

Massage

Honolulu School of Massage, Inc.
1123 11th Avenue, Suite 102
Honolulu, HI 96816
(808) 733-0000
e-mail: hsminc@msn.com

Illinois

Chiropractic Doctor

National College of Chiropractic
200 East Roosevelt Road
Lombard, Illinois 60148-4583
(630) 629-2000 or (800) 826-NATL (toll-free)

Massage

Wellness and Massage Training Institute
618 Executive Drive
Willowbrook, IL 60521
(630) 325-3773
http://www.wmti.com

Osteopathic Doctor

Chicago College of Osteopathic Medicine
Midwestern University
555 31st Street
Downers Grove, IL 60515
(708) 969-4400 or (800) 458-6253 (toll-free)

Indiana

Massage

Alexandria School of Scientific Therapeutics
809 S. Harrison
Alexandria, IN 46001
(317) 724-9152

Iowa

Chiropractic Doctor

Palmer College of Chiropractic
1000 Brady Street
Davenport, Iowa 52803
(319) 326-9656 or (800) 722-3648 (toll-free)

Massage

Carlson College of Massage Therapy
11809 Country Road
Box 28
Anamosa, IA 52205
(319) 462-3402
e-mail: carlc@inav.net

Osteopathic Doctor

University of Osteopathic Medicine and Health Sciences
College of Osteopathic Medicine and Surgery
3200 Grand Avenue
Des Moines, IA 50312
(515) 271-1450

Maine

Massage

Downeast School of Massage
PO Box 24
99 Moose Meadow Lane
Waldoboro, ME 04572
(207) 832-5531
e-mail: dsm@midcoast.com

Midwifery

Birthwise Midwifery Training
66 S. High Street
Bridgton ME 04009
(207) 647-5968

Osteopathic Doctor

University of New England
College of Osteopathic Medicine
11 Hills Beach Road
Biddeford, ME 04005
(800) 477-4863 (toll-free)

Maryland

Acupuncture

Maryland Institute of Traditional Chinese Medicine
4641 Montgomery Avenue, Suite 415
Bethesda, MD 20814
(301) 718-7373

Traditional Acupuncture Institute
American City Building
10227 Wincopin Circle, Suite 100
Columbia, MD 21044-3422
(301) 596-6006

Massage

Baltimore School of Massage
6401 Dogwood Road
Baltimore, MD 21207
(410) 944-8855
http://www.bsom.com

Massachusetts

Acupuncture

The New England School of Acupuncture
30 Common Street
Watertown, MA 02172
(617) 926-1788

Massage Therapy

Bancroft School of Massage Therapy
333 Shrewsbury Street
Worcester, MA 01604
(508) 757-7923
http://members.aol.com/bsmttank/bsmtcontents.htm

Massage Institute of New England, Inc.
22 McGrath Highway, Suite 11
Somerville, MA 02143
(617) 666-3700

Muscular Therapy Institute
122 Rindge Avenue
Cambridge, MA 02140
(617) 576-1300
http://www.mtti.com

Energy Work

Polarity Institute
17 Spring Street
Watertown, MA 02172
(617) 924-9150

Macrobiotics

Kushi Institute
PO Box 7
Becket, MA 01223
(413) 623-5741

Yoga

Kripalu Center for Yoga and Health
Box 793
Lenox, MA 01240
(800) 741-7353 (toll-free)

Michigan

Osteopathic Doctor

Michigan State University
College of Osteopathic Medicine
East Fee Hall
East Lansing, MI 48824
(517) 353-7740

Minnesota

Acupuncture

Minnesota Institute of Acupuncture and Herbal Studies
1821 University Avenue, Suite 278-S
St. Paul, MN 55104
(612) 603-0994

Chiropractic Doctor

Northwestern College of Chiropractic
2501 West 84th Street
Bloomington, MN 55431
(612) 888-4777 or (800) 888-4777 (toll free)

Missouri

Chiropractic Doctor

Cleveland Chiropractic College
6401 Rockhill Road
Kansas City, MO 64131
(816) 333-8230 or (800) 467-CCKC (toll-free)

Logan College of Chiropractic
1851 Schoettler Road
PO Box 1065
Chesterfield, MO 63006-1065
(314) 227-2100 or (800) 533-9210 (toll-free in the
    United States and Canada)

Osteopathic Doctor

Kirksville College of Osteopathic Medicine
800 West Jefferson
Kirksville, MO 63501
(816) 626-2237
http://www.kcom.edu

The University of Health Sciences
College of Osteopathic Medicine
1750 Independence Boulevard
Kansas City, MO 64106-1453
(816) 283-2000 or (800) 234-4UHS (toll-free)
http://worldmall.com/erf/uhscom.htm

New Jersey

Massage

Healing Hands Institute for Massage Therapy
41 Bergenline Avenue
Westwood, NJ 07675
(201) 722-0099
e-mail: HH1@aol.com

Somerset School of Massage Therapy
7 Cedar Grove Lane
Somerset, NJ 08873
(732) 356-0787
http:// www.massagecareer.com

Osteopathic Doctor

University of Medicine and Dentistry of New Jersey
School of Osteopathic Medicine
Academic Center
One Medical Center Drive
Stratford, NJ 08084
(609) 566-7050

New Mexico

Acupuncture

International Institute of Chinese Medicine
PO Box 4991
Santa Fe, NM 87502
(505) 473-5233

Southwest Acupuncture College
325 Paseo de Peralta, Suite 500
Santa Fe, NM 87501
(505) 988-3538

Massage

New Mexico Academy of Healing Arts
501 Franklin Street
Santa Fe, NM 87501
(505) 982-6271

New Mexico School of Natural Therapeutics
117 Richmond NE, Suite A
Albuquerque, NM 87106
(505) 268-6870 or (800) 654-1675 (toll-free)
http://www.nmsnt.org/nathealth

Scherer Institute of Natural Healing
935 Alto Street
Santa Fe, NM 87501
(505) 982-8398

Ayurvedic Medicine and Yoga

The Ayurvedic Institute
11311 Menaul NE
Albuquerque, NM 87112
(505) 291-9698

Herbalism

National College of Phytotherapy
120 Aliso SE
Albuquerque NM 87108
(505) 265-0795

New York

Acupuncture, Massage, and Holistic Medicine

The New Center College for Wholistic Health
    Education and Research
6801 Jericho Turnpike
Syosset, NY 11791-4465(516) 364-0808
http://www.newcenter.edu

Acupuncture

Pacific Institute of Oriental Medicine
915 Broadway, 3rd Floor
New York, NY 10010
(212) 982-3456

Chiropractic Doctor

New York Chiropractic College
2360 Route 89
Seneca Falls, New York 13148-0800
(315) 568-3040 or (800) 234-6922 (toll-free)

Osteopathic Doctor

New York College of Osteopathic Medicine
New York Institute of Technology
Box 170
Old Westbury, NY 11568
(516) 626-6947
http://www.nyit/nycom

Herbalism

Northeast School of Botanical Medicine
PO Box 6626
Ithaca, NY 14851
(607) 564-1023

Nutrition

Natural Gourmet Cookery School
48 West 21st Street
New York, NY 10010
(212) 627-COOK

North Carolina

Massage

Body Therapy Institute
South Wind Farm
300 South Wind Road
Siler City, NC 27344
(919) 663-3111 or (888) 500-4500

Carolina School of Massage Therapy
103 W. Weaver Street
Carrboro, NC 27510
(919) 933-2212

Ohio

Massage

Central Ohio School of Massage (COSM)
1120 Morse Road, Suite 250
Columbus, OH 43229
(614) 841-1122
http://www.cosm.org

Osteopathic Doctor

Ohio University
College of Osteopathic Medicine
Grosvenor Hall
Athens, OH 45701
(800) 345-1560 (toll-free)
http://www.tcom.ohiou.edu/oucom

Oklahoma

Osteopathic Doctor

Oklahoma State University
College of Osteopathic Medicine
1111 West 17th Street
Tulsa, OK 74107
(918) 582-1972 or (800) 677-1972 (toll-free)

Oregon

Acupuncture

Oregon College of Oriental Medicine
10525 SE Cherry Blossom Drive
Portland, OR 97216
(503) 253-3443
http://www.infinite.org/oregon.acupuncture

Chiropractic

Western States Chiropractic College (WSCC)
2900 NE 132nd Avenue
Portland, OR 97230
(503) 256-5723 or (800) 641-5641 (toll-free)
http://www.wschiro.edu

Massage

East-West College of the Healing Arts
4531 SE Belmont Street
Portland, OR 97215-1635
(503) 231-1500 or (800) 635-9141 (toll-free)

Midwifery

Birthingway Midwifery Center
5731 North Williams Avenue

Portland OR 97217
(503) 283-4996

Oregon School of Midwifery
342 East 12th Avenue
Eugene OR 97401
(541) 338-9778
http://www.efn.org/~osm

Naturopathic Doctor

National College of Naturopathic Medicine (NCNM)
1049 SW Porter Street
Portland, OR 97201
(503) 499-4343
http://www.ncnm.edu

Pennsylvania

Massage

Career Training Academy
ExpoMart, 105 Mall Boulevard, Suite 300 W
Monroeville, PA 15146-2230
(412) 372-3900 or (800) 491-3470 (toll-free)
http://www.careerta.com

Pennsylvania School of Muscle Therapy, Ltd.
994 Old Eagle School Road, Suite 1005
Wayne, PA 19087
(610) 687-0888
http://www.psmt.com

Osteopathic Doctor

Lake Erie College of Osteopathic Medicine
1858 West Grandview Boulevard
Erie, PA 16509
(814) 866-6641

Philadelphia College of Osteopathic Medicine
4170 City Avenue
Philadelphia, PA 19131
(215) 871-6770 or (800) 999-6998 (toll-free)

South Carolina

Chiropractic Doctor

Sherman College of Straight Chiropractic
PO Box 1452
Spartanburg, SC 29304
(803) 578-8770 or (800) 849-8771 (toll-free)

Tennessee

Energy Work (Reiki)

Reiki Plus Institute
130 Ridge Road
Celina, TN 38551
(615) 243-3712

Texas

Acupuncture

Academy of Oriental Medicine
PO Box 9446
Austin, TX 78766-9446
(512) 454-1188
http://www.holistic.com

American College of Acupuncture and Oriental Medicine
9100 Park West Drive
Houston, TX 77063
(713) 780-9777
http://www.acaom.edu

Texas College of Traditional Chinese Medicine
4005 Manchaca Road, Suite 200
Austin, TX 78704
(512) 444-8082
http://www.ccsi.com/~texastcm

Chiropractic Doctor

Parker College of Chiropractic
2500 Walnut Hill Lane
Dallas, Texas 75229-5668
(214) 438-6932 or (800) GET-MY-DC (toll-free)
http://www.parkercc.edu

Texas Chiropractic College
5912 Spencer Highway
Pasadena, TX 77505
(713) 487-1170 or (800) GO-TO-TEX (toll-free)

Massage

Asten Center of Natural Therapeutics
797 N. Grove Road, Suite 101
Richardson, TX 75081-2761
(972) 669-3245

Lauterstein-Conway Massage School and Clinic
4701-B Burnet Road
Austin, TX 78756
(512) 374-9222 or (800) 474-0852 (toll-free)

Midwifery

Maternidad La Luz
1308 Magoffin
El Paso, TX 79901
(915) 532-5895

Osteopathic Doctor

University of North Texas
Health Sciences Center at Fort Worth
Texas College of Osteopathic Medicine
3500 Camp Bowie Boulevard
Fort Worth, TX 76107-2970
(817) 735-2204
http://www.hsc.unt.edu

Utah

Massage

Utah College of Massage Therapy, Inc.
25 South 300 East
Salt Lake City, UT 84111
(801) 521-3330 or (800) 617-3302 (toll-free)
http://www.ucmt.com

Virginia

Massage

Harold J. Reilly School of Massotherapy
215 67th Street
Virginia Beach, VA 23451
(757) 437-7202
http://www.are-cayce.com

Virginia School of Massage
2008 Morton Drive
Charlottesville, VA 22903
(904) 293-4031 or (888) 599-2001 (toll-free)
http://www.vasaom.com

Veterinary (Equine Massage)

Equissage
PO Box 447
Round Hill, VA 22141
(800) 843-0224 (toll-free)

Washington

Acupuncture, Naturopathic Doctor, and Nutrition

Bastyr University
14500 Juanita Drive, NE
Bothell, Washington 98011
(425) 823-1300
http://www.bastyr.edu

Acupuncture

Northwest Institute of Acupuncture and Oriental Medicine
1307 North 45th Street, Suite 300
Seattle, WA 98103
(206) 633-2419
http://www.halcyon.com/niaom

Seattle Institute of Oriental Medicine
916 NE 65th, Suite B
Seattle, WA 98115
(206) 517-4541

Massage

Brenneke School of Massage
160 Roy Street
Seattle, WA 98109
(206) 282-1233

Brian Utting School of Massage
900 Thomas Street
Seattle, WA 98109
(206) 292-8055 or (800) 842-8731 (toll-free)

Seattle Massage School
7120 Woodlawn Avenue NE
Seattle, WA 98115
(206) 527-0807

Midwifery

Seattle Midwifery School
2524 16th Avenue South, Room 300
Seattle, WA 98144
(206) 322-8834

Yoga

Yoga Centers
2255 140th Ave NE #1
Bellevue, WA 98005
http://www.yogacenters.com
(206) 746-7476

West Virginia

Osteopathic Doctor

West Virginia School of Osteopathic Medicine
400 North Lee Street
Lewisburg, WV 24901
(301) 647-6251

Wisconsin

Acupuncture

Midwest Center for the Study of Oriental Medicine
6226 Bankers Road, Suites 5 and 6
Racine, WI 53403
(414) 554-2010
http://www.acupuncture.edu

CANADA

Alberta

Herbalism

Wild Rose College of Natural Healing
1228 Kensington Road NW
Calgary, Alberta T2N 4P9
(403) 270-0936

British Columbia

Acupuncture

Academy of Classical Oriental Sciences
533 Baker Street
Nelson, British Columbia V1L 5R2
(250) 352-5887 or (888) 333-8868 (toll-free)
http://www.acos.org

Canadian College of Acupuncture and Oriental Medicine
855 Cormorant Street
Victoria, British Columbia, V8W 1R2
(250) 384-2942

Massage

West Coast College of Massage Therapy
Box 12110
555 West Hastings Street
Vancouver, British Columbia V6B 4N6
(604) 689-3854
e-mail: wccmt@wccmt.edu

Acupressure and Shiatsu

Canadian Acupressure Institute
301 - 733 Johnson Street
Victoria, British Columbia V8W 3C7
(250) 388-7475

Ontario

Acupuncture

Ontario College of Acupuncture and Chinese Medicine
658 Danforth Avenue Suite 413
Toronto, Ontario M4J 1L1
(416) 560-2340

Chiropractic

Canadian Memorial Chiropractic College
1900 Bayview Avenue
Toronto, Ontario M4G 3E6
(416) 482-2340

Massage

Sutherland-Chan School and Teaching Clinic
300 Dupont Street, 4th Floor
Toronto, Ontario M5R 1V9
(416) 924-1107

Midwifery

Ryerson Polytechnic University
350 Victoria Street
Toronto, Ontario M5B 2K3
(416) 979-5000
http://www.ryerson.ca

Naturopathic Doctor

Canadian College of Naturopathic Medicine
60 Berl Avenue
Toronto, Ontario M8Y 3C7
(416) 251-5261
http://www.ccnm.edu

Shiatsu and Acupressure

Shiatsu Institute of Canada
47 College Street
Toronto, Ontario M6G-1A9
(416) 323-1818 or (800) 263-1703 (toll-free in Canada or United States)
http://www.shiatsucanada.com

Homeopathy

Canadian Academy of Homeopathy
3044 Bloor Street West, Suite 203
Toronto, Ontario M8X 1C4
(416) 503-4003

Nutrition

Canadian School of Natural Nutrition
10720 Yonge Street #220
Richmond Hill, Ontario L4C 3C9
(905) 737-0284 or (800) 569-9938 (toll-free)

Quebec

Homeopathy

Centre de Techniques Homeopathiques, Inc.
910 Boulanger
Montreal, Quebec H2S 3P4
(514) 277-1007

APPENDIX B

Professional Organizations, Useful Resources, and Internet Sites

Unless otherwise noted, the organizations and other educational resources listed in this appendix are more fully described in the chapters in parts 2 and 3.

National Organizations

UNITED STATES

American Academy of Environmental Medicine
Box CN 1001-2001
New Hope, PA 18938
(215) 862-4544

American Association of Oriental Medicine
433 Front Street
Catasauqua, PA 18032
(610) 266-1433

The American Academy of Medical Acupuncture
5820 Wilshire Boulevard, Suite 500
Los Angeles, CA 90036

American Alliance of Aromatherapy
PO Box 309
Depoe Bay, OR 97341
(800) 809-9850 (toll-free)

American Association of Naturopathic Physicians (AANP)
601 Valley #105
Seattle, WA 98109
(206) 298-0126
http://www.infinite.org/naturopathic.physician

American Botanical Council
PO Box 201660
Austin, TX 78720
(512) 331-8868

American Chiropractic Association
1701 Clarendon Boulevard
Arlington VA 2209
(703) 276-8800

American Herbalists Guild (AHG)
PO Box 746555
Arvada, CO 80006
(303) 423-8800
http://www.healthy.net/herbalists

American Herbal Products Association
4733 Bethesda Avenue, Suite 345
Bethesda, Maryland 20814

American Massage Therapy Association (AMTA)
820 Davis Street, Suite 100
Evanston, IL 60201
(847) 864-0123
http://www.amtamassage.org

American Oriental Bodywork Therapy Association (AOBTA)
AOBTA National Headquarters
Glendale Executive Campus, Suite 510
1000 White Horse Road
Voorhees, NJ 08043
(609) 782-1616

American College of Nurse-Midwives
1522 K Street, Suite 1000
Washington, DC 20005

American Holistic Nurses' Association (AHNA)
PO Box 2130
Flagstaff AZ 86003-2130
http://www.ahna.org

American Holistic Medical Association
4101 Lake Boone Trail, Suite 201
Raleigh, NC 27607
(919) 787-5181
http://www.ahmaholistic.com

American Osteopathic Association
142 East Ontario Street
Chicago, IL 60611
(800) 621-1773
http://www.aacom.org

American Reflexology Certification Board
PO Box 620607
Littleton, CO 80162
(303) 933-6921

Associated Bodywork and Massage Professionals (ABMP)
28677 Buffalo Park Road
Evergreen, CO 80439-7347
(303) 674-8478
http://www.abmp.com

The Association for Applied Psychophysiology and Biofeedback
10200 W. 44th Avenue, Suite 304
Wheat Ridge, CO 80033-2840
(303) 422-8436 or (800) 477-8892 (toll free)

Association of Labor Assistants and Childbirth Educators (ALACE)
PO Box 382724
Cambridge, MA 02238
(617) 441-2500
http://www.alace.org

CANI
1300 26th Avenue, Suite 605
San Francisco, CA 94122

Council on Chiropractic Education (CCE)
7975 North Ayden Road, #A-210
Scottsdale, AZ 85258

Doulas of North America (DONA)
Connie Sultana, Certification Chair
1106 Hamilton Way
Columbia, MO 65203
http://www.dona.com

Federation of Chiropractic Licensing Boards
901 54th Avenue #101
Greeley, CO 80634

The Feldenkrais Guild
PO Box 489
Albany, OR 97321
(503) 926-0981 or (800) 775-2118 (toll-free)
e-mail: feldngld@peak.org

The Flower Essence Society (FES)
PO Box 459
Nevada City, CA 95959
(916) 265-9163 or (800) 736-9222
    (toll-free in United States and Canada)

Foundation for Chiropractic Education and Research
1701 Clarendon Boulevard
Arlington, VA 22209
(703) 276-7445

Herb Research Foundation
1007 Pearl Street, #200
Boulder, CO 80302
(303) 449-2265 or (800) 748-2617 (toll-free)

Hellerwork International, LLC
406 Berry Street
Mount Shasta, CA 96067
(916) 926-2500 or (800) 392-3900 (toll-free)
http://www.hellerwork.com

Holistic Dental Association
PO Box 5007
Durango, CO 81301
e-mail: hda@frontier.net

Homeopathic Academy of Naturopathic Physicians
12132 S.E. Foster Place
Portland, OR 97266
(503) 761-3298
e-mail: hanp@igc.apc.org

International Association of Colon Hydrotherapy (I-ACT)
2204 NW Loop 410
San Antonio, TX 78230
(210) 366-2888
e-mail: iact@healthy.net

I-ACT offers information about continuing and progressive education in the field of colon hydrotherapy for its members. I-ACT–certified instructors must have a minimum of 1,000 hours of training or three years of practice; have already achieved certification, by I-ACT at the intermediate level; demonstrate teaching in a prearranged regional or other I-ACT meeting with a minimum of eight students; submit an outline of teaching to headquarters one month before the seminar; and write a satisfactory test of fifty questions and answers (on separate pages).

The International Society for the Study of Subtle Energies and
Energy Medicine (ISSSEEM)
356 Goldco Circle
Golden, CO 80401
(303) 278-2228
e-mail: 74040.1273@compuserve.com
http://www.vitalenergy.com/issseem

International Association of Infant Massage
1720 Willow Creek #516
Eugene, OR 97402
(800) 248-5432

International Alliance of Healthcare Educators
11211 Prosperity Farms Road
Palm Beach Gardens, FL 33410
(800) 311-9204 (toll-free)

This coalition of health-care instructors and curriculum developers currently coordinates 700 workshops per year in major cities throughout the world in support of more than twenty modalities.

The International Foundation for Homeopathy
PO Box 7
Edmonds, WA 98020
(206) 776-4417

International Herb Growers and Marketers Association
P.O. Box 281
Silver Springs, PA 17575
(717) 285-4252

International Massage Association
3000 Connecticut Avenue, NW., Suite 308
Washington, DC, 20008
(202) 387-6555
http://www.internationalmassage.com

International Medical and Dental Hypnotherapy Association
4110 Edgeland #800
Royal Oak, MI 48073
(810) 549-5594

International Institute of Reflexology
PO Box 12642
St. Petersburg, FL 33733
(813) 343-4811

International Veterinary Acupuncture Society
PO Box 2074
Nederland, CO 80466
(303) 258-3767

Midwives Alliance of North America
PO Box 175
Newton, KS 67114
http://www.mana.org

National Acupuncture Detoxification Association
3220 N Street NW, Suite 275
Washington, DC 20007
(503) 222-1362

National Acupuncture and Oriental Medicine Alliance
14637 Starr Road SE
Olalla, WA 98359
(206) 851-6896

National Association for Holistic Aromatherapy (NAHA)
PO Box 17622
Boulder, CO 80308
(415) 731-4634

The National Center for Homeopathy
801 North Fairfax Street, Suite 306
Alexandria, VA 22314
(703) 548-7790

National Association of Nurse Massage Therapists
PO Box 1150
Abita Springs, LA 70420
(888) 462-6686

North American Registry of Midwives (NARM)
PO Box 15
Linn, WV 26384

North American Society of Teachers of the Alexander Technique
3010 Hennepin Avenue South, Suite 10
Minneapolis, MN 55408
(612) 824-5066 or (800) 473-0620 (toll-free)

North American Society of Homeopaths
10700 Old County Road 15 #350
Plymouth, MN 55441
(612) 595-0459

The Physicians Association for Anthroposophical Medicine (PAAM)
7953 California Avenue
Fair Oaks, CA 95628
(916) 967-8250

Trager Institute
21 Locust
Mill Valley, CA 94941
(415) 388-2688

Yoga and Health Studios
US Contact: Yoga For Health
7918 Bolling Drive
Alexandria, VA 22308

The Zero Balancing Association
PO Box 1727
Capitola, CA 95010
http://www.zerobalancing.com

CANADA

Canadian Childbirth Education
2043 Ferndale Street
Vancouver, British Columbia V5L 1Y2

Canadian Chiropractic Association
1396 Eglinton Avenue W.
Toronto, Ontario M6R 2H2

Canadian Council on Chiropractic Education
130-10100 Shellbridge Way
Richmond, British Columbia V6W 2W7
(604) 270-1332

Canadian Medical Acupuncture Society
9904-106 Street N.W.
Edmonton, Alberta T5K 1C4
(403) 426-2760

Canadian Massage Therapist Alliance
365 Bloor Street East, Suite 1807
Toronto, Ontario M4W 3L4P
(416) 968-2149

Canadian Naturopathic Association
PO Box 4520, Station C
Calgary, Alberta, T2T 5N3
(403) 244-4487

Canadian Osteopathic Association
575 Waterloo St
London, Ontario N6B 2R2
(519) 439-5521

International Society for Orthomolecular Medicine
16 Florence Avenue
Toronto, Ontario M2N 1E9 Canada
(416) 733-2117

Canadian Provincial Massage Associations

Massage Therapist Association of Alberta (MTAA)
Box 24031 RPO Plaza Centre
Red Deer, Alberta T4N 6X6
(403) 340-1913

Massage Therapists' Association of British Columbia (MTA of BC)
34 East 12th Avenue, 3rd Floor
Vancouver, British Columbia V5T 2G5
(604) 873-4467

Massage Therapy Association of Manitoba (MTAM)
Riverview PO Box 63030
Winnipeg, Manitoba R3L 2V8
(204) 254-0406

New Brunswick Massotherapy Association Inc. (NBMA)
PO Box 21009
Fredericton, New Brunswick E3B 7A3
(506) 459-5788

Newfoundland Massage Therapists' Association (NMTA)
PO Box 5032, Station C
St. John's, Newfoundland A1C 5V3
(709) 726-4006

Massage Therapists' Association of Nova Scotia (MTA of NS)
PO Box 33103, Quinpool Post Office
Halifax, Nova Scotia B3L 4T6
(902) 429-2190

Ontario Massage Therapist Association (OMTA)
365 Bloor Street East, Suite 1807
Toronto, Ontario M4W 3L4
(416) 968-6487 or (800) 668-2022 (toll-free)

Federation Quebecoise des Masseurs et Massotherapeutes
1265 Mont-Royal est. bureau 204
Montreal, Quebec H2J 1Y4
(514) 597-0505 or (800) 363-9609 (toll-free)

Saskatchwan Massage Therapist Association (SMTA)
PO Box 1551
Regina, Saskatchewan S4P 3C4
(306) 924-4441

Other Useful Resources

Feldenkrais Resources
PO Box 2067
Berkeley, CA 94702
(510) 540-7600 or (800) 765-1907 (toll-free)

Feldenkrais Resources sells books, cassettes, and videotapes related to the teaching of Moshe Feldenkrais.

Healing Pages Bookstore
600 W. McGraw #2
Seattle, WA 98119
(206) 283-7621
http://members.aol.com/healingpgs/index.htm

Healing Pages specializes in both popular press and textbooks related to the natural medicine field, particularily herbs, homeopathy, nutrition, traditional Chinese medicine, and therapeutic protocols for specific conditions. Free newsletter and mail-order service available.

Minimum Price
250 H Street
PO Box 2187
Blaine, WA 98231
e-mail: greg_cooper@minimum.com

This mail-order bookstore specializes in the homeopathy, the art of the "minimum dose." Catalog available by request.

Internet Sites

Acupuncture.com
http://www.acupuncture.com

This web site has long listings of acupuncture schools (accredited and unaccredited), hot links related to acupuncture, and various articles of interest to practitioners.

Feldenkrais Web Site
http://www.feldenkrais.com

> This web site contains international listings of instructors, educational materials, professional organizations, and other information related to the teachings of Moshe Feldenkrais.

Massagetherapy.com
http://www.massagetherapy.com

> Like Acupuncture.com, this site keeps track of schools, organizations, and issues of interest to massage therapists and students.

Ontario College of Reflexology (OCR)
http://www.nt.net/ocr/index.html

> This professional organization seeks to organize reflexologists in the province of Ontario to help establish legal recognition for the profession. OCR offers workshops conducted on weekends, or private courses taught by OCR-qualified teachers. In 1997 the average cost was $150 to $200 CDN. Some home study or correspondence courses may be available. OCR's website also contains lists of other schools recognized by them to provide professional standard reflexology courses.

OsteopathicNet
http://www.osteopathic.net

> This web site has an interactive bulletin board for questions about osteopathic schools, paying back loans, and residency opportunities. The PreMed FAQ covers frequently asked questions about osteopathic medicine and medical schools.

Phoenix Rising Yoga Therapy
http://www.pyrt.com
(800) 288-9642 (toll-free)

> Classes take place at yoga schools around the country. In 1997 the cost ranged from $495 (Level 1) to $1,895 (Level 3). Call or check the web site for current location of workshops.

Internet Newsgroups

Access to certain newsgroups may depend on your internet server. If you're interested in the politics, debates, and hot issues, this is where they tend to get aired. Check Dejanews (www.dejanews.com) for other newsgroups in the natural therapies.

> alt.healing.flower-essence
> alt.health
> alt.health.ayurveda
> alt.folklore.herbs
> alt.hypnosis
> alt.meditation
> alt.med.nutrition

The America Online keyword is `altmed`.

APPENDIX C

More Schools

Information on the following schools was received from the accrediting agencies or practitioners after the publication deadline for this edition.

UNITED STATES

Acupuncture

The following schools were accredited or under consideration for accreditation during the 1996/97 school year.

Academy for Five Element Acupuncture
(Worsley Institute of Classical Acupuncture)
6175 NW 153rd Street, Suite 324
Miami Lakes, FL 33014
(305) 823-7270

Florida Institute of Traditional Chinese Medicine
5335 66th Street North
St. Petersburg, FL 33709
(813) 546-6565 or (800) 565-1246 (toll-free)

National Institute of Oriental Medicine
1724 S. Bumby Avenue
Orlando, FL 32806
(407) 895-9443

Traditional Chinese Medical College of Hawaii
Parker Ranch Office Center, Bldg. 3
PO Box 2288
Kamuela, Hawaii 96743
(808) 885-9226

Tri-State Institute of Traditional Chinese Acupuncture
80 - 8th Avenue, 4th Floor
New York, NY 10011
(212) 496-7869

Ayurveda and Yoga

International Yoga Studios
13833 South 31st Place
Phoenix, AZ 85048
(602) 759-1972

Iyengar Yoga Institute of San Francisco
2404 27th Avenue
San Francisco, CA 94116
(415) 753-0909

Herbalism

Connecticut Institute for Herbal Studies
87 Market Square
Newington, CT 0611
(860) 666-5064

The Rocky Mountain Herbal Institute
PO Box 579
Hot Springs MT 59845
(406) 741-3811
http://www.ronan.net/~rmhi

Sage Mountain Herbal Center (Rosemary Gladstar)
PO Box 420
East Barre, VT 05649
(802) 479-9825

Massage

The following progams were accredited or approved by the AMTA in 1996/97.

Blue Cliff School of Therapeutic Massage
1919 Veterans Boulevard, Suite 310
Kenner, LA 70062
(504) 471-0294

Central California School of Body Therapy
1330 Southwood Drive, #7
San Luis Obispo, CA 93401
(805) 783-2200

Chicago School of Massage Therapy
2918 N. Lincoln Avenue
Chicago, IL 60657-4109
(773) 477-9444

Connecticut Center for Massage Therapy, Inc.
75 Kitts Lane
Newington, CT 06111
(860) 667-1886

Connecticut Center for Massage Therapy, Inc.
25 Sylvan Road S.
Westport, CT 06880
(203) 221-7325

Educating Hands School of Massage
120 SW 8th Street
Miami, FL 33130
(305) 285-6991

Health Enrichment Center, Inc.
1820 N. Lapeer Road
Lapeer, MI 48446-7771
(810) 667-9453

Humanities Center Institute of Allied Health
School of Massage
4045 Park Boulevard
Pinellas Park, FL 34665
(813) 541-5200

Institute of Natural Healing Sciences
4100 Felps Road, Suite E
Colleyville, TX 76034
(817) 498-0716

Integrative Therapy School
3000 T Street, Suite 104
Sacramento, CA 95816
(916) 739-8848

Lakeside School of Natural Therapeutics, Inc.
1726 N. First Street, Suite 300
Milwaukee, WI 53212
(414) 372-4345

Lewis School and Clinic of Massage Therapy, Inc.
3400 Michigan Street
Hobart, IN 46342
(219) 962-9640

New Hampshire Institute for Therapeutic Arts School
    of Massage Therapy
39 Main Street
Bridgton, ME 04009
(207) 647-3794
Fax: (603) 598-9101

New Hampshire Institute for Therapeutic Arts School
    of Massage Therapy
153 Lowell Road
Hudson, NH 03051
(603) 882-3022

Northern Lights School of Massage Therapy
1313 SE Fifth Street, Suite 202
Minneapolis, MN 55414
(612) 379-3822
Fax: (612) 379-5971

S.H.I., Integrative Medical Massage School
130 Cook Road
Lebanon, OH 45036
(513) 932-8712

Stillpoint Center School of Massage, Inc.
PO Box 15
60 Main Street
Hatfield, MA 01038
(413) 247-9322

Swedish Institute, Inc.
School of Massage Therapy and Allied Health Sciences
226 W. 26th Street, 5th floor
New York, NY 10001
(212) 924-5900

Tri-City School of Massage
26 E. Third Avenue
Kennewick, WA 99336
(509) 586-6434

Nurse-Midwifery

The following certificate or master's programs meet the standards of the America College of Nurse-Midwives. Check with the ACNM (Appendix B) for new programs, accreditation information, and current admissions requirements. Some programs allow combined RN/CNM; some require you to already be an RN before entering. Most phone numbers listed are for the main switchboards at the college or university.

CERTIFICATE PROGRAMS:
Baylor College of Medicine
Midwifery Education Program
Dept. of OB/GYN
Smith Towers, 7th Floor
6550 Fannin
Houston, TX 77030
(715) 798-4951

Charles R. Drew University of Medicine and Science
Nurse-Midwifery Education Program
College of Allied Health Services
1621 E. 120th Street
Los Angeles, CA 90059
(213) 563-4987

Marquette University
College of Nursing
Milwaukee, WI 53201
(414) 288-3808

State University of New York
Health Sciences Center
Brooklyn College of Health Related Professions
Nurse-Midwifery Educational Program
Box 93
450 Clarkson Avenue
Brooklyn, NY 11203
(718) 270-1000

University of Medicine and Denistry of New Jersey
School of Health Related Professionals
Nurse-Midwifery Program
65 Bergen Street
Newark, NJ 07107-3006
(201) 982-4300

University of Southern California
Nurse-Midwifery Program
Women's Hospital, Room 8K51
240 North Mission Road
Los Angeles, CA 90033
(213) 740-2311

MASTER'S DEGREE PROGRAMS:

Boston University, School of Public Health
MPH/CNM Program
80 E Concord Street
Boston, MA 02118
(617) 353-2000

Case Western Reserve University
Frances Payne Bolton School of Nursing
Nurse-Midwifery Program
2121 Abington Road
Cleveland, OH 44106
(216) 368-2000

Columbia University
School of Nursing
Graduate Program in Nurse-Midwifery

617 W 168th Street
New York, NY 10032
(212) 854-1754

Emory University
Nell Hodgson School of Nursing
Atlanta, GA 30322
(404) 727-7980

Medical University of South Carolina
Nurse-Midwifery Program
College of Nursing
171 Ashley Avenue
Charleston, SC 29425
(803) 792-3281

Oregon Health Sciences University
School of Nursing, Department of Family Nursing
Nurse-Midwifery Program
3181 SW Sam Jackson Park Road
Portland, OR 97201
(503) 494-7725

University of Colorado Health Sciences Center
School of Nursing Graduate Program
Nurse-Midwifery Program
4200 E 9th Avenue, Box C 288
Denver, CO 80262
(303) 399-1211

University of Illinois at Chicago
College of Nursing, Nurse-Midwifery Program
Department of Maternal Child Nursing
845 S. Damen Avenue
Chicago, IL 60612
(312) 996-2159

University of Miami, School of Nursing
D2-5, Royce Bldg.
PO Box 016960
1755 NW 12th Avenue
Miami, FL 33136
(305) 284-2211

University of Michigan
Nurse-Midwifery Program
School of Nursing
400 N Ingalls, Room 4320
Ann Arbor, MI 48109
(313) 764-1817

University of Minnesota
School of Nursing
6-101 Unit F308 Harvard Street SE
Minneapolis, MN 55455
(612) 625-5000

University of New Mexico
College of Nursing
Nurse-Midwifery Program
Albuquerque, NM 87131
(505) 277-0111

University of Pennsylvania
School of Nursing Nursing Education Bldg.
420 Service Drive
Philadelphia, PA 19104-6096
(215) 898-5000

University of Texas at El Paso
Collaborative Nurse-Midwifery Program
Texas Tech University HSC, Department of OB/GYN
4800 Alberta Avenue
El Paso, TX 79905
(915) 747-5000

University of Utah
College of Nursing
Graduate Program in Nurse-Midwifery
25 S Medical Drive
Salt Lake City, UT 84112
(801) 581-7200

Vanderbilt University
School of Nursing
Nashville, TN 37240
(615) 322-3800

Yale University
School of Nursing
Maternal-Newborn Nursing/Nurse-Midwifery Program
25 Park Street
New Haven, CT 06536-0740
(203) 432-4771

Osteopathic Doctor

Pikeville College School of Osteopathic Medicine
214 Sycamore Street
Pikeville, KY 41501
(606) 432-9200

Feldenkrais

The following institutions offered Feldenkrais Professional Training Program during 1996/97.

Carl Ginsburg Institute for Awareness in Motion
PO Box 50624
Columbia, SC 29250
(803) 799-6258

Mind in Motion/Vie et Mouvement
307 North McKinley Avenue
Champaign, IL 61821
(217) 398-6683

Reese Movement Institute
160 Chesterfield Drive, Suite 8
Cardiff-by-the-Sea, CA 92007
(619) 436-9087 or (800) 500-9807 (toll-free)

Semio Physics
2747 Woolsey Street
Berkeley, CA 94705
(510) 655-6530

CANADA

Acupuncture

Check with provincial authorities or professional organizations to make sure these schools will meet the requirements of the location in which you want to practice.

The Canadian College of Traditional Chinese Medicine
#202 - 560 West Broadway
Vancouver, British Columbia V5Z 1E9
(604) 879-2365

Can-Orient Culture Academy
279 Highglen Avenue
Markham, Ontario L3S 3W2
(905) 305-9558

College de Rosemont
Departement d'acupuncture
6400, 16eme Avenue
Montreal, Quebec H1X 2S9
(514) 376-1620

SSC Acupuncture Institute
547 College Street
Toronto, Ontario M6G 1A9
(416) 323-1818

Toronto School of Traditional Chinese Medicine
2010 Eglinton Avenue West #302
Toronto, Ontario M6E 2K3
(416) 782-9682

Herbalism

Dominion Herbal College
7527 Kingsway Avenue
Burnaby, British Columbia V3N 3C1
(604) 521-5822

Massage

Schools usually concentrate on providing an education that satisfies the provincial or local requirements of the area in which they are located. Check with the school or your professional massage organization if you plan to practice in another province.

Alberta Institute of Massage
7644 Gaetz Avenue
Red Deer, Alberta T4P 2A8
(403) 346-1018

Canadian College of Massage and Hydrotherapy
5160 Yonge Street
North York, Ontario M2N 6L9
(416) 250-8690

Canadian Therapeutic College
760 Brant Street
Burlington, Ontario L7R 4B7
(905) 632-3200

Centennial College of Applied Arts and Technology
PO Box 631, Station "A"
Scarborough, Ontario M1K 5E9
(416) 694-3241

The D'Arcy Lane Institute
627 Maitland Street
London, Ontario N5Y 2V7
(519) 673-4421

Edmonton College of Swedish Massage
290 Kaska Road
Sherwood Park, Alberta T8A 4G7
(403) 464-8548

Foothills College of Massage Therapy
7220 Fisher Street SE, Suite 130
Calgary, AB, T2H 2H8
(403) 255-4445

Grant MacEwan Community College
7319-29 Avenue
Edmonton, Alberta T6K 2P1
(403) 497-4040

Kikkawa College
1 Riverview Gardens
Toronto, Ontario M6S 4E4
(416) 762-4857

Kine-Concept Inc.
760 St-Zotique Street E.
Montreal, Quebec, H2S 1M5
(514) 272-5463

The Maritime School of Health and Well Being
RR1, Site 3B, Box 14
Waverly, Nova Scotia BON 2S0
(902) 435-0432

Mount Royal Community College
4825 Richard Road SW
Calgary, Alberta T3E 6K6
(403) 240-6875

Northern Institute of Massage
5016 - 50 Street
Clyde, AB, T0G 0P0
(403) 348-5385

Northwestern School of Massage
8 Floor, 2424 - 4 Street SW
Calgary, Alberta T2S 2T9
(403) 228-6307

Okanagan Valley College of Massage Therapy
3317 39th Avenue
Vernon, British Columbia V1T 2C9
(604) 558-3748

Rocky Mountain Academy
The Burns Building
401, 237 - 8 Avenue SE
Calgary, Alberta T2G 5C3
(403) 266-5226

Sault College of Applied Arts and Technology
School of Health Sciences
PO Box 60
Sault Ste. Marie, Ontario P6A 5L3
(705) 759-6773

Sir Sanford Fleming College
Lakeshore Campus
1005 William Street
Cobourg, Ontario K9A 5J4
(905) 372-6865

Veterinary: Equine Massage

D'Al School of Equine Massage Therapy
627 Maitland Street
London, Ontario N5Y 2V7
(519) 637-4420

BIBLIOGRAPHY

The books used in researching this volume are noted in the recommended reading at the end of each chapter.

American Association of Naturopathic Physicians. "Naturopathic Medicine: Contributions to Health Care Reform." Proposal submitted to the Task Force on National Health Reform (April 1993): 13.

Barrett, Jennifer. "U.S. Yoga Teachers Consider National Standards." *Yoga Journal* (September/October 1997): 21.

Beauchamp, Natasha. "Choosing a Certified Nurse-Midwifery Program." In *Getting an Education, A Book for Aspiring Midwives*. Oregon: Midwifery Today Inc., 1995.

Corio, Carol. "Dollars & Scents: Essential Ingredients for Energizing Aromatherapy Sales." *New Age Retailer* (September 1997): 46.

Frishberg, Manny. "Alternative Medicine Gaining Acceptance." *Common Ground* 81 (January 1998): 10.

Frishberg, Manny. "Can Clinic Survive?" *Common Ground* 74 (June 1997): 7.

Jerome, Tom. "Zero Balancing: Bodywork of Relationship." *Massage Magazine* 69 (September/October 1997): 35.

Lamphear, Fred. "Acupuncture Across America." *The Meridian* 8, no. 2 (Spring/Summer 1997): 4.

Manahan, Tim. "Holistic Health in Medical School: A Growth Spurt." Paper presented at the 20th Annual Conference of AHMA, May 1997, Bellevue WA. Published on the AHMA web site.

Mower, Melissa, "Massage Returns to Nursing." *Massage Magazine* 69 (September/October 1997): 46.

These popular magazines carry many articles on natural therapies as well as news about new types of practices:

Natural Health, 17 Station Street, Brookline, MA 02146

New Age, 42 Pleasant, Watertown, MA 02172

AUTHOR BIOGRAPHY

Rosemary Jones owns Healing Pages Bookstore, a Seattle bookstore that specializes in natural medicine literature for the lay person and the professional. She is a regular contributor to AltMed, the AOL forum on alternative medicine, the *Well-Being Journal,* and *Common Ground,* as well as many other publications. She coauthored two books on collecting children's books, *The Collector's Guide to Children's Books: 1850 to 1950,* volume 1 and volume 2, and is currently working on the third in the series. Questions may be sent to her at the following address: Healing Pages Bookstore, 600 W. McGraw #2, Seattle, WA 98119, e-mail: hpedu@aol.com. Please enclose a self-addressed, stamped envelope for reply.

INDEX

ALSO FROM PRIMA

It's Like Having the World's Most Respected Health Experts at Your Fingertips

Imagine having some of the world's most respected natural health experts talk to you about your health concerns. Now, with this extraordinary reference tool, you can! In this, easy-to-use volume, some of today's most highly regarded clinical practitioners in the field have teamed together to provide timely, practical, and fully integrated advice on treating troublesome health conditions in a safe, natural way. *The Natural Pharmacy* is your most trusted guide to the conditions, supplements, herbs, and homeopathic remedies available to date.

In Association with HealthNotes™ Online

THE NATURAL PHARMACY

From the World's Most Trusted Experts

Covers All Major Ailments and Conditions

Includes Herbs, Nutritional Supplements, and Homeopathy

SKYE LININGER, D.C., EDITOR-IN-CHIEF
JONATHAN WRIGHT, M.D.   STEVE AUSTIN, N.D.
DONALD BROWN, N.D.   ALAN GABY, M.D.

U.S. $19.99 / Can. $26.95
ISBN 0-7615-1227-6
paperback / 464 pages

To order, call (800) 632-8676 or
visit us online at www.primapublishing.com

OVER 300,000 COPIES SOLD!

The Perfect Balance Between the Latest Research and Age-Old Wisdom

You'll want to consult this handy, reader-friendly book again and again! It presents effective, natural treatments for 100 different health problems in an easy-to-use, A-to-Z format. Written by two of the leading naturopathic doctors working today, *Encyclopedia of Natural Medicine*, also features a guide to basic principles of good health and offers a comprehensive overview of natural medicine.

This modern classic is recognized as the definitive resource for maintaining vibrant good health naturally. Completely revised and updated, it's the most balanced and professional guide to natural medicine available, yet it's written with the general reader in mind.

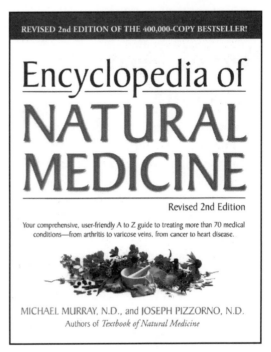

REVISED 2nd EDITION OF THE 400,000-COPY BESTSELLER!

Encyclopedia of NATURAL MEDICINE

Revised 2nd Edition

Your comprehensive, user-friendly A to Z guide to treating more than 70 medical conditions—from arthritis to varicose veins, from cancer to heart disease.

MICHAEL MURRAY, N.D., and JOSEPH PIZZORNO, N.D.
Authors of *Textbook of Natural Medicine*

U.S. $20.00 / Can. $26.95
ISBN 0-7615-1157-1
paperback / 640 pages

**To order, call (800) 632-8676 or
visit us online at www.primapublishing.com**

Your Guide to the Best of Alternative Medicine

One person in three now relies on some form of alternative medical care, from dietary supplements and herbal remedies to chiropractic and Eastern medicines. If you are one of these people, this ground-breaking new book is for you. In *The Alternative Medicine Ratings Guide*, 20 of the world's leading health experts review and rate the most popular alternative treatments for more than 90 common ailments. Each entry provides you with a detailed review of the treatment's effectiveness, potential side effects, clinical research, ease of use, and cost.

U.S. $19.95 / Can. $25.95
ISBN 0-7615-1278-0
paperback / 340 pages

**To order, call (800) 632-8676 or
visit us online at www.primapublishing.com**

ALSO FROM PRIMA

Your Guide to Health and Healing with Vitamins, Minerals, and Other Supplements

Nutritional supplements promote overall health and well-being, minimize the effects of aging, strengthen the immune system, and encourage the body's natural ability to heal itself. In this easy-to-use, comprehensive guide, bestselling author Dr. Michael T. Murray introduces you to key vitamins, minerals, nutrients, oils, enzymes, and extracts. He describes in detail the healing properties of each and explains symptoms that may indicate a deficiency. Most important, he details the health conditions that each supplement can improve. With recommendations for use and dosage, this essential healing resource gives you the power to improve your health naturally.

"This book will be powerful medicine for everyone who reads it." —*Natural Health*

MICHAEL T. MURRAY, N.D.
Co-author of the bestselling *Encyclopedia of Natural Medicine*

Encyclopedia of NUTRITIONAL SUPPLEMENTS

Includes detailed profiles of all major nutritional supplements—vitamins, minerals, essential fatty acids, accessory nutrients, and glandular extracts.

Discover how supplements can help you live longer, feel better, and fight the effects of aging.

Learn which nutritional supplements to take for high cholesterol, depression, fatigue, arthritis, heart disease, allergies, immune deficiencies, and many other health concerns.

U.S. $19.95 / Can. $26.95
ISBN 0-7615-0410-9
paperback / 576 pages

**To order, call (800) 632-8676 or
visit us online at www.primapublishing.com**

To Order Books

Please send me the following items:

Quantity	Title	Unit Price	Total
_____	**The Natural Pharmacy**	$ 19.99	$ _____
_____	**Encyclopedia of Natural Medicine**	$ 20.00	$ _____
_____	**The Alternative Medicine Ratings Guide**	$ 19.95	$ _____
_____	**Encyclopedia of Nutritional Supplements**	$ 19.95	$ _____
_____	_____	$ _____	$ _____

Subtotal	$ _____
Deduct 10% when ordering 3–5 books	$ _____
7.25% Sales Tax (CA only)	$ _____
8.25% Sales Tax (TN only)	$ _____
5% Sales Tax (MD and IN only)	$ _____
7% G.S.T. Tax (Canada only)	$ _____
Shipping and Handling*	$ _____
Total Order	$ _____

*Shipping and Handling depend on Subtotal.

Subtotal	Shipping/Handling
$0.00–$14.99	$3.00
$15.00–$29.99	$4.00
$30.00–$49.99	$6.00
$50.00–$99.99	$10.00
$100.00–$199.99	$13.50
$200.00+	Call for Quote

Foreign and all Priority Request orders:
Call Order Entry department
for price quote at 916-632-4400

This chart represents the total retail price of books only
(before applicable discounts are taken).

By Telephone: With MC, Visa or American Express, call 800-632-8676
or 916-632-4400. Mon–Fri, 8:30-4:30.
WWW: http://www.primapublishing.com

By Internet E-mail: sales@primapub.com
By Mail: Just fill out the information below and send with your remittance to:

**Prima Publishing
P.O. Box 1260BK
Rocklin, CA 95677**

Name _____

Address _____

City _____ State _____ ZIP _____

MC/Visa# _____ Exp. _____

Check/money order enclosed for $ _____ Payable to Prima Publishing

Daytime telephone _____

Signature _____